The TIME
of the END

Tim Warner

"Although I heard, I did not understand. Then I said, 'My lord, what shall be the end of these things?' And he said, 'Go your way, Daniel, for the words are closed up and sealed till **the TIME of the END***. Many shall be purified, made white, and refined, but the wicked shall do wickedly; and none of the wicked shall understand, but the wise shall understand.'"* Daniel 12:8-10

To my wife, Diane – my best friend and partner: Without your loving support, encouragement, and help, this book could never have been written.

Copyright © 2012 by Tim Warner

Contents

Part I

Part II
A Complete Chronology

Charts & Tables

INTRODUCTION

TEOTWAWKI – no it's not a Greek word. It's a modern acronym for "the end of the world as we know it," a term used by many doomsayers, survivalists, and your average "Chicken Little." Most of us still remember the Y2K hysteria over a decade ago – a complete bust. Yet, TEOTWAWKI hysteria is on the increase, despite a long record of failures.

It is not that some proposed end-of-the-world event on the horizon is so compelling. Rather, there is a general mood of anxiety and fear. This is driven in part by the apparent breakdown of world economies, increase in terrorism, looming wars, rapid decline of morality, massive corruption in governments, an agenda-driven news media spewing propaganda, crumbling societies, and a growing sense of entitlement by the masses who are increasingly embracing anarchy. Add to this a religious – prophetic – Messianic component, and you have the perfect storm. People living in fear will easily latch on to popular TEOTWAWKI scenarios without much critical thinking or research because they fear the unknown and being caught unprepared.

December 21, 2012 was the latest TEOTWAWKI non-event to fizzle. According to the Mayan calendar, well, … nothing really. The calendar just doesn't go beyond the winter solstice of 2012. Why all the fuss about an ancient calendar? Who were the Mayans anyway? And why would they have some special knowledge of the distant future? They were pagans.

According to the Bible, all of the pagan gods are demons masquerading as gods.[1] The Mayans are hardly a reliable source for predicting the future. Yet many people bought into it, again without critical analysis.

Closely associated with the Mayan calendar devotees are the Planet X enthusiasts. Haven't you heard? There is a giant inhabited planet in a highly elliptical orbit of our sun. Every few thousand years it approaches from the farthest reaches of our solar system making a close pass to Earth, and causing great disturbances from the close encounter. NASA is trying to cover it all up! The aliens of Planet X have been visiting earth for thousands of years, and are about to arrive again![2]

Christians are not immune from getting carried away with fantastic predictions of the end of the world. Many are often more gullible than non-Christians and may be more susceptible to TEOTWAWKI deception. After all, the Bible predicts the second coming of Christ, the mother of all TEOTWAWKI events.

The most noteworthy example in recent times is the sad story of Harold Camping, president of Family Radio, and former host of the network's "Open Forum." Camping guaranteed that the rapture would occur on May 21, 2011 and the whole universe would be destroyed on October 21, 2011. His many followers promoted his ideas without critical analysis of his methods or testing his claims of special "spiritual" revelation. Many sold their possessions to support the media blitz, and

---

[1] Deut. 32:17; 1 Cor. 10:20

[2] http://www.xfacts.com

quit their jobs to spend their last days on Earth promoting Camping's prognostication.

Following the complete failure on May 21 and October 21, Camping tried hard to maintain the loyalty of his followers, claiming that the failed predictions were not his fault. God misled Camping for His own grand and mysterious purpose.[3] For several months after the final failure, Camping continued to release messages which deflected his responsibility for this mess with no sincere apology. All that changed, however, in May 2012.

A loyal supporter of Camping and host of one of Family Radio's regular radio programs was Gunter von Harringa. Gunter's son, Guy, worked at Family Radio headquarters as an internet technician and labored hard to get the message of May 21 and October 21 to as many as possible.[4] In the aftermath of Camping's failed predictions Guy became very despondent, according to acquaintances.[5] On May 14, 2012,

---

[3] Harold Camping, Family Radio website, 12-04-2011: *"We now believe God led us to those dates, but did not give us complete understanding."* Audio Message #1 (10-28-2011) *"God was in charge of everything. … He allowed everything to happen the way it did without correction, He could have stopped everything if He had wanted to. … God is in charge of this whole business, and we are not."* Audio Message #2 (11-06-2011) *"No one has treated a subject with greater care than we have treated this subject. We have been so careful. But, God didn't open up everything to us."* Audio Message #3 (11-08-2011) *"God has done to us similarly to what He did to a couple of other great men of faith, one being Abraham."*

[4] http://www.youtube.com/watch?v=fjBHWbLpzJc

[5] Matt Tuter posted on Facebook: *"The day before yesterday a despondent young man who worked for Family Radio, and was very close to Harold Camping took his own life. Members of his family blame Harold Camping and the Board of Directors of Family Stations, Inc. That's a good place to start. I may have more to say about this later, but this issue should be put in the face of the people running Family Radio every day until they*

Guy von Harringa committed suicide at the young age of 26.[6] The Delaware County coroner's report said his death was suicide by hanging.[7] In the wake of this tragedy, Harold Camping's messages on Family Radio seem to have taken a much more repentant tone, admitting that he was wrong and the error was his own fault, not God's.

Most Christians gave no heed to Camping's ludicrous interpretations of Scripture or his numerology. He was never seen as within the mainstream of Evangelical Christianity. Yet, many who are considered in the mainstream have given credence to supposed seers of no better repute than Camping: Nostradamus, the Fatima visions of a Catholic teenager, and St. Malachy's alleged list of future popes. Jack Van Impe has made a career out of peddling these kinds of pseudo-seers to predict the time of the "rapture." His track record is no better than Harold Camping's.

The modern Charismatic movement has been spewing out a constant stream of "prophets" with their latest "word from the Lord" or prophetic dream. Scripture says that there will be a great apostasy in the last days brought about by many false prophets using lying signs and wonders.[8] Yet, for decades the Charismatic "prophets" have been promising a great revival which has no basis in Scripture and never seems to materialize (unless you count the laughing-hyena, barking-dog, clucking-chicken, drunken-stupor revivals). There are

---

leave and hand the organization to some people who will run it as intended. Not as the mess from Hell it has become."

[6] http://delgazette.com/2012/05/guy-von-harringa/
[7] https://docs.google.com/file/d/0BzCBYlZYMzxuV0NBbTFybnZLLUk/edit?pli=1
[8] Matt. 7:22-23; Matt. 24:9-15; 2 Thess. 2:9-12

many TEOTWAWKI prophecies and dreams coming from the restored apostles and prophets movement. Many are so bizarre as to boggle the mind. Yet, even the most outrageous modern prophets seem to have his or her own devoted following.[9]

The lunacy is not only on the fringe of the Charismatic movement. Even well-respected pastors of large Charismatic churches have been caught up in it. On March 14, 1993, John J. Hinkle, Charismatic pastor-prophet of Christ Church, Los Angeles, California, created quite a stir in the Charismatic community. Hinkle made the following startling announcement on TBN:

> *"I ask you to open your hearts and souls now and invite the Spirit of the Living God within the depths of your being to listen to the message He gave me. On Thursday night, March 4th, at about two o'clock in the morning, the Lord spoke to me in a very loud firm voice, as clear as a ringing bell and with such power and clarity there was no way to doubt it. I heard it both outside and inside, and I was amazed that it did not wake up my wife Bonnie as well, but it didn't. This is the startling message that He gave me, 'ON THURSDAY, JUNE THE 9TH, I WILL RIP THE EVIL OUT OF THIS WORLD.' There was no doubt that this was the voice of God speaking. But my human mind asked a question, and I asked the Lord, 'Lord, you said in your Word that no man would know the hour of the Second Coming.' Instantly the voice spoke and said to me, 'I did not say the Second Coming,' and in that moment I knew it was going to*

---

[9] Example: Apostle-Prophet, Elizabeth Elijah Nikomia, www.amightywind.com

be a great cleansing and destruction of evil forces and powers in the world. It is not the rapture, but God's love and glory overcoming all evil. … As I sat there shaken by the glory of the Lord, the thought came to check on the date. So I got out of bed and went into the other room, turned on the light and checked the calendar that I had on my desk, and at first I was shocked, for June 9th is on a Wednesday, not Thursday. I thought, 'Is Satan trying to play some kind of trick?' But before I could complete the thought, that great wonderful voice spoke again and said: 'Check 1994.' I did, and there it was, Thursday, June 9th, 1994. The hair on the back of my neck literally stood up and the power of the Lord just shook me as I stood there."[10]

Needless to say, when Friday, June 10, 1994 finally arrived, evil was still in business. Nothing was ripped out of the world except Hinkle's "prophet" credentials.

Even the respected late pastor-prophet, David Wilkerson, has offered his own dreams and visions of the end times. All of his prognostications have, so far, failed to materialize as he foresaw. Since 1992 Wilkerson has repeatedly predicted the imminent burning of New York City and cities all across America in widespread race riots and mayhem.[11] These were not long term prognostications, but alleged imminent disasters for which his followers were instructed to

---

[10] Hinkle, John J, Sermon: "Thy Kingdom Come," Christ Church TV, broadcast on TBN, 3-14-1993,
http://www.triumphalrestoration.com/kingdomcome.html
[11] http://www.garynorth.com/public/4712.cfm
http://asterisktom.xanga.com/695057610/david-wilkerson-false-prophecies--unscriptural-teaching/

immediately store up food and supplies. No one would dispute the great evangelistic work Wilkerson has done in New York City. But, his wrong views on eschatology – claiming that America is Mystery Babylon[12] – combined with his Charismatic excesses seem to have led him astray. In turn, he has led others astray with his repeated false predictions.

Ronald Weinland's book, "2008, God's Final Witness," has recently become compost fodder. Weinland is the head of the Church of God, PKG,[13] a splinter group from Herbert W. Armstrong's World-Wide Church of God, former publisher of "The Plain Truth" magazine. In 1956, Armstrong predicted the second coming would occur in 1975.[14] Weinland is following in his mentor's footsteps.

Weinland claimed that the last 3.5 years of great tribulation began in 2008. His deadline for the second coming of Christ was May 27, 2012.[15] How did he arrive at this date? God told Him, of course.

> *"It is now with boldness, confidence and great clarity that I give to you what God has given me. I am to announce, through God's direct revelation, that I am one of those two witnesses. The other witness will be revealed to the world*

---

[12] In Wilkerson's book, "Set the Trumpet to Thy Mouth," he wrote, *"I believe modern Babylon is present-day America, including its corrupt society and its whorish church system. No other nation on earth fits the description in Revelation 18 but America, the world's biggest fornicator with the merchants of all nations."* (pg. 3-4)

[13] http://www.the-end.com/RonaldWeinland.asp

[14] Armstrong, Herbert W., 1975 in Bible Prophecy, Radio Church of God, 1956

[15] http://the-end.com *"The year 2008 marked the last of God's warnings to mankind and the beginning in a countdown of the final three and one-half years of man's self-rule that will end by May 27, 2012."*

11

during the time of the great tribulation—within the final three and one-half years of man's era. During that period of time, we will, together, completely fulfill all that God has given us to witness to this whole earth. Then, at the end, we will die in the streets of Jerusalem; and finally, exactly three and one-half days later, we will be resurrected (Revelation 11). The world will see this resurrection via television. At this same time Jesus Christ will appear in the heavens above the earth as He is returning to take the reigns [sic] of man's government on earth."[16]

*"For that matter, none of the Book of Revelation was written so that just anyone reading it could understand. It has to be revealed through God's servants, and most of it was reserved to be revealed at this end-time through God's end-time prophet—**me**."[17]*

Weinland's prophesied day of Christ's return came and went without event. So he borrowed a page from Harold Camping's playbook, claiming that the coming was "spiritual" instead of physical.

"May 27th has come and gone, so how can I say this is still the day of Christ's return? The answer is a matter of God's revelation which is spiritual in nature, but having a definite physical outcome. It is prophetic. I did not know that when I stated this was the "day" of Christ's coming. I viewed it in a physical manner until God revealed that it was spiritual."[18]

---

[16] Weinland, Ronald, 2008, God's Final Witness, pp. 16-17

[17] Weinland, Ronald, 2008, God's Final Witness, p. 87

[18] Ronald Weinland's blog, May 30 entry. http://www.ronaldweinland.com/

Just like Harold Camping, Weinland blamed God instead of himself.

> *"As God inspired what was recorded in this book, He also revealed the date He wanted the world to have that would be the time of His Son coming to earth as King of kings. It is a prophetic day that God gave. It was the day of Pentecost, 2012. But, **we were not told by God that this was a prophetic day**, so we prepared for a literal one-day event on a physical plane. May 27, 2012, has come and gone, but it is the prophetic day of Christ's coming."*[19]

It is hard to believe that anyone of sound mind would give such "prophecies" the time of day. But what is even more mind-boggling is that many of the followers of these false prophets are gullible enough to buy their excuses and continue following them.

The throngs of disillusioned devotees in the wake of these failed predictions have no one to blame but themselves. All of these failures can be traced to one thing: **placing confidence in unreliable sources**. So many Christians seem to have taken up dumpster-diving to find any scraps of information on when Christ will return. One wonders what happened to the old-fashioned idea of relying on the genuine Apostles and Prophets in the Bible!

For those who are convinced that Christians will remain on earth through the final seven years of tribulation, the desire to know how close we are is very powerful indeed. The recent

---

[19] ibid

reelection of Barack Obama is being seen by many Christians as the point of no return for America. And it very well may be. The hope of deliverance from the avalanche of filth and corruption through Christian political activism has been crushed. Our hope ought to be in the coming of Jesus Christ and His righteous Kingdom. Yet, turning to dubious and unreliable sources to discern the time of His coming is a huge mistake, a sure recipe for disaster.

Deception is Satan's greatest tool.[20] If *"the truth shall make you free,"*[21] then the lie will make you its prisoner. Our enemy obscures the truth by flooding the field with counterfeits. There is counterfeit science, and there are counterfeit spiritual gifts, counterfeit prophets, counterfeit gospels, counterfeit christs, and counterfeit TEOTWAWKI scenarios. And of course, there are counterfeit claims to have discovered the time of Christ's return. And many Christians are prisoners to these lies.

In promoting many erroneous dates for Christ's return, Satan's goal is no doubt to get as much mileage as possible out of the "Boy Who Cried Wolf" effect. If enough people cry "wolf" prematurely few will pay any heed when the real wolf is spotted. The vast majority of Christians will be caught unprepared. That is Satan's goal. So, he offers many false eschatological viewpoints and many false TEOTWAWKI scenarios to occupy those who intuitively know that we are approaching the end of the age. He discourages others from

---

[20] 2 Cor. 4:4
[21] John 8:32

following this line of inquiry by pointing to the long list of failed date-setters of the past.

Many great minds have pursued the Holy Grail of biblical prophecy – the date of Christ's return. Sir Isaac Newton was a brilliant scientist and biblical scholar. He spent many years pursuing the date of Christ's return by studying both Bible prophecy and biblical chronology. But in the end, he too failed.

Even Daniel himself pursued this line of inquiry, seeking to know the time of Christ's coming Kingdom. He quizzed *"one like a Son of Man"*[22] about the time of the coming Kingdom and was told why it was being withheld from him. *"Go your way, Daniel, for the words are closed up and sealed till the time of the end. Many shall be purified, made white, and refined, but the wicked shall do wickedly; and none of the wicked shall understand, but the wise shall understand."*[23] It was not yet the "time of the end" in Daniel's day, nor in Newton's day. God was keeping this information sealed up and out of reach. Why? It is because this information is very, very dangerous.

Satan knows that the end of his reign of terror is near. He intends to go out with a bang and take as many with him as possible into the flames.[24] He knows that those things which were sealed up in Daniel's day will indeed be unsealed in the

---

[22] The same person who appeared to Daniel as a human (Dan. 10:16,18) is the one who gave him the information in Dan. 10-12. This was almost certainly Christ Himself, whom Daniel spoke of previously using the same language (Dan. 7:13).

[23] Dan. 12:9-10

[24] Rev. 12:12

last days, and *"the wise shall understand."*[25] So, he has been busy preempting the revelation of this critical information at the proper time by spinning fables, by making a mockery of truth, and by offering "revelation" through demonic encounters for those all too eager for something mystical.

The rest of Christendom – those too sophisticated for inquiry into this line of questioning – Satan dissuades from pursuing the time of Christ's return by insisting that it is wrong and sinful to do so. Without fail, modern nay-sayers wheel out their standard "proof text" to refute any attempt to discern the time of Christ's return – *"But of that day and hour no one knows, not even the angels of heaven, but My Father only."*[26] This verse is called upon to instantly stop in their tracks anyone who has the audacity to try to discover when the Master is coming, and to dissuade the sheep from paying attention to anything that smacks of "date setting."

Yet, the student of early Christian literature will find just the opposite opinion among the earliest Christian writers, those who had close linkage to the Apostles. They unanimously believed and taught that the second coming of Jesus Christ to establish His Kingdom on the earth would occur exactly six thousand years from creation.[27] According to this system, knowing what year it is on a continuous calendar that begins with creation is all that is necessary to know the year of Christ's return. A few early Christian writers attempted to develop a chronology from creation to their day. But,

---

[25] Daniel 12:10
[26] Matt 24:36
[27] See chapter 2

unfortunately, they had defective source material for their chronology work.[28]

How do we account for the disparity between what the disciples of the Apostles taught and what modern Evangelical Christians teach about the possibility of knowing the time? First, the early Christians did not hold to either of the popular contemporary eschatological systems: dispensationalism (with its imminent pretribulation rapture) or amillennialism (with its imminent end of the world).

The eschatology of the earliest Christians is called "chiliasm" (kill'-ee-az-um), from the Greek word "chilia" which means "a thousand." The term "chiliasm" is equivalent to our modern term, "millennialism." However, it does not only refer to the "millennium" of Christ's reign mentioned in Revelation 20. It refers to the division of man's time on earth into a series of six millennia of living under the curse followed by the Millennial Sabbath – Christ's reign in Jerusalem. This view was simpler than modern dispensational premillennialism, holding all of the following truths:

- All of the redeemed, both Jew and Gentile, form a single body of God's people with a single inheritance.
- The inheritance of Christians after the resurrection is not heaven, but the restored Land that God promised to Abraham and to his 'Seed' on the restored earth.
- The 70th week of Daniel is entirely future, a seven-year period of trouble just before Jesus returns. This period consists of 3.5 years for the two prophets of Revelation

---

[28] See chapter 7

11 to preach repentance, followed by 3.5 years of the Antichrist's reign of terror.

- The resurrection and gathering of Christians to meet Christ is after the great tribulation.
- The future reign of Christ on earth from Jerusalem over the nations is the seventh millennium, after exactly six millennia from creation have been completed.

The earliest Christian writers defended these points of doctrine using many passages of Scripture. Contrary to what is claimed by modern prophecy experts, the early Christians had a well-developed systematic eschatology. Yet, the standard reaction by modern Christian leaders to chiliasm is to either dismiss it or disparage it. They claim the earliest Christian writers were not as sophisticated as modern scholars and prophecy experts.[29] Why? It is simply because modern commentators do not like what they had to say; primitive Christianity does not look like modern Christianity. There are major differences between what the earliest

---

[29] Disparaging the earliest Christian writers because of disagreement with their chiliasm is nothing new. When amillennialism began to displace the ancient eschatology just a few centuries after the Apostles, writers actually disparaged some of the early Christian martyrs and students of the Apostles who had taught it. For example, when writing about Papias (a student of John's who had interviewed many of the hearers of Jesus), Eusebius (AD 263 – 339) wrote: *"The same writer [Papias] gives also other accounts which he says came to him through unwritten tradition, certain strange parables and teachings of the Savior, and some other more mythical things. To these belong his statement that there will be a period of some thousand years after the resurrection of the dead, and that the kingdom of Christ will be set up in material form on this very earth. I suppose he got these ideas through a misunderstanding of the apostolic accounts, not perceiving that the things said by them were spoken mystically in figures. For he appears to have been of very limited understanding, as one can see from his discourses."* (Eusebius, Church History, Bk. III, ch. xxxix)

Christians taught and what most Evangelical Christian leaders teach. These differences touch on many important topics, including the nature of the Trinity, baptism, the security of the believer, the nature of free will, the fate of the wicked, and of course eschatology. Someone must be wrong. Our scholarly veneer and sophistication (as well as our modern world view) drive us to conclude that the early Christians must have been wrong. Yet, such a supposition seems highly suspect given the fact that these primitive Christian apologists were personally acquainted with the Apostles and/or their oral tradition.

Perhaps, instead of chasing the latest TEOTWAWKI fad, Charismatic self-appointed prophet, or prophecy hype from Jack and Rexella, we ought to take a second look at the primitive Christian works, this time with a humbler attitude. Why not, given all the tomfoolery spewing from all these other sources?

The early Christian apologists were intimately familiar with the historical context and culture in which the New Testament was written, and with many very ancient manuscripts of the Old Testament which we do not have. They spoke the same Greek language in which the New Testament was written. The Apostles and their associates placed some of these men in leadership of the early churches they founded. Should we not consider what the most ancient Christian pastors had to say about the end of the age given the great advantages they possessed, rubbing shoulders with the Apostles? If we assume that they were misguided and largely in error, would that not strongly imply that the Apostles failed in their primary mission to make disciples and ground them in the teachings of Christ?[30] The Apostles claimed to have done just that, delivering to the next generation the perfected Christian Faith. Paul wrote, *"For I have not shunned to declare to you the whole counsel of God."*[31] This was *"the Faith once for all delivered to the saints,"* for which Jude insisted that the early Christians must "earnestly contend."[32] And contend they did! This is why we have so much of their written apologetic material which scrutinized the many Gnostic heresies, and defended what had been handed down by the Apostles and was universally believed in all of the apostolic churches.

We humans tend to place far too much trust in our own intellect and the work of modern scholarship. We neglect to consider the wisdom of the ancient Christians who stared down wild beasts and stood unflinching as they were burned at the stake for their faithfulness to Christ. We cannot see our own flaws in thinking. We cannot discern the fact that we are basing our views on certain unproven presuppositions and a great deal of accumulated theological baggage. Are we so arrogant as to think that we can discern the Apostles' teaching from evaluating the New Testament in a vacuum? Why do we suppose that the men personally trained by the Apostles, who were entrusted with the apostolic writings and oral tradition, whom the Apostles gave the responsibility to lead the local congregations, were unsophisticated and ignorant men? Yes, that is precisely what most modern Christian leaders do, brushing aside these ancient witnesses as irrelevant and naïve

---

[30] Matt. 28:18-20
[31] Acts 20:27
[32] Jude 1:3

simply because they may not happen to agree with some of their denomination's distinctive doctrines. A humbler approach would be to admit that we are the ones who are naïve. We are the ones separated from the Apostles by nearly two millennia, living in a far different culture and speaking a completely different language. Yet we often act arrogantly and full of ourselves, like the teenager who thinks the wisdom of his parents and grandparents is outdated.

This book is a call to take a second look at the most ancient Christian eschatology – chiliasm – which places Christ's return at the end of the sixth millennium, at the dawning of the Millennial Sabbath.

The first part of this book will show that the Millennial Week concept was unanimously taught by the earliest Christians, those with direct and indirect linkage to the Apostles. Next, it will be shown that this view is indeed apostolic, holding up under the test of inspired Scripture. Why this view was eventually abandoned and replaced with amillennialism's "Kingdom now" theory will be fully explained and documented. Finally, the ancient Millennial Week eschatology will be taken to its logical conclusion. A continuous chronology and calendar spanning from creation to the second coming of Christ will be presented. The chronology will be based exclusively on chronological information from the Bible, which is the only reliable chronological data available. This is something unique to this book. Previous attempts to establish such a chronology have typically used a combination of biblical and secular historical data. Finally, this chronology will narrow down the timeframe when the Millennial Sabbath will begin.

The author realizes that he is treading treacherous waters, and is not anxious to be lumped in with the long list of failed prognosticators. He claims no supernatural prophetic gift or "word from the Lord." This book is the result of many years of research, both of the early Church as well as biblical chronology. Therefore, everything presented in this book can be objectively tested. As with any human endeavor, mistakes are always possible. The reader is encouraged to be skeptical, to check out the things presented here against original sources. Plenty of footnotes have been provided to help verify claims. Do not accept the conclusions of this book unless you are compelled to do so by overwhelming evidence which you have verified independently. Ultimately, God's Word will judge us all, including our motives. *"Test all things; hold fast what is good."*[33]

---

[33] 1 Thess. 5:21

Chapter 1
KNOWING the DAY and HOUR

Before we begin any attempt to discern the time of the Lord's return, we first need to clear the most important major hurdle. Is this information indeed something that God wants His people to possess as we near the time of the end? Or does God want us to be completely surprised by the coming of Jesus Christ? Is seeking such knowledge misguided or even sinful as many claim?

Certainly, desiring to know when the Messiah's Kingdom would appear was not sinful, but honorable. This information was sought by all the holy prophets and by the Apostles.

> *1 Peter 1:10-12*
> *10 Of this salvation the prophets have **inquired and searched carefully**, who prophesied of the grace that would come to you, 11 searching what, **or what manner of time**, the Spirit of Christ who was in them was indicating when He testified beforehand the sufferings of Christ **and the glories that would follow**. 12 To them it was revealed that, not to themselves, but to us they were ministering the things which now have been reported to you through those who have preached the gospel to you by the Holy Spirit sent from heaven — **things which angels desire to look into**.*

Daniel is a perfect example of a prophet's search for such knowledge. He was given time-related information about both Christ's first and second comings in response to his inquiries. In the Seventy Weeks prophecy of Daniel 9, he was told exactly how long it would be until the Messiah came and was crucified almost 500 years before it occurred! This information was intended to give the Jews adequate warning of when the Messiah would appear. Yet, they did not heed Daniel, they did not keep up a continuous biblical calendar, and consequently, they did not recognize the Messiah when He came. If they had heeded Daniel's prophecy and kept a continuous calendar they would have known the exact year of Jesus' crucifixion.

Jesus condemned them for not knowing the time of His appearance from Daniel's prophecy. *"For days will come upon you when your enemies will build an embankment around you, surround you and close you in on every side, and level you, and your children within you, to the ground; and they will not leave in you one stone upon another, **because you did not know the time of your visitation**."*[34] God held the Jews accountable for understanding the prophecies, keeping an accurate chronology, and knowing the time when Jesus would appear the first time. Why would He expect anything less from us regarding His second coming? He has given us in Scripture all of the necessary information to know when it will occur. According to Daniel, it will be uncovered at the proper time to the "wise" who will understand and prepare.

In Daniel 12, Daniel was told that there would be 1290 days from the "abomination of desolation" until the "end" (when Daniel would be resurrected and receive his allotted

---

[34] Luke 19:43-44

24

inheritance). When pressing the "Son of Man"[35] further concerning the time of the end, Daniel was told by Him: *"Go your way, Daniel, **for the words are closed up and <u>sealed till the time of the end</u>**. Many shall be purified, made white, and refined, but the wicked shall do wickedly; and none of the wicked shall understand, **<u>but the wise shall understand</u>**."*[36] The time of Christ's return was to be revealed at some point just prior to the end, and the wise[37] will indeed understand.

Referring to this same chapter, the "Son of Man" told His disciples, *"when you therefore shall see the abomination of desolation spoken of by Daniel the Prophet standing in the holy place, **<u>let the reader understand</u>**."*[38] Thus, Jesus was pointing all of His followers to Daniel 12 to understand the exact time of His return after this major event occurs. It is obvious, then, that knowing the time of Jesus' return is not impossible at any time before Jesus appears. Christians will certainly know the exact date once this event occurs if they are "wise" and have paid the least attention to Jesus' instructions, Daniel's prophecy, and can count to 1290. If Daniel's prophecy is to be unsealed in the last days, we ought to be just as eager as Daniel himself was to gain this knowledge at the appropriate time.

How then should we understand Jesus' statement, *"But of that day and hour no one knows, not even the angels of heaven, but My Father only"*?[39] First, we need to understand what Jesus meant

---

[35] Daniel 10:16,18

[36] Dan 12:9-10

[37] The Hebrew word translated "wise" actually means "perceptive."

[38] Matt. 24:15

[39] Matt 24:36

by the terms, "day" and "hour." Most take both terms literally. Yet, the word "hour" does not necessarily refer to the position of the little hand on the clock. On several other occasions Jesus used the term "hour" to refer to an extended period of time.[40] In fact, He used the term "hour" to describe the whole time of great tribulation. *"Because you have kept My command to persevere, I also will keep you from the **hour** of trial which shall come upon the whole world, to test those who dwell on the earth."*[41] Revelation also refers to this as the "hour of His judgment."[42] It also indicates that the ten kings will reign for "one hour with the Beast,"[43] referring to the final 3.5 years of great tribulation.

"No one knows" does not necessarily mean "no one can ever know," as we have been led to believe by the prophecy talking heads. The misrepresentation of this passage comes from both pretribulationists (whose entire eschatological system depends on the "rapture" being "imminent") and amillennialists (who also teach an "imminent" end of the world). The modern understanding of this verse is supposed to prove that Jesus' coming could occur at any moment. Yet, this is a completely unbiblical view, since the very same passage places Christ's coming after a long sequence of signs, ending with a cosmic display beyond imagination.[44] Until that whole sequence of events plays out, Jesus is not coming back to earth, period. But, once the sequence begins with the

---

[40] John 4:21,23; John 12:23,27; John 16:32
[41] Rev. 3:10
[42] Rev. 14:7
[43] Rev. 17:12
[44] Matt. 24:29-31

26

"abomination of desolation," we will know exactly when He is coming.

When Jesus said this, no one had seen or discovered "that day and hour." The "day" is the specific day of His coming. The "hour" is the general timeframe of tribulation events in which this entire series of signs will play out including His coming *"immediately after the tribulation of those days."*[45] Obviously, Jesus was not speaking of a pretribulation rapture. Pretribulationists who use this passage to prove that the rapture is "imminent" are grossly mishandling the text. Let's consider this passage carefully, in context.

> *Matt. 24:36, 42-44*
> *36 "But of that day and hour no one knows, not even the angels of heaven, but My Father only. ...*
> *42 Watch therefore, for you do not know what hour your Lord is coming. 43 But know this, that if the master of the house had known what hour the thief would come, he would have watched and not allowed his house to be broken into. 44 Therefore you also be ready, for the Son of Man is coming at an hour you do not expect.*

Two things need our attention here. The first is the English translation which is imprecise in virtually all English translations. The second is the illustration Jesus used to drive His point home to the disciples. Let's take the translation issue first. Below is my literal translation from the Greek text.

---

[45] Matt. 24:29

Matt 24:36, 42-44

*36 "Yet about that day and the hour no one **has seen**,[46] not the messengers of the heavens, except My Father only." …*

*42 "Watch then, because **you have not seen**[47] which hour your Master is coming.*

*43 Yet, know this: that if the home owner **had seen**[48] which watch the thief is coming, he would have watched and would not have permitted his house to be plundered. 44 **Through this**[49] **you also become ready**,[50] because you do not know which hour the Son of Man is coming."*

First, notice that Jesus did not say that no one knows (present tense) the time. Nor did He say that no one will know (future tense). And He certainly did not say that it was impossible to discover the time. He said that no one had discovered (seen or perceived) the time. He used the perfect tense of the verb "see." The perfect tense refers to a past completed action with the results continuing to the present. The result of observing something in the past is the present knowledge of what was seen. This verb refers to current knowledge based on past observation or discovery. When Jesus said this, no one had yet seen or discovered either the specific day or the general timeframe when Jesus would come.

---

[46] οιδεν – is the Greek verb for "see" in the perfect tense. The perfect tense in Greek indicates a past completed action with results that continue to the present.

[47] Same as previous note

[48] Here the same verb is in the pluperfect tense.

[49] δια τουτο

[50] γινεσθε - Strong's #1096, refers to something coming into being. The noun "genesis" comes from this root verb. The verbs for "generate" and "beget" are also closely related. Here it is in the imperative mood – a command.

Verse 42 begins with a command to watch because they had not yet discovered the "hour" (meaning the whole tribulation timeframe).

Verse 43 begins with a command to pay attention to something very important – "Yet know this." Jesus then gave a hypothetical parable. *"Because if the home owner had seen* __*which watch*__ *the thief is coming, he would have watched and would not have permitted his house to be plundered."*

Notice carefully that this parable does not concern knowing the exact time, but knowing the timeframe (which watch). The term "watch" as a measurement of time refers to three-hour periods in which the night was divided so that the Roman soldiers could change shifts. The first "watch" was from 6pm to 9pm; the second watch was from 9pm to midnight; the third "watch" was from midnight to 3am; and the fourth "watch" was from 3am to 6am. Thus, in Jesus' parable, the fault of the householder was his ignorance of the three-hour timeframe in which the thief was coming, not the exact time of his arrival.

Also, notice the association between KNOWING and WATCHING. In Jesus' statement, "watching" depends on first "knowing" the timeframe. If the householder had known the timeframe (three-hour watch), he would have watched during it. And if he had watched, he would have avoided disaster by confronting the thief the moment of his arrival. Knowing the timeframe is therefore a prerequisite to watching. And watching is necessary to avoid the plundering of the house. The plundering of his house was the result of not knowing the timeframe, and therefore neglecting to watch during the critical three-hour period. On the other hand, if he had known the timeframe, he would have watched and his house would not have been plundered.

Jesus' parable demonstrates that knowing the timeframe beforehand is good and even essential. Ignorance of the timeframe beforehand is portrayed as being extremely dangerous and potentially disastrous.

Since the disciples had not yet perceived when this timeframe of the tribulation events would occur, they too were vulnerable to the same kind of disaster.

Jesus then gave them this critical command: *"Through this (that is, through this illustration[51]) you also become ready, because you do not know which hour the Son of Man is coming."* Jesus commanded the disciples to use this parable as a mechanism to "become ready." He did not say "be ready," as many translations have it. The Greek words are "γινεσθε ετοιμοι." The verb literally means, *"to cause to be, generate, to become, come into being."*[52] It does not refer to continuing in a static state of readiness, but achieving something they did not yet possess. Jesus told them to achieve a state of readiness which they did not yet possess due to their incomplete knowledge. He meant that His followers must not be like this man (who did not know the timeframe in which

---

[51] Jesus began the parable saying, *"But know **this**: ..."* The pronoun "this" is neuter in gender and points ahead to the whole parable. Immediately after the parable He said, *"through **this** you become ready."* Again, "this" is a neuter pronoun, pointing back to the whole parable.

[52] Strong's #1096

the thief was coming; therefore he did not watch; therefore he suffered great loss). To "become ready" means to discover the timeframe of the tribulation events so that you know when to watch for His coming. When the "abomination of desolation" actually occurs within that timeframe, you will know precisely when He is coming. By doing this, you will avoid the calamity of having your house ransacked.

In the verses which immediately follow, Jesus spoke about His servants whom the Master puts in charge of His other servants, *"to give them their food at the proper time."* What food? He had just commanded them to discover the timeframe of the tribulation events! Thus, if the servants who have been charged with feeding Christ's flock do as Jesus commanded, and they actually discover the critical information in time to prepare their subordinates, (to give them their proper food at the proper time), they will be blessed by the Lord when He returns. Luke's parallel account[53] makes it quite clear that Jesus was addressing these two parables to future Christian pastors and elders who would be charged with shepherding Christ's flock.

Upon hearing Jesus' parable of the man surprised by the thief, and Jesus' command to "become ready," Peter asked Him a critical question. *"Lord, do You speak this parable only to us, or to all?"* Peter wanted to know whether Jesus' parable was meant generally, that each of Christ's followers must discern the time for himself, or specifically for the twelve disciples. Jesus' answer to Peter's question was, neither. It was for the future

---

[53] Luke 12:35-48

pastors and elders who would be appointed to shepherd Jesus Christ's congregations at some time in the future.

> *Luke 12:42*
> *42 And the Lord said, "Who then is that faithful and wise steward, whom his master __will make__ ruler over his __household__, to give them their portion of food in due season?*

Jesus' answer speaks of future appointments of "rulers." These are the elders of the churches who would be charged with both ruling and feeding Christ's flock.[54] His command to discover the timeframe was neither for the Apostles nor for Christians in general. It was for future pastors and elders. These are the ones Jesus commanded to discover the timeframe of end-time events, and feed this necessary food to the flock at the proper time.

Jesus then went on to describe the various rewards and punishments that will be meted out to pastors and elders based on how well they take to heart this parable, preparing Christ's household under their care at the proper time.

> *Luke 12:43-48*
> *43 "Blessed is that servant whom his master will find so doing when he comes. 44 Truly, I say to you that he will make him ruler over all that he has. 45 But if that servant says in his heart, 'My master is delaying his coming,' and begins to beat the male and female servants, and to eat and drink and be drunk, 46 the master of that servant will come on a day when he is not looking for him, and at an hour*

---

[54] Acts 20:28; 1 Peter 5:1-4

when he is not aware, and will cut him in two and appoint him his portion with the unbelievers. 47 And that servant who knew his master's will, and did not prepare himself or do according to his will, shall be beaten with many stripes. 48 But he who did not know, yet committed things deserving of stripes, shall be beaten with few. For everyone to whom much is given, from him much will be required; and to whom much has been committed, of him they will ask the more."

According to Jesus' own words some of the Christian pastors will be *"cut in two and appointed their portion with the unbelievers."* Other pastors will be *"beaten with many stripes"*; others will be *"beaten with few stripes."* But, the *"faithful and wise stewards"* will heed Jesus' parable. They will discern the timeframe of tribulation events and will give His other servants under their care the necessary food at the proper time. And when Jesus returns, He will make them *"ruler over all that he has."*

The servant who says, *"My Master is delaying His coming"* is the Christian pastor who does not heed Jesus' warning. He refuses to discern the time of tribulation in advance and prepare the flock under his care. Instead, he abuses the flock; he "eats and drinks," implying an extravagant lifestyle or business as usual. And he becomes drunk. Drunkenness is a metaphor in Scripture for self-deception.[55] This Christian pastor is condemned for not knowing when the Master is coming. *"The Master of that servant will come on a day when he is not looking for him, and at an hour when he is not aware, and will cut him in two and appoint him his portion with the unbelievers."*

---

[55] Isaiah 19:13-14; Isaiah 28:7-8; Isaiah 29:9-10

This is not an idle threat. And Christian pastors would be prudent to take it very, very seriously. Notice the contrast between the command to "become ready" by discovering the timeframe, and the manner in which Christ's return will catch the unprepared pastor off guard, coming *on a day when he is not looking for him, and at an hour when he is not aware."*

This raises the question of how one is to discover the time of the Lord's coming. The answer is within the context. Jesus had just given them a series of signs that will precede His coming. These are divided into two sections. The first group is called "the beginning of birth pains,"[56] and the second group is called "intense travail."[57] These terms were borrowed from the parable in Isaiah 66. God likened the restoration of Jerusalem and the Promised Land to a woman giving birth.[58] Jesus also likened the "the beginning of birth pains" (the first 3.5 years of the final week) and the "intense travail" (the last 3.5 years) to a fig tree budding.[59] When the tree buds, they knew that summer was near. He then said, *"So you also, when you see all these things, know that it is near — at the doors!"*[60] Thus, Jesus did not tell them exactly when He was coming, but He equipped them with the necessary tools to discover it in plenty of time to give believers "their necessary food at the proper time."

---

[56] Matt. 24:8
[57] Matt. 24:21
[58] Isaiah 66:5-16
[59] Matt. 24:32-33
[60] Matt 24:33

When Paul referred to Jesus' parable of the thief, he indicated that his readers were already equipped to know when the time came.

> *1 Thess. 5:1-6*
> *1 But concerning the times and the seasons, brethren, you have no need that I should write to you. 2* **_For you yourselves know perfectly that the day of the Lord so comes as a thief in the night_**. *3 For when they say, "Peace and safety!" then sudden destruction comes upon them, as labor pains upon a pregnant woman. And they shall not escape. 4* **_But you, brethren, are not in darkness, so that this Day should overtake you as a thief_**. *5 You are all sons of light and sons of the day. We are not of the night nor of darkness. 6 Therefore let us not sleep, as others do, but let us watch and be sober.*

Paul expected that the Thessalonians were perfectly capable of discovering the time since they were "not in darkness" – ignorant of the signs and instructions Jesus gave. He had already instructed them about these things orally.

A short time later, Paul had to readdress this issue because some of the Thessalonian Christians were not nearly as well versed in Jesus' teaching as Paul had supposed. In the second epistle, he got much more specific, describing the two primary signs Jesus had given, the "falling away" (which occurs throughout the "birth pains"[61]) and the revealing of the Man

---

[61] Matt. 24:8-12

35

of Sin (which occurs at the beginning of the "intense travail"[62]).

> *2 Thess. 2:1-5*
> *1 Now, brethren, concerning* **the coming of our Lord Jesus Christ and our gathering together to Him**, *we ask you, 2 not to be soon shaken in mind or troubled, either by spirit or by word or by letter, as if from us, as though the day of Christ had come.*[63]
> *3 Let no one deceive you by any means; for* **that Day will not come unless the falling away comes first, and the man of sin is revealed, the son of perdition**, *4 who opposes and exalts himself above all that is called God or that is worshiped, so that he sits as God in the temple of God, showing himself that he is God.*
> *5 Do you not remember that when I was still with you I told you these things?*

Verse 5 was somewhat of a rebuke for their failing to retain what Paul had taught them. In the previous epistle he expressed confidence that they knew all these things by saying, "*But concerning the times and the seasons, brethren, you have no need that I should write to you. For you yourselves know perfectly that the day of the Lord so comes as a thief in the night.*" Yet, here he had to re-teach something he taught them before, and assumed that they had retained.

Jesus spoke specifically about the revelation of the Man of Sin which would actually reveal the exact date of Christ's return.

---

[62] Matt. 24:15-21

[63] Lit. "has come near" (The KJV renders it, "is at hand.")

Matt 24:15
15 "Therefore when you see the 'abomination of desolation,' spoken of by Daniel the prophet, standing in the holy place (whoever reads, let him understand), …"

Daniel described this event, and was told how long it would be from this event until the resurrection and inheritance. The clause, "whoever reads, let him understand," means whoever reads Daniel's prophecy about this should understand from Daniel how much time there is left.

In the 12th chapter of Daniel, he was told about the coming time of "great travail," much worse than anything before or after. Yet, the Messenger also promised that many would be delivered from the intense trouble by Michael's standing up on their behalf.[64] This was to be followed by the resurrection of the dead to enjoy their inheritance. Daniel then questioned the Messenger about when the "end" of these things would come. He was told: *"Go your way, Daniel, for the words are closed up and sealed till the time of the end. Many shall be purified, made white, and refined, but the wicked shall do wickedly; and none of the wicked shall understand, but the wise shall understand. And from the time that the daily sacrifice is taken away, and the abomination of desolation is set up, there shall be one thousand two hundred and ninety days."[65]*

---

[64] This is the same promise found in Revelation 12. The "woman" is given two wings to fly into the wilderness where God has prepared a place for the angels to provide for her during the last 3.5 years of "intense travail." This woman is the true Church of Jesus Christ. Psalm 91 refers to this as well.

[65] Dan 12:9-11

Therefore, when Paul wrote, *"You yourselves know perfectly that the Day of the Lord so comes as a thief in the night,"* and when he reminded the Thessalonians that our gathering to Christ will not occur until after the Man of Sin has been revealed (as described by Daniel), he was implicitly reminding them that they were aware of the information necessary to calculate the exact day of Christ's return once the sequence of end-time events began to occur. What was needed was to discern the timeframe of tribulation in which one is supposed to "watch" for that critical event, the "abomination of desolation."

It is quite clear from all of these passages that the early Christians had been fully equipped by the Apostles to discern when Christ's coming would become imminent. It is a shame that so many modern Christians are ignorant of these things, and that so many pastors do not teach these essential truths.

Pastors in the end times are commanded by Jesus to discover the timeframe of these events and to prepare the flock under their care. Daniel said that knowledge of the time had been sealed up until "the time of the end." That time is now! Daniel said that the "wicked" will continue to do wickedly. These are some of the servants whom Christ appointed over His flock. They become "wicked servants" by continuing to teach their eschatological fables. Yet, the "wise" will understand. These are the pastors in Jesus' parable who heed His command, discern the time, and prepare the flock under their care.

Why is the penalty so severe for the "wicked servants?" These men are entrusted with the well-being of the Christ's flock, something as precious to God as the blood of His own Son.

*"Therefore take heed to yourselves and to all the flock, among which the Holy Spirit has made you overseers, to shepherd the church of God **which He purchased with His own blood**."*[66] When pastors maliciously fail Jesus' flock, He takes it very seriously. *"Then He said to the disciples, 'It is impossible that no offenses should come, but woe to him through whom they do come! It would be better for him if a millstone were hung around his neck, and he were thrown into the sea, than that he should offend one of these little ones'."*[67]

---

[66] Acts 20:28
[67] Luke 17:1-2

Chapter 2
EARLY CHRISTIAN ESCHATOLOGY

As stated in the introduction, the earliest Christian writers, whose eschatology can be determined with certainty, consistently held to chiliasm – six millennia followed by the Millennial Sabbath.[68] These early writers lived contiguous with the age of the Apostles. Some of them were personally instructed by the Apostles and others who had seen the Lord. They were the early apologists for the Christian Faith, fiercely attacking and overthrowing the emerging Christian-Gnostic cults that sprang up like tares among the wheat. They took seriously the warning of Jude to *"earnestly contend for the Faith which was once for all delivered to the saints."*[69] Their weapons were the sacred Scriptures and the united testimony of apostolic oral tradition preserved by the elders within all the churches personally founded by the Apostles.[70] And many of them sealed their testimony with their own blood.

The earliest Christians' hope was the one found throughout the Old Testament Scriptures and reiterated in the New

---

[68] All of the earliest writers who had any kind of connection to the Apostles or their associates specifically endorsed chiliasm. We have no clear examples of any first or second century writers opposing chiliasm, or offering any theological points which are incompatible with chiliasm. Justin Martyr called the opponents of chiliasm "heretics" (referring to the Gnostic cults) and indicated that they denied the resurrection of the body, which was a cardinal tenet of the Apostolic Faith.

[69] Jude 1:3

[70] See: Irenaeus, Bk I, ch. x; Bk. III, ch. iii-iv; Bk. III, ch. xii; Bk. V, ch. xxxiii

Testament – the resurrection of the flesh and gathering to the permanent Land inheritance, the millennium of Christ's reign over the nations from Jerusalem. The prophets predicted that God would come to live among His people perpetually.[71] Rather than expecting to fly away to heaven at the second coming, the early Christians expected to be caught up in the air to greet Christ at His coming, escort Him back to earth, and receive their inheritance on the restored Land.

Unlike modern dispensationalists who look only to the New Testament for their "blessed hope," the early Christians looked to the Old Testament Scriptures, viewing the New Testament hope as being perfectly compatible with the prophets. According to the earliest Christians, the future hope of the inheritance for Christ's followers is described most clearly in the prophecies of Isaiah and Ezekiel. This hope was found in the coming Kingdom of the Messiah, the resurrection of the body, the restoration of Jerusalem and the Promised Land, the curse removed from the earth, and the redeemed from all ages and nations rejoicing in Jerusalem. This hope came from passages such as the following:

> *Isaiah 66:10-16, 22-24*
> *10 "Rejoice with Jerusalem, And be glad with her, all you who love her; Rejoice for joy with her, all you who mourn for her;*
> *11 That you may feed and be satisfied with the consolation of her bosom, That you may drink deeply and be delighted with the abundance of her glory."*

---

[71] Jer. 3:17; Ezek. 43:7; Ezek. 48:35; Rev. 21:3; Rev. 22:3

12 For thus says the LORD: "Behold, I will extend peace to her like a river, And the glory of the Gentiles like a flowing stream. Then you shall feed; On her sides shall you be carried, And be dandled on her knees.

13 As one whom his mother comforts, So I will comfort you; And you shall be comforted in Jerusalem."

14 When you see this, your heart shall rejoice, And your bones shall flourish like grass; The hand of the LORD shall be known to His servants, And His indignation to His enemies.

15 For behold, the LORD will come with fire and with His chariots, like a whirlwind, To render His anger with fury,

And His rebuke with flames of fire. 16 For by fire and by His sword the LORD will judge all flesh; And the slain of the LORD shall be many. ...

22 "For as the new heavens and the new earth which I will make shall remain before Me," says the LORD, "So shall your descendants and your name remain.

23 And it shall come to pass that from one New Moon to another, And from one Sabbath to another, All flesh shall come to worship before Me," says the LORD.

24 "And they shall go forth and look upon the corpses of the men who have transgressed against Me. For their worm does not die, And their fire is not quenched. They shall be an abhorrence to all flesh."

Ezekiel's closing chapters provide a detailed description of the division of the restored Land among the tribes of Israel after having been brought out of their graves, and a vivid account of restored Jerusalem. *"And the name of the city from that day shall be: 'THE LORD IS THERE.'"*[72]

The early Christians saw harmony between these promises and the New Testament prophecies, including Revelation. They saw themselves as being adopted into Israel, becoming *"heirs according to the promise"* through being baptized into Christ.[73] Consequently, the eternal Land promises were for the faithful of Israel and the Gentile nations, all who belong to Christ.

The Land Promise Hope of the Abrahamic Covenant

The hope of Israel was the hope of Abraham, to finally receive the Promised Land as an eternal inheritance. Israel's inheritance under the Law was temporary and conditional. Moses repeatedly recorded God as saying that Israel's tenancy in the Land was only as long as they kept His Law.[74] They were merely tenants in God's Land. *"The land shall not be sold permanently, for the land is Mine; for you are strangers and sojourners with Me."*[75] He reserved the right to evict them. But the Abrahamic promise of the Land was unconditional and forever. After Israel's temporary inheritance of the Land under Joshua, Scripture promised a second permanent inheritance of the same Promised Land under the new "Joshua" (Yeshua).

---

[72] Ezekiel 48:35
[73] Gal. 2:26-29
[74] Lev. 18:24-29; Lev. 20:22-24; Deut. 4:25-27,40; Deut. 5:32-33; Deut. 28:20-21, 63-68
[75] Lev 25:23-24

Isaiah 60:18-21

18 Violence shall no longer be heard in your land, Neither wasting nor destruction within your borders; But you shall call your walls Salvation, And your gates Praise.

19 "The sun shall no longer be your light by day, Nor for brightness shall the moon give light to you; But the LORD will be to you an everlasting light, And your God your glory. 20 Your sun shall no longer go down, Nor shall your moon withdraw itself; For the LORD will be your everlasting light, And the days of your mourning shall be ended. 21 Also your people shall all be righteous; **They shall inherit the land forever**, *The branch of My planting, The work of My hands, That I may be glorified.*

Isaiah 61:1-7 LXX

1 The Spirit of the Lord is upon me, because he has anointed me; he has sent me to preach glad tidings to the poor, to heal the broken in heart, to proclaim liberty to the captives, and recovery of sight to the blind; 2 to declare the acceptable year of the Lord, and the day of recompense; to comfort all that mourn; 3 that there should be given to them that mourn in Sion glory instead of ashes, the oil of joy to the mourners, the garment of glory for the spirit of heaviness: and they shall be called generations of righteousness, the planting of the Lord for glory.

4 And they shall build the old waste places, they shall raise up those that were before made desolate, and shall renew the desert cities, even those that had been desolate for many generations. 5 And strangers shall come and feed thy flocks, and aliens shall be thy ploughmen and vine-dressers.

6 But ye shall be called priests of the Lord, the ministers of God: ye shall eat the strength of nations, and shall be admired because of their wealth.

*7 **Thus shall they inherit the land a second time**,[76] and everlasting joy shall be upon their head."*

Psalm 37 also spoke of this second, permanent Land inheritance.

Psalm 37:9-11

9 For evildoers shall be cut off; But those who wait on the LORD, They shall inherit the earth.

10 For yet a little while and the wicked shall be no more; Indeed, you will look carefully for his place, But it shall be no more.

11 But the meek shall inherit the earth, And shall delight themselves in the abundance of peace.

Jesus quoted this Psalm in His Sermon on the Mount, and applied it to His disciples.[77]

The early Christians based their hope of inheritance squarely on the permanent and unconditional Land promise of the Abrahamic Covenant. Irenaeus,[78] disciple of Polycarp, disciple of John, articulated this hope plainly.

---

[76] This is the literal translation of the Greek Septuagint. The Hebrew text can be translated either, "they will inherit double" or "they will inherit twice." Since the Jewish translators of the LXX rendered the Hebrew as "a second time," this is the preferred translation.

[77] Matt. 5:5

[78] Irenaeus (AD 120-202) was a student of Polycarp, who was a student of John. Polycarp was appointed bishop of the Church in Smyrna by the Apostles

"Thus, then, the promise of God, which He gave to Abraham, remains steadfast. For thus He said: 'Lift up thine eyes, and look from this place where now thou art, towards the north and south, and east and west. For all the earth which thou seest, I will give to thee and to thy seed, even forever.' And again He says, 'Arise, and go through the length and breadth of the land, since I will give it unto thee;' and [yet] he did not receive an inheritance in it, not even a footstep, but was always a stranger and a pilgrim therein. And upon the death of Sarah his wife, when the Hittites were willing to bestow upon him a place where he might bury her, he declined it as a gift, but bought the burying-place (giving for it four hundred talents of silver) from Ephron the son of Zohar the Hittite. Thus did he await patiently the promise of God, and was unwilling to appear to receive from men, what God had promised to give him, when He said again to him as follows: 'I will give this land to thy seed, from the river of Egypt even unto the great river Euphrates.' If, then, God promised him the inheritance of the land, yet he did not receive it during all the time of his sojourn there, it must be, that together with his seed, that is, those who fear God and believe in Him, he shall receive it at the resurrection of the just. For his seed is the Church, which receives the adoption to God through the

---

(Irenaeus, Bk. III, Ch. iii, 4). He led that congregation when Jesus dictated the letter to Smyrna contained in Rev. 2. Jesus had no criticism, only praise for the faithfulness of this church. His prophetic exhortation to this church, *"Do not fear any of those things which you are about to suffer. … Be faithful until death, and I will give you the crown of life,"* (Rev. 2:10) was certainly heeded by Polycarp. He stood boldly and confidently on the pyre, without being bound to the stake, while he was burned to death for his faithfulness to Christ. His pupil, Irenaeus, carried on his master's teachings and included some of them in his own works. Irenaeus also died for his faith along with many of the members of the church he pastored in Lyons, Gaul.

Lord, as John the Baptist said: 'For God is able from the stones to raise up children to Abraham.' Thus also the apostle says in the Epistle to the Galatians: 'But ye, brethren, as Isaac was, are the children of the promise.' And again, in the same Epistle, he plainly declares that they who have believed in Christ do receive Christ, the promise to Abraham thus saying, 'The promises were spoken to Abraham, and to his seed. Now He does not say, And of seeds, as if [He spake] of many, but as of one, And to thy seed, which is Christ.' And again, confirming his former words, he says, 'Even as Abraham believed God, and it was accounted to him for righteousness. Know ye therefore, that they which are of faith are the children of Abraham. But the Scripture, fore-seeing that God would justify the heathen through faith, declared to Abraham beforehand, That in thee shall all nations be blessed. So then they which are of faith shall be blessed with faithful Abraham.' Thus, then, they who are of faith shall be blessed with faithful Abraham, and these are the children of Abraham. Now God made promise of the land to Abraham and his seed; yet neither Abraham nor his seed, that is, those who are justified by faith, do now receive any inheritance in it; but they shall receive it at the resurrection of the just. For God is true and faithful; and on this account He said, 'Blessed are the meek, for they shall inherit the earth.'"[79]

The Land promise was not only to Abraham's Seed, but to Abraham personally.[80] Therefore, its fulfillment absolutely requires the resurrection of Abraham. The promise of God to Abraham, then to Isaac, then to Jacob, that they would receive

---

[79] Irenaeus, *Against Heresies*, Bk. V, ch. xxxii
[80] Genesis 13:15,17; Genesis 17:8

the Land as a permanent possession could not be fulfilled by the Israelites merely inheriting the Land under Joshua. God's promise absolutely required the resurrection of Abraham, Isaac, and Jacob, because they did not inherit the Land while they were alive, but only lived in it as pilgrims and aliens.[81]

As the previous quotation of Irenaeus shows, the early Christians believed that Abraham's Seed, which Genesis states was to be the heir of the Land permanently along with Abraham, is Christ and all who are baptized into Him. This was derived from Galatians 3:16-29, which makes this exact claim.

The first few generations of post-Apostolic Christians held the hope of the Abrahamic permanent possession of the Land. It was for Abraham and his Seed through Jesus Christ; and it was to be realized at the resurrection. Justin[82] agreed with Irenaeus on the destiny of the redeemed.

> *"What larger measure of grace, then, did Christ bestow on Abraham? This, namely, that He called him with His voice by the like calling, telling him to quit the land wherein he dwelt. And He has called all of us by that voice, and we have left already the way of living in which we used to spend our days, passing our time in evil after the fashions of the other inhabitants of the earth;* **and along with Abraham we shall inherit the holy Land, when we shall receive the**

---

[81] Acts 7:1-5

[82] Justin Martyr (AD 110-165) was a former philosopher turned Christian. He became the earliest apologist for the Christian Faith, defending Christianity to the Roman Senate and to the Greek pagans. He was born only about 15 years after John wrote Revelation.

inheritance for an endless eternity, being children of Abraham through the like faith."[83]

"But why do you not similarly investigate the reason why the name of Oshea the son of Nave (Nun), which his father gave him, was changed to Jesus [Joshua]? But since not only was his name altered, but he was also appointed successor to Moses, being the only one of his contemporaries who came out from Egypt, he led the surviving people into the Holy Land; and as he, not Moses, led the people into the Holy Land, and as he distributed it by lot to those who entered along with him, so also Jesus the Christ will turn again the dispersion of the people, and will distribute the good Land to each one, though not in the same manner. For the former gave them a temporary inheritance, seeing he was neither Christ who is God, nor the Son of God; but the latter, after the holy resurrection, shall give us the eternal possession."[84]

A Posttribulation Resurrection and Gathering

There was absolutely no debate among the early Christians whether the resurrection and gathering of Jesus' elect was pretribulational or posttribulational. All of them were posttribulational, seeing Christians enduring the brief tribulation under Antichrist prior to Christ's second coming.

Irenaeus: (AD 120-202)

"In a still clearer light has John, in the Apocalypse, indicated to the Lord's disciples what shall happen in the last times,

---

[83] Justin, Dialogue with Trypho, ch. cxix
[84] Justin, Dialogue with Trypho, ch. cxiii

and concerning the ten kings who shall then arise, ... 'These have one mind, and give their strength and power to the beast. These shall make war with the Lamb, and the Lamb shall overcome them, because He is the Lord of lords, and King of kings. ... And they shall lay Babylon waste, and burn her with fire, and shall give their kingdom to the beast, and put the Church to flight. After that they shall be destroyed by the coming of our Lord.'"[85]

"For all these and other words were unquestionably spoken in reference to the resurrection of the just, which takes place after the coming of Antichrist, and the destruction of all nations under his rule; in [the times of] which [resurrection] the righteous shall reign on the earth, waxing stronger by the sight of the Lord: and through Him they shall become accustomed to partake in the glory of God the Father, and shall enjoy in the kingdom intercourse and communion with the holy angels, and union with spiritual beings; and those whom the Lord shall find in the flesh, awaiting Him from heaven, and who have suffered tribulation, as well as escaped the hands of the Wicked one."[86]

Tertullian:[87] (AD 145-220)

"In the Revelation of John, again, the order of these times is spread out to view, which 'the souls of the martyrs' are taught to wait for beneath the altar, whilst they earnestly

---

[85] Irenaeus, Against Heresies V, XXVI, 1

[86] Irenaeus, Against Heresies V, XXXV, 1

[87] Tertullian (AD 145-220) was a presbyter of the North African Church of Carthage. He is considered the founder of Latin Christianity, being the first to write a defense of Christianity in the Latin language.

pray to be avenged and judged: (taught, I say, to wait), in order that the world may first drink to the dregs the plagues that await it out of the vials of the angels, and that the city of fornication may receive from the ten kings its deserved doom, and that the beast Antichrist, with his false prophet may wage war on the Church of God; and that, after the casting of the devil into the bottomless pit for a while, the blessed prerogative of the first resurrection may be obtained from the thrones; and then again, after the consignment of him to the fire, that the judgment of the final and universal resurrection may be determined out of the books. Since, then, the Scriptures both indicate the stages of the last times, and concentrate the harvest of the Christian hope in the very end of the world."[88]

"Now the privilege of this favor [the resurrection] awaits those who shall at the coming of the Lord be found in the flesh, and who shall, owing to the oppressions of the time of Antichrist, deserve by an instantaneous death, which is accomplished by a sudden change, to become qualified to join the rising saints; as he writes to the Thessalonians: 'For this we say unto you by the word of the Lord, that we which are alive and remain unto the coming of the Lord shall not prevent them which are asleep. For the Lord Himself shall descend from heaven with a shout, with the voice of the archangel, and with the trump of God: and the dead in Christ shall rise first: then we too shall ourselves be caught up together with them in the clouds, to meet the Lord in the air: and so shall we ever be with the Lord.'"[89]

---

[88] Tertullian, On the Resurrection of the Flesh, XXV
[89] Tertullian, On the Resurrection of the Flesh, XLI

Hippolytus:[90] (AD 170-236)

"It is proper that we take the Holy Scriptures themselves in hand, and find out from them what, and of what manner, the coming of Antichrist is; on what occasion and at what time that impious one shall be revealed; and whence and from what tribe (he shall come); and what his name is, which is indicated by the number in Scripture; and how he shall work error among the people, gathering them from the ends of the earth; and (how) he shall stir up tribulation and persecution against the saints; and how he shall glorify himself as God; and what his end shall be; and how the sudden appearing of the Lord shall be revealed from heaven; and what the conflagration of the whole world shall be; and what the glorious and heavenly kingdom of the saints is to be, when they reign together with Christ; and what the punishment of the wicked by fire."[91]

"With respect to his name, it is not in our power to explain it exactly, as the blessed John understood it and was instructed about it, but only to give a conjectural account of it; for when he appears, the blessed one will show us what we seek to know. ... Wherefore we ought neither to give it out as if this were certainly his name, nor again ignore the fact that he may not otherwise be designated. But having the mystery of God in our heart, we ought in fear to keep faithfully what has been told us by blessed prophets, in order that when

---

[90] Hippolytus (AD 170-236) was a student of Irenaeus, who was a student of Polycarp, who was a student of John. He was a presbyter and possibly bishop of the church in Rome. He was martyred in AD 236.

[91] Hippolytus, Treatise on Christ and Antichrist, 5

those things come to pass, we may be prepared for them, and not be deceived. For when the times advance, he too, of whom these things are said, will be manifest."[92]

Cyprian:[93] (AD 200-258)

"[T]he Lord hath foretold that these things would come. With the exhortation of His forseeing word, instructing, and teaching, and preparing, and strengthening the people of His Church for all endurance of things to come. He predicted and said that wars, and famines, and earthquakes, and pestilences would arise in each place; and lest an unexpected and new dread of mischiefs should shake us, He previously warned us that the adversary would increase more and more in the last times."[94]

"For you ought to know and to believe, and hold it for certain, that the day of affliction has begun to hang over our heads, and the end of the world and the time of Antichrist to draw near, so that we must all stand prepared for the battle;'"[95]

"Nor let any one of you, beloved brethren, be so terrified by the fear of future persecution, or the coming of the threatening Antichrist, as not to be found armed for all things by the evangelical exhortations and precepts, and by the heavenly warnings. Antichrist is coming, but above him

---

[92] Hippolytus, Treatise on Christ and Antichrist, 50

[93] Cyprian was bishop of Carthage (N. Africa), and was martyred for his faith in AD 258.

[94] Cyprian, Treatise VII, 2

[95] Cyprian, Epistles of Cyprian, LV, 1,2

comes Christ also. The enemy goeth about and rageth, but immediately the Lord follows to avenge our sufferings and our wounds."[96]

Victorinus:[97] (AD ?-304)

"He speaks of Elias the prophet, who is the precursor of the times of Antichrist, for the restoration and establishment of the churches from the great and intolerable persecution."[98]

"The woman clothed with the sun, and having the moon under her feet, and wearing the crown of twelve stars upon her head, and travailing in her pains, is the ancient Church of fathers, and prophets, and saints, and apostles ..."[99]

"He shall cause also that a golden image of Antichrist shall be placed in the temple at Jerusalem, and that the apostate angel should enter, and thence utter voices and oracles. ... [T]he Lord, admonishing His churches concerning the last times and their dangers, says: 'But when ye shall see the contempt which is spoken of by Daniel the prophet standing in the holy place, let him who readeth understand.'"[100]

---

[96] Cyprian, Epistles of Cyprian, LV, 7,8

[97] Victorinus was bishop of the church in Poetovio (modern Ptuj in Slovenia), who flourished about AD 270. His surviving works are commentaries on Genesis and Revelation. He was martyred during the persecutions of Diocletian in AD 304.

[98] Victorinus, Commentary on the Apocalypse, 7:2

[99] Victorinus, Commentary on the Apocalypse, 12:1

[100] Victorinus, Commentary on the Apocalypse, 13:13

"The little season signifies three years and six months, in which with all his power the devil will avenge himself under Antichrist against the Church."[101]

The 70th Week of Daniel

Like modern dispensationalists, the chiliast interpretation of the 70th week of Daniel was a seven year period at the close of this age. The first half contains the preaching of the two witnesses, and the last half contains the Antichrist's rule. They believed that the Temple would be rebuilt, and the Antichrist would defile it in the middle of the 70th week.

Irenaeus: (AD 120-202)

"This he does, in order that they who do [now] worship the devil by means of many abominations, may serve himself by this one idol, of whom the apostle thus speaks in the second Epistle to the Thessalonians: 'Unless there shall come a failing away first, and the man of sin shall be revealed, the son of perdition, who opposeth and exalteth himself above all that is called God, or that is worshipped; so that he sitteth in the temple of God, showing himself as if he were God.' The apostle therefore clearly points out his apostasy, and that he is lifted up above all that is called God, or that is worshipped — that is, above every idol — for these are indeed so called by men, but are not [really] gods; and that he will endeavor in a tyrannical manner to set himself forth as God.

"Moreover, he (the apostle) has also pointed out this which I have shown in many ways, that the temple in Jerusalem was made by the direction of the true God. For the apostle

---

[101] Victorinus, Commentary on the Apocalypse, 20:1-3

himself, speaking in his own person, distinctly called it the temple of God. Now I have shown in the third book, that no one is termed God by the apostles when speaking for themselves, except Him who truly is God, the Father of our Lord, by whose directions the temple which is at Jerusalem was constructed for those purposes which I have already mentioned; in which [temple] the enemy shall sit, endeavoring to show himself as Christ, as the Lord also declares: 'But when ye shall see the abomination of desolation, which has been spoken of by Daniel the prophet, standing in the holy place (let him that readeth understand), then let those who are in Judea flee into the mountains; and he who is upon the house-top, let him not come down to take anything out of his house: for there shall then be great hardship, such as has not been from the beginning of the world until now, nor ever shall be.'"[102]

"[T]hat is, the earthly Jerusalem, … Which also he shall do in the time of his kingdom: he shall remove his kingdom into that city, and shall sit in the temple of God, leading astray those who worship him, as if he were Christ. To this purpose Daniel says again: 'And he shall desolate the holy place; and sin has been given for a sacrifice, and righteousness been cast away in the earth, and he has been active, and gone on prosperously.' … And then he points out the time that his tyranny shall last, during which the saints shall be put to flight, they who offer a pure sacrifice unto God: 'And in the midst of the week,' he says, 'the sacrifice and the libation shall be taken away, and the abomination of desolation shall be brought into the temple: even unto the consummation of

---

[102] Irenaeus, Against Heresies, Book V, XXV,1&2

the time shall the desolation be complete.' Now three years and six months constitute the half-week."[103]

Hippolytus: (AD 170-236)

"For when the threescore and two weeks are fulfilled, and Christ is come, and the Gospel is preached in every place, the times being then accomplished, there will remain only one week, the last, in which Elias will appear, and Enoch, and in the midst of it the abomination of desolation will be manifested, viz., Antichrist, announcing desolation to the world...."[104]

"But it becomes us further diligently to examine and set forth the period at which these things shall come to pass, and how the little horn shall spring up in their midst. For when the legs of iron have issued in the feet and toes, according to the similitude of the image and that of the terrible beast, as has been shown in the above, (then shall be the time) when the iron and the clay shall be mingled together. Now Daniel will set forth this subject to us. For he says, 'And one week will make a covenant with many, and it shall be that in the midst (half) of the week my sacrifice and oblation shall cease.' By one week, therefore, he meant the last week which is to be at the end of the whole world of which week the two prophets Enoch and Elias will take up the half. For they will preach 1,260 days clothed in sackcloth, proclaiming repentance to the people and to all the nations. For John says, 'And I will give power unto my two witnesses, and they shall prophesy a

---

[103] Irenaeus, Against Heresies, Book V, XXV, 2
[104] Hippolytus, On Daniel, II, 22

thousand two hundred and threescore days, clothed in sackcloth.' That is the half of the week whereof Daniel spake. 'These are the two olive trees and the two candlesticks standing before the Lord of the earth. And if any man will hurt them, fire will proceed out of their mouth, and devour their enemies; and if any man will hurt them, he must in this manner be killed.'"[105]

"Now concerning the tribulation of the persecution which is to fall upon the Church from the adversary, John also speaks thus, 'And I saw a great and wondrous sign in heaven; a woman clothed with the sun, ... And to the woman were given two wings of a great eagle, that she might fly into the wilderness, where she is nourished for a time, and times, and half a time, from the face of the serpent.' That refers to the one thousand two hundred and threescore days (the half of the week) during which the tyrant is to reign and persecute the Church.... These things then, being come to pass, beloved, and the one week being divided into two parts, and the abomination of desolation being manifested then, and the two prophets and forerunners of the Lord having finished their course, and the whole world finally approaching the consummation, what remains but the coming of our Lord and Saviour Jesus Christ from heaven, for whom we have looked in hope."[106]

"For he says, 'I shall make a covenant of one week, and in the midst of the week my sacrifice and libation will be removed.' For by one week he indicates the showing forth of the seven

---

[105] Hippolytus, Treatise on Christ and Antichrist, 43, 47
[106] Hippolytus, Treatise on Christ and Antichrist, 60, 61, 64

years which shall be in the last times. And the half of the week the two prophets, along with John, will take for the purpose of proclaiming to all the world the advent of Antichrist, that is to say, for a thousand two hundred and sixty days clothed in sackcloth; and they will work signs and wonders with the object of making men ashamed and repentant, even by these means, on account of their surpassing lawlessness and impiety. And if any man will hurt them, fire will proceed out of their mouth, and devour their enemies. 'These have power to shut heaven, that it rain not' in the days of the advent of Antichrist, 'and to turn waters into blood, and to smite the earth with all plagues as often as they will.' And when they have proclaimed all these things they will fall on the sword, cut off by the accuser. And they will fulfill their testimony, as Daniel also says; for he foresaw that the beast that came up out of the abyss would make war with them, namely with Enoch, Elias, and John, and would overcome them, and kill them, because of their refusal to give glory to the accuser. That is the little horn that sprang up. And he, being lifted up in heart, begins in the end to exalt himself and glorify himself as God, persecuting the saints and blaspheming Christ."[107]

"And at first, indeed, that deceitful and lawless one, with crafty deceitfulness, will refuse such glory; but the men persisting, and holding by him, will declare him king. And thereafter he will be lifted up in heart, and he who was formerly gentle will become violent, and he who pursued love will become pitiless, and the humble in heart will become haughty and inhuman, and the hater of unrighteousness will

---

[107] Hippolytus, Appendix to the Works of Hippolytus, XXI

persecute the righteous. Then, when he is elevated to his kingdom, he will marshal war; and in his wrath he will smite three mighty kings, — those, namely, of Egypt, Libya, and Ethiopia. And after that he will build the temple in Jerusalem, and will restore it again speedily, and give it over to the Jews. And then he will be lifted up in heart against every man; yea, he will speak blasphemy also against God, thinking in his deceit that he shall be king upon the earth hereafter forever; not knowing, miserable wretch, that his kingdom is to be quickly brought to nought, and that he will quickly have to meet the fire which is prepared for him, along with all who trust him and serve him. For when Daniel said, 'I shall make my covenant for one week,' he indicated seven years; and the one half of the week is for the preaching of the prophets, and for the other half of the week — that is to say, for three years and a half — Antichrist will reign upon the earth. And after this his kingdom and his glory shall be taken away. Behold, ye who love God, what manner of tribulation there shall rise in those days, such as has not been from the foundation of the world, no, nor ever shall be, except in those days alone. Then the lawless one, being lifted up in heart, will gather together his demons in man's form, and will abominate those who call him to the kingdom, and will pollute many souls."[108]

The Millennial Week & Sabbath Rest

The primary component of chiliasm, which is critical to our study of chronology and discovering the time of Jesus' return, is the belief in the Millennial Week. The whole time of man's struggle under the curse was confined to six millennia. The

---

[108] Hippolytus, Appendix to the Works of Hippolytus, XXV

seventh millennium, the Sabbath Rest, was the one thousand year reign of Christ over the nations from Jerusalem. In fact, the term "chiliasm" (meaning "millennialism") referred to these seven millennia, not just the "Millennium" of Christ's reign over the nations. The Millennial Week eschatology was an inseparable part of early Christian eschatology. In the following quotation from Irenaeus, all of the essential elements of chiliasm can be seen tied together. This is early Christian eschatology in a nutshell:

- the future gathering of Jesus' elect after a brief period of persecution by the Antichrist
- the future hope of the Abrahamic Land inheritance
- the future millennium, *"the rest, the hallowed seventh day,"* after six millennia of man's struggle under the curse.

"But when this Antichrist shall have devastated all things in this world, he will reign for three years and six months, and sit in the temple at Jerusalem; and then the Lord will come from heaven in the clouds, in the glory of the Father, sending this man and those who follow him into the lake of fire; but bringing in for the righteous the times of the kingdom, that is, **the rest, the hallowed seventh day***; and* **restoring to Abraham the promised inheritance***, in which kingdom the Lord declared, that 'many coming from the east and from the west should sit down with Abraham, Isaac, and Jacob.'"*[109]

One can clearly see in this quotation the connection between chiliasm's "seventh day" (seventh millennium) and the

---

[109] Irenaeus, Against Heresies Bk. V, ch. xxx

ultimate fulfillment of the Abrahamic Land inheritance, which includes the gentiles who have become Abraham's seed through Jesus Christ.

The early Christians believed that the seven-day creation week in Genesis one was an accurate historical record. God created everything in six twenty-four hour days. Yet they also understood the creation week to be prophetic. God's six days of labor and His rest on the Sabbath formed a precedent and pattern for His entire plan of redemption. God would instruct and discipline humanity for six millennia, bringing mankind to completion and perfection in the seventh Millennium.

Man's destiny was to take full dominion over the earth, just as He commanded Adam.[110] *"Then God blessed them, and God said to them, 'Be fruitful and multiply; fill the earth and subdue it; have dominion over the fish of the sea, over the birds of the air, and over every living thing that moves on the earth'."*[111] Yet, because of man's sin and the curse placed on the creation, man is not yet fit to reign over God's creation. As Hebrews says, *"For in that He put all in subjection under him, He left nothing that is not put under him. But now we do not yet see all things put under him."*[112] Christ came to make man fit for his destiny, *"leading many sons to glory."*[113] Man will ultimately enjoy God's "rest" in the

---

[110] Barnabas, VI, *"But He said above, 'Let them increase, and rule over the fishes.' Who then is able to govern the beasts, or the fishes, or the fowls of heaven? For we ought to perceive that to govern implies authority, so that one should command and rule. If, therefore, this does not exist at present, yet still He has promised it to us. When? When we ourselves also have been made perfect [complete] to become heirs of the covenant of the Lord."*

[111] Gen 1:28

[112] Heb. 2:8

[113] Heb. 2:9-10

Millennial Sabbath, when Jesus Christ returns to restore Jerusalem, rule the nations, and rid the Earth of its curse at the end of the sixth millennium.

The week of six millennia plus the Sabbath millennium was held by virtually all of the earliest writers who had any connection whatsoever to the Apostles.

Clement of Rome[114] (AD 30-100) & Justin (AD 110-165)

> *"And the fact that it was not said of the seventh day equally with the other days, 'And there was evening, and there was morning,' is a distinct indication of the consummation which is to take place in it before it is finished, as the fathers declare, especially St. Clement, and Irenaeus, and Justin the martyr and philosopher."*[115]

Papias[116] (AD 70-155)

> *"Taking occasion from Papias of Hierapolis, the illustrious, a disciple of the apostle who leaned on the bosom of Christ, and Clemens, and Pantaenus ... of the Alexandrians, and the wise Ammonius, the ancient and first expositors [of Scripture], who agreed with each other, who understood the*

---

[114] Clement of Rome knew the Apostle Paul, being called by him a "fellow worker" in Phil. 4:3 (Eusebius, History, Book III, ch. iv)

[115] Justin, Frag. XV, Comments by Anastasius about Clement, Irenaeus, and Justin

[116] Papias was one of the Apostle John's students. He was a bishop in the church at Hierapolis while John lived at Ephesus (just a few miles to the north) after his release from Patmos. Papias also had personal contact with others who had heard Jesus teach. He wrote a great deal about chiliasm. Unfortunately, all of his original works are lost. All that remains are references to him and quotations from his works by later writers.

work of the six days as referring to Christ and the whole Church."[117]

Barnabas[118] *(AD 100?)*

"'And God made in six days the works of His hands, and made an end on the seventh day, and rested on it, and sanctified it.' Attend, my children, to the meaning of this expression, 'He finished in six days.' This implieth that the Lord will finish all things in six thousand years, for a day is with Him a thousand years. And He Himself testifieth, saying, 'Behold, today will be as a thousand years.' Therefore, my children, in six days, that is, in six thousand years, all things will be finished. 'And He rested on the seventh day.' This meaneth: when His Son, coming [again], shall destroy the time of the wicked man, and judge the ungodly, and change the sun, and the moon, and the stars, then shall He truly rest on the seventh day."[119]

---

[117] Fragments of Papias, IX

[118] Early Christian writers attributed this epistle to Barnabas, Paul's companion (see: Tertullian, On Modesty, ch. xx; Clement of Alexandria, Stromata, Bk II, ch. xx). It was held in extremely high regard, so much so, that it was included along with the inspired New Testament books in some early Christian copies of the Scriptures (e.g. Codex Siniaticus). In general, the book seems to have been written to counter the Judaizing tendencies by Jewish Christians. One striking feature of this epistle is its clear dependence on the book of Hebrews, using very similar arguments and terminology. As will be demonstrated in later chapters, chiliasm itself was rooted largely in the teaching of the fourth chapter of Hebrews.

[119] Epistle of Barnabas, XV

Irenaeus: (AD 120-202)

"[He gives this] as a summing up of the whole of that apostasy which has taken place during six thousand years.[120] For in as many days as this world was made, in so many thousand years shall it be concluded. And for this reason the Scripture says: 'Thus the heaven and the earth were finished, and all their adornment. And God brought to a conclusion upon the sixth day the works that He had made; and God rested upon the seventh day from all His works.' This is an account of the things formerly created, as also it is a prophecy of what is to come. For the day of the Lord is as a thousand years; and in six days created things were completed: it is evident, therefore, that they will come to an end at the sixth thousandth year ... the whole apostasy of six thousand years, and unrighteousness, and wickedness, and false prophecy, and deception; for which things' sake a cataclysm of fire shall also come [upon the earth]."[121]

"These are [to take place] in the times of the kingdom, that is, upon the seventh day, which has been sanctified, in which God rested from all the works which He created, which is the true Sabbath of the righteous, which they shall not be engaged in any earthly occupation; but shall have a table at hand prepared for them by God, supplying them with all sorts of dishes."[122]

---

[120] The 6,000 years are counted from the fall of man, when the curse was put into force and Adam and Eve were expelled from Eden.

[121] Irenaeus, Against Heresies, Bk. V, xxviii

[122] Irenaeus, Against Heresies, Bk. V, xxxiii

Hippolytus: *(AD 170-236)*

"And six thousand years must needs be accomplished, in order that the Sabbath may come, the rest, the holy day on which God rested from all His works. For the Sabbath is the type and emblem of the future kingdom of the saints, when they shall reign with Christ, when He comes from heaven, as John says in his Apocalypse. 'For a day with the Lord is as a thousand years.' Since, then, in six days God made all things, it follows that six thousand years must be fulfilled."[123]

Commodianus:[124] *(AD 240)*

"Adam was the first who fell, and that he might shun the precepts of God, Belial was his tempter by the lust of the palm tree. And he conferred on us also what he did, whether of good or of evil, as being the chief of all that was born from him; and thence we die by his means, as he himself, receding from the divine, became an outcast from the Word. We shall be immortal when six thousand years are accomplished."[125]

"This has pleased Christ, that the dead should rise again, yea, with their bodies; and those, too, whom in this world the fire has burned [martyrs], when six thousand years are completed, ... Those who are more worthy, and who are begotten of an illustrious stem, and the men of nobility

---

[123] Hippolytus, On the HexaËmeron, (Or Six Days' Work), Fragments from Commentaries on Various Books of Scripture

[124] Commodianus was a bishop of a church in North Africa.

[125] Commodianus, Christian Discipline, xxxv

under the conquered Antichrist, according to God's command living again in the world for a thousand years, ... They who make God of no account when the thousandth year is finished shall perish by fire, ... "[126]

Cyprian: *(AD 200-258)*

"It is an ancient adversary and an old enemy with whom we wage our battle: six thousand years are now nearly completed since the devil first attacked man.[127] *All kinds of temptation, and arts, and snares for his overthrow, he has learned by the very practice of long years. If he finds Christ's soldier unprepared, if unskilled, if not careful and watching with his whole heart; he circumvents him if ignorant, he deceives him incautious, he cheats him inexperienced. But if a man, keeping the Lord's precepts, and bravely adhering to Christ, stands against him, he must needs be conquered, because Christ, whom that man confesses, is unconquered. "*[128]

---

[126] Commodianus, Instructions of Commodianus, lxxx

[127] A few writers spoke of the 6,000 years as being nearly complete in their day. These writers thought that the Antichrist was about to appear, after which Christ would return. (Other writers, such as Irenaeus and Hipploytus, expected a considerable delay before Antichrist would appear). The error was based on their use of the Septuagint's erroneous ages of the patriarchs in the Genesis genealogies. The LXX has been systematically altered, adding 100 years per generation to most of the people mentioned when they had their child. The use of such calculations necessarily placed the end of the 6,000 years within a hundred or so years of some of the later writers.

[128] Cyprian, Treatise xi

Methodius:[129] (AD 260-312)

"For since in six days God made the heaven and the earth, and finished the whole world, and rested on the seventh day from all His works which He had made, and blessed the seventh day and sanctified it, so by a figure in the seventh month, when the fruits of the earth have been gathered in, we are commanded to keep the feast to the Lord,[130] which signifies that, when this world shall be concluded in the seventh thousand years, when God shall have completed the world, He shall rejoice in us. ... Then, when the appointed times shall have been accomplished, and God shall have ceased to form this creation, in the seventh month, the great resurrection-day, it is commanded that the Feast of our Tabernacles shall be celebrated to the Lord, of which the things said in Leviticus are symbols and figures."[131]

"For I also, taking my journey, and going forth from the Egypt of this life, ... celebrate with Christ the millennium of rest, which is called 'the seventh day,' even 'the true Sabbath.'"[132]

---

[129] Methodius was a bishop of the churches of Olympus and Patara in Lycia (Turkey), and was martyred for the Faith in AD 312. He was an outspoken opponent and critic of Origen – the enemy of chiliasm. The philosophical speculations and allegorical approach to Scripture made popular by Origen eventually led to the decline and eventual extinction of chiliasm in Christianity.

[130] Feast of Tabernacles

[131] Methodius, Discourse IX, ch. i

[132] Methodius, Discourse IX, ch. v

Lactantius:[133] *(AD 260-330)*

> *"Therefore let the philosophers, who enumerate thousands of ages from the beginning of the world, know that the six thousandth year is not yet completed, and that when this number is completed the consummation must take place, and the condition of human affairs be remodeled for the better ... Therefore, since all the works of God were completed in six days, the world must continue in its present state through six ages, that is, six thousand years. ... And again, since God, having finished His works, rested the seventh day and blessed it, at the end of the six thousandth year all wickedness must be abolished from the earth, and righteousness reign for a thousand years; and there must be tranquility and rest from the labors which the world now has long endured. ... For six thousand years have not yet been completed, and when this number shall be made up, then at length all evil will be taken away, that justice alone may reign."[134]*

Victorinus: *(AD 300?)*

> *"And in Matthew we read, that it is written Isaiah also and the rest of his colleagues broke the Sabbath — that that true*

---

[133] Lactantius *"boldly confessed the Faith amid the fires of the last and most terrible of the great persecutions"* (editor of his works). Justin had written to the Roman Emperor in his day, defending Christianity and overthrowing the pagan gods of the Empire. Lactantius followed in Justin's footsteps, writing to instruct the Emperor Constantine himself in the Christian Faith. He was a Christian teacher of great renown, being charged with the personal instruction of the Emperor Constantine's son, Crispus.

[134] Lactantius, The Epitome of the Divine Institutes, LXX

and just Sabbath should be observed in the seventh millenary of years. Wherefore to those seven days the Lord attributed to each a thousand years; for thus went the warning: 'In Thine eyes, O Lord, a thousand years are as one day.' Therefore in the eyes of the Lord each thousand of years is ordained, for I find that the Lord's eyes are seven. Wherefore, as I have narrated, that true Sabbath will be in the seventh millenary of years, when Christ with His elect shall reign."[135]

"So great a cloud of witnesses" have testified to the eschatology handed down by the Apostles of Jesus Christ. Many were pastors entrusted with the early churches; many were martyrs who sealed their testimony with their own blood. They all believed and taught the same eschatology – chiliasm.

The question that begs to be asked is, why? Where did chiliasm originate? The proverbial elephant in the room is that chiliasm was taught by the Apostles, just as Irenaeus indicated, *"the presbyters, the disciples of the Apostles"* repeated what they had heard from the Apostles.[136] Chiliasm was and is a part of *"the Faith once for all delivered to the saints."*

---

[135] Victorinus, On the Creation of the World
[136] Irenaeus, Against Heresies, Bk. V, ch. xxxvi

Chapter 3
The MILLENNIAL WEEK
in SCRIPTURE

The pervasiveness of the Millennial Week chronology among the early Christian writers close to the Apostles cannot be denied. Many writers mentioned it as fact, but none gave a very full explanation of the biblical support for such a calendar. The primary justification offered was the claim that the creation week was both history and prophecy, and that God reckoned a day as a thousand years based on Psalm 90:4, cited by Peter in 2 Peter 3:8-10.

Why would the early Christians so universally accept this as fact on such apparently flimsy evidence? It is not readily apparent that the seven days of creation in Genesis are both history and a prophetic pattern. The statement in the Psalms, that a day with God is as a thousand years, is insufficient evidence in itself for such a theory. If the Millennial Week chronology was evident from the creation account and Psalm 90:4 alone, surely the Jews would have discerned it from the Hebrew Scriptures or from the Septuagint. Yet, it seems they knew nothing of it. Here is the Septuagint's rendering.

> *Psalm 90:4 LXX My translation*
> *4 Because **a thousand years** in Your sight are as **the day**, the previous day which is past, and a watch in the night.*

This passage draws a correlation between a millennium and *"the day"* from God's perspective. David's intent was that God does not reckon time as do humans. The correlation between a millennium and *"the day"* could just be hyperbole.

Yet, if we take this verse literally it implies that God indeed acknowledges a millennial *"Day."* But there is nothing here to directly suggest that this principle relates to creation, or to a calendar counting down to the coming of Messiah. If there was, surely the Jews would have discovered it.

If Psalm 90:4 is meant literally, that God does indeed reckon time in millennial *"Days,"* where would David have gotten such an idea? The answer is to be found in Genesis.

> *Gen. 2:16-17*
> *16 And the LORD God commanded the man, saying, "Of every tree of the garden you may freely eat; 17 but of the tree of the knowledge of good and evil you shall not eat, <u>for in the DAY that you eat of it you shall surely die</u>."*

Adam did not die within a twenty-four hour "day" of eating the forbidden fruit. Some have tried to explain away God's warning by claiming that only a *sentence* of death was passed on Adam that day, or that he only *began* to die that day. Yet, that is not what the text says. The Hebrew literally says, *"in the day you eat of it, dying you shall die."* The Septuagint renders it, *"in the day you eat of it you shall die by death."*

Some Christian interpreters, realizing the text demands the full execution (not only sentence) of death on that very day, appeal to allegorical interpretation, claiming Adam died "spiritually" that day. Such an interpretation denies any connection to physical death in God's threat. Yet, this clashes with Paul's commentary on the passage. *"Therefore, just as through one man sin entered the world, **and death through sin, and thus death spread to all men**, because all sinned … Nevertheless **death reigned from Adam to Moses**."*[137] Paul was referring to physical death (which reigned from Adam to the Law) as the result of Adam's sin, which was based on God's judgment predicted in Genesis 2:16-17. Paul understood the threat of "death" to Adam to be physical death.

Notice the result of Adam's defiance of God's threat. *"Then to Adam He said, "Because you have heeded the voice of your wife, and have eaten from the tree of which I commanded you, saying, 'You shall not eat of it': … In the sweat of your face you shall eat bread till you return to the ground, for out of it you were taken; **for dust you are, and to dust you shall return**."*[138] There can be no doubt that the last statement, *"for dust you are, and to dust you shall return,"* is precisely the same judgment predicted in God's prior warning: *"for in the day that you eat of it **you shall surely die**."*

Paul was therefore correct in understanding this as a threat of physical death. God stated emphatically that Adam would die physically in the same day that he ate the forbidden fruit. This fact presents us with a conundrum for which there are only two possible solutions: Either God lied to Adam, or the "Day"

---

[137] Rom. 5:12,14
[138] Gen. 2:17,19

that God was referring to was greater than 930 years, the span of Adam's life.

The only way to maintain God's integrity and Paul's interpretation is to understand that the "Day" God spoke of was the first millennium. Adam died just short of the end of the first millennium. The oldest man to ever live, Methuselah, died at 969 years old, also within the millennium in which he was born.

This was the ancient Jewish interpretation of this passage. It is articulated in the Jewish apocryphal book called, "Jubilees," written about 150 years before Christ's birth.[139]

> "… Adam died, and all his sons buried him in the land of his creation, … And he lacked seventy years of one thousand years; **for 'one thousand years are as one day'** in the testimony of the heavens and therefore was it written concerning the tree of knowledge: '**On the day that ye eat thereof ye will die**.' **For this reason he did not complete the years of this day; for he died during it**."[140]

Notice the author's quotation of David's Psalm as the explanation for the "Day" in God's threat to Adam. This connection between the two passages was already well known to Jews long before Jesus' birth.

Early Christians had the same understanding as the Jews — that "the Day" in this passage referred to a millennium, based

---

[139] Machiela, Daniel, The Dead Sea Genesis Apocryphon, p. 16
[140] Book of Jubilees, IV, 29-30

on the same Psalm, as the following quotations from Justin and Irenaeus illustrate.

> "For as Adam was told that **in the day he ate of the tree he would die**, we know that he did not complete a thousand years. We have perceived, moreover, that the expression, **'The day of the Lord is as a thousand years**,' is connected with this subject. And further, there was a certain man with us, whose name was John, one of the apostles of Christ, who prophesied, by a revelation that was made to him, that those who believed in our Christ would dwell a thousand years in Jerusalem."[141]

> "Thus then, **in the day that they did eat, in the same did they die**, ... for since 'a day of the Lord is as a thousand years,' **he did not overstep the thousand years, but died within them, thus bearing out the sentence of sin**. ... [T]hat he [Adam] did not overstep the thousand years, but died within their limit, it follows that, in regard to all these significations, God is indeed true. "[142]

Since God's warning to Adam was true, the opening chapters of Genesis have already defined a "Day" as being equivalent to a millennium from God's perspective. David discerned this from the Genesis account and therefore wrote, *"because a thousand years in Your sight are as the day,"* taking this principle from God's carrying out his threat to Adam in Genesis. It is evident therefore that David's statement is not hyperbole, but was meant literally. God indeed does reckon time in

[141] Justin, Dialogue with Trypho, ch. LXXXI
[142] Irenaeus, Against Heresies V, XXIII, 2

millennial "Days." The first millennial "Day" is to be counted from creation.

However, there is nothing in either Genesis or the Psalms that justifies interpreting the seven days of creation as not only literal history, but also prophecy of a Millennial Week. This is apparently why the Jews did not discover the Millennial Week chronology. To understand the creation week to be prophecy, one needs the teaching of the Apostles in the New Testament.

The Millennial Week was Later Apostolic Teaching

We know that the Apostles spent their lives teaching the early Christians the things Jesus taught, and the things progressively revealed to them by the Holy Spirit after Jesus' ascension.[143] The vast majority of the Apostles' teaching was oral, and never written down. And there is no record of the oral teaching of most of the Apostles. The New Testament only contains small fragments of the teaching and preaching of a few of Jesus' Apostles, primarily Peter, John, and Paul.

There are statements in the New Testament that refer to specific oral teaching by the Apostles for which we have no direct written record. Paul reminded the Thessalonians of his previous oral teaching concerning the one who restrains the revelation of Antichrist.[144] Yet, nothing of this apostolic teaching has survived. He reminded them of things they already knew. Yet we have no record of his prior teaching to them about that subject or the details of that teaching.

---

[143] John 16:12-13
[144] 2 Thess. 2:5-6

In the first chapter, we examined Jesus' instructions to those whom He would appoint over His flock, to discover the time of His coming. He used the hypothetical parable of a man caught off guard by the "thief in the night." Had he known the time the thief was coming, he would have watched and avoided disaster. Watching was something that one could only do once he knew the time. Jesus them told them, "*Through this* [the parable of the man surprised by the thief] *you also become ready, because you do not know which hour the Son of Man is coming.*"

Did the Apostles obey Jesus' command? Did they "become ready" by discovering the time of Jesus' coming? Did they transmit this critical information to their hearers orally? The answer is yes. Both Peter and Paul referred to Jesus' parable of the thief in the night, and in both cases they were reminding their readers of their prior oral teaching – teaching which has not been written down.

The Millennial Week According to Peter

Peter's second epistle was written just before his martyrdom. It was intended to prepare his readers for "*an abundant entrance into the age-enduring Kingdom of our Lord and Savior, Jesus Christ.*"[145]

Peter set out to do this through a brief reminder of what the prophets had spoken about the arrival of Christ's Kingdom and the oral apostolic preaching concerning it.

---

[145] 2 Peter 1:11 my translation

2 Peter 1:12-15

*12 For this reason I will not be negligent to **remind** you always of these things, though **you know** and are established in the present truth. 13 Yes, I think it is right, as long as I am in this tent, to **stir you up by reminding you**, 14 knowing that shortly I must put off my tent, just as our Lord Jesus Christ showed me. 15 Moreover I will be careful to ensure that you always have **a reminder** of these things after my decease.*

2 Peter 3:1-2

*1 Beloved, I now write to you this second epistle (in both of which I stir up your pure minds **by way of reminder**), 2 that you may be mindful of the words which were spoken before by the holy prophets, and of the commandment of us, the apostles of the Lord and Savior.*

Peter's second epistle was a reminder of previous apostolic oral preaching. Peter deemed his last words to be critically important for his readers. This epistle was merely a brief reminder of all the oral apostolic preaching. And this preaching was necessary to ensure *"an abundant entrance into the age enduring Kingdom of our Lord and Savior, Jesus Christ."*[146]

Peter did not even attempt to give a full accounting of the apostolic preaching. That was not the purpose for his written works. He expected a brief reminder to be sufficient to refresh the memories of his hearers. The much larger body of apostolic oral preaching was left by the Apostles in the custody of those faithful chosen men – the elders of the

---

[146] 2 Peter 1:11 my translation

various congregations – to be guarded and faithfully transmitted orally.[147] Thus, it is apparent that Peter trusted these faithful men completely as conduits for the inspired teachings.

Peter reminded his readers that *"the prophetic word"* (the words of the prophets) had been *"confirmed"* when Jesus gave Peter, James, and John a brief glimpse of His coming Kingdom on the Mount of Transfiguration. This confirmation to the Apostles, having been chosen by Jesus to be eyewitnesses of a special preview of His coming Kingdom, was the basis of the apostolic preaching which Peter wanted his readers to recall. It was to assure them of the certainty of the prophecies which had been confirmed through the Transfiguration experience. Let's review Mark's account of that incident before considering Peter's commentary.

> *Mark 8:38 – 9:7 KJV*
> *38 Whosoever therefore shall be ashamed of me and of my words in this adulterous and sinful generation; of him also shall the Son of man be ashamed, **when he cometh in the glory of his Father with the holy angels**.*
> *9:1 And he said unto them, Verily I say unto you, That there be some of them that stand here, which shall not taste of death, **till they have seen the kingdom of God come with power**.*
> *2 And **after six days** Jesus taketh with him Peter, and James, and John, and leadeth them up into an high mountain apart by themselves: and he was transfigured before them. 3*

---

[147] 2 Tim. 2:2

And his raiment became shining, exceeding white as snow; so as no fuller on earth can white them. ...
*7 And there was a cloud that overshadowed them: and a voice came out of the cloud, saying, **This is my beloved Son**: hear him.*

The Mount of Transfiguration experience was a preview of the coming of Christ's Kingdom meant to confirm the prophets' predictions to these disciples. In particular, the voice which came from heaven, *"This is My beloved Son..."* was God's announcing that Jesus was the "Son" of God, the King to be installed on Mount Zion prophesied in Psalm 2.

> *Psalm 2:6-9 LXX (My translation)*
> *6 "But I have been made King by him on Sion his holy mountain, 7 declaring the decree of the Lord: **the Lord said to me, 'You are my Son**, today have I begotten You. 8 Ask of me, and I will give You the nations as Your inheritance, and the ends of the Land for Your possession. 9 You shall shepherd[148] them with a rod of iron; thou shalt shatter them like a potter's vessel."*

In this Psalm, God called Christ His "Son," and announced to Him the inheritance which would be His – to govern all the nations, and to inherit the whole Land. This is Christ's Kingdom, the inheritance, promised to Him by the Father.

Daniel also prophesied that the sovereignty of the whole world would be transferred from the "Ancient of Days" to the "Son of Man."

---

[148] See also the Greek text of Rev. 12:5 & 19:15

Dan. 7:13-14, 27

13 "I was watching in the night visions, And behold, One like the Son of Man, Coming with the clouds of heaven! He came to the Ancient of Days, And they brought Him near before Him.

14 Then to Him was given dominion and glory and a kingdom, That all peoples, nations, and languages should serve Him. His dominion is an everlasting dominion, Which shall not pass away, And His kingdom the one Which shall not be destroyed. ...

27 Then the kingdom and dominion, And the greatness of the kingdoms under the whole heaven, Shall be given to the people, the saints of the Most High. His kingdom is an everlasting kingdom, And all dominions shall serve and obey Him."

On the Mount of Transfiguration, the disciples were given a preview of the Father's transferring the sovereignty of the earth to His Son – a vision of the coming Kingdom.

Immediately after Jesus announced to the disciples that some among them would see the coming of His Kingdom, Mark recorded the fulfillment of that promise: *"after six days Jesus took Peter, James, and John up into a high mountain ... and was transfigured before them."* On the Mount of Transfiguration Peter, James, and John received a vision of the future fulfillment of Psalm 2, vividly experiencing a preview of the coming of Christ and the transfer of the Kingdom to Him. Their experience was not unlike John's later visions on Patmos where he also saw this transfer of sovereignty to Christ in much greater detail.

It is significant that the vision of Jesus' coming Kingdom took place *"after six days"* according to both Matthew and Mark. However, Luke's account seems to present a real problem. *"Now it came to pass, **about eight days after these sayings**, that He took Peter, John, and James and went up on the mountain to pray."*[149] This is sometimes presented as a discrepancy in the Bible. But, it is not; it is deliberate.

Luke was dating the event from the time when Jesus made the prediction. It was literally eight days from the time Jesus made the prediction until they went up to the mountain. Why then do Matthew and Mark say "after six days?" The answer is that Matthew and Mark were counting from the first day of the week – Sunday. Jesus made the statement on a Friday. "After eight days" would be the following Saturday. But Matthew and Mark chose to record the actual day of the week – Saturday – when this vision took place. "After six days" means after the first six days of the week, on the Sabbath Day. Thus both passages are correct. This apparent discrepancy actually shows that the Transfiguration experience occurred on the seventh day of the week, the Sabbath.

The mountaintop transfiguration experience of Peter, James, and John was modeled after Moses' experience on Mount Sinai.

> *Exodus 24:16-18*
> *16 Now the glory of the LORD rested on Mount Sinai, and the cloud covered it six days. And **on the seventh day** He called to Moses out of the midst of the cloud. 17 The sight of*

---

[149] Luke 9:28

the glory of the LORD was like a consuming fire on the top of the mountain in the eyes of the children of Israel. 18 So Moses went into the midst of the cloud and went up into the mountain. And Moses was on the mountain forty days and forty nights.

The seventh day on which Moses ascended Mount Sinai into the midst of the cloud was the weekly Sabbath. This can be shown from Exodus 16. On the 15th day of the second month after the exodus, God promised to provide manna for the Israelites on the morning of the following day.[150] This would continue for six days. On the Sabbath, they were forbidden from collecting the manna. Thus, the 16th day of the month was a Sunday, and the 22nd day was the following Sabbath. The following week was from the 23rd through the 29th. The last day of the second month was the 30th, a Sunday. Exodus 19 tells us that the Israelites arrived at Mount Sinai on the first day of the third month,[151] which would be a Monday.

Moses went part way up the mountain on the same day (Monday) and heard from God.[152] The next day (Tuesday) he climbed down the mountain and told the people what God said.[153] The following day (Wednesday), Moses climbed the mountain again and reported to God what the people had said.[154] God then sent him back down (Thursday) to instruct the people to prepare themselves for His appearance in power on the mountain. Moses descended and instructed the people

---

[150] Exodus 16:1,7
[151] Exodus 19:1
[152] Exodus 19:3-6
[153] vss. 7-8
[154] vss. 8-13

on Thursday that God would come down on Mount Sinai in their sight in a thick cloud on the "third day."[155] On the "third day" (Sunday), God's presence appeared in the thick cloud on the top of Mount Sinai.[156] For six days (Sunday – Friday) the cloud covered the top of Mount Sinai.[157] But, on the seventh day (Saturday), God called Moses to come up into the cloud in the top of the mountain to meet with Him face to face.

In the Transfiguration experience, Jesus took Peter, James, and John up into the mountain on the Sabbath day, into the thick cloud.[158] Why would both of these mountaintop experiences occur on a Sabbath day, when the text in both cases explicitly indicates the concluding of the six previous days of the week? In both cases, man met with God face to face on the Sabbath day and lived. Perfection was completed on the seventh day. The similarity to the six days of creation and Sabbath rest is hard to miss.

Peter himself explained how the Apostles understood what occurred on that *seventh day*. It was a preview of Jesus' coming Kingdom.

> *2 Peter 1:16-19 (My literal translation)*
> *16 For not by following cunningly devised myths did we make known to you the **power** and **coming** of our Lord Jesus Christ, but having become eyewitnesses of His **majesty**. 17 For having received from God the Father honor*

---

[155] vss. 14-15
[156] vs. 16
[157] Exodus 24:16-18
[158] Luke 9:34

*and glory from the voice which came to Him from the magnificent glory: "**This is My beloved Son** in whom I am well pleased." 18 And we heard this voice carried from heaven when we were with Him on the holy mountain.*

*19 And [so] we have the prophetic word confirmed, which you are rightly heeding as a lamp appearing in a dark place **until the Day dawns** and the One clothed with light[159] arises.[160]*

Peter understood that in the Transfiguration experience he had witnessed *"the **power** and **coming** of our Lord Jesus Christ"* in *"His majesty."* The words "power" and "coming" were part of Jesus' initial promise: *"there be some of them that stand here, which shall not taste of death, till they have seen the kingdom of God **come** with **power**."*[161] Mark's Gospel was written from Peter's recollections.[162] Peter obviously thought it necessary to have

---

[159] The Greek word φωσφορος is incorrectly rendered "Daystar" in many translations. The word is not φωσφερος - derived from φως (light) and φερω (bearer) as many lexicons incorrectly suppose. It is φωσφορος derived from φως (light) and φορεω (to be clothed – see: Matt. 11:8; James 2:3). The English word "phosphorus" (a luminescent element) is the direct transliteration of this Greek word, and has precisely the same meaning – to be clothed with light. In the masculine singular form, as it appears in 2 Peter 1:19, it literally means, *"the One clothed with light."* When Peter wrote, *"until that Day dawns, and the One clothed in light arises,"* he was referring to the coming of Christ's Kingdom (the dawning of the "Day"), and to Jesus as He appeared to the three disciples on the Mount of Transfiguration – *"His clothes became shining, exceedingly white, like snow, such as no launderer on earth can whiten them."* The "dawning" and "arising" metaphor Peter used is based on Malachi's prophecy of Christ's Kingdom (that Day), and the arising of the "Sun of Righteousness," who is Jesus Christ, (Mal. 4:1-3).

[160] Most translations add "in your hearts" to the end of verse 20. However, this prepositional phrase is better understood as beginning the next verse. *"In your hearts knowing this first, that no prophecy of Scripture is of any private interpretation."*

[161] Mark 9:1 KJV

[162] Eusebius, Church History, Book II, ch. 15

Mark record that their preview of Jesus' Kingdom took place *"after six days,"* on *the seventh day.*

The Greek word translated "coming" in Peter's explanation is "παρουσια" (par-oo-see'-ya). This is a Greek word that is not found in the Greek Old Testament. It is a special term borrowed from the Greeks and Romans. It did not merely refer to any "arrival," but to the arrival of a dignitary in pomp and celebration. It was the normal term used in secular Greek for the triumphal return of kings from conquering their enemies.[163] Such processions would be accompanied by many people who went out to meet and greet him, and then escort him into the city. This word became a technical term referring to Jesus' second coming in glory as King.[164] It is never used of His first coming. Thus, when Peter wrote that he, James, and John had witnessed *"the power and παρουσια of our Lord Jesus Christ"* in "His majesty," they were plainly saying that they had been eyewitnesses of the triumphal return of the King to take the Kingdom, when they *"were with Him on the holy mountain."*

Peter then referred to the future arrival of the Kingdom as the dawning of *"that Day."*[165] Like Genesis 2, Peter established a precedent, using the word *"Day"* in reference to the Kingdom, which Revelation identifies as a millennium.[166] The apostolic eyewitness testimony to this event was "the prophetic word confirmed." That is, the prophecies of Psalm 2 and Daniel 7

---

[163] Kittle, Gerhard, Theological Dictionary of the New Testament, Vol. V, 859-860
[164] Matt. 24:3,27,37,39; 1 Cor. 15:23; 1 Thess. 2:19; 1 Thess. 3:13; 1 Thess. 4:15; 1 Thess. 5:23; 2 Thess. 2:1,8,9; James 5:7-8; 2 Pet. 3:4,12; 1 Jn. 2:28
[165] 2 Pet. 1:19
[166] Rev. 20:1-5

were confirmed to these three disciples through this unique experience. The Apostles' eyewitness testimony to this fact was intended to provide for Christians *"a lamp appearing in a dark place **until the Day dawns** and the One clothed with light arises."* The dawning of "the Day" is the arrival of Christ's Millennial reign over the nations. Thus, "the Day" in this passage also refers to a thousand years.

In the third chapter Peter went beyond merely referring to Christ's reign over the nations as "the Day." He also applied the same principle outlined Psalm 90:4, that a day is as a thousand years, to the period between Jesus' ascension and His second coming. He gave a countdown to the Messianic "Day" in millennial "Days."

> *2 Peter 3:3-4, 8-10*
> *3 knowing this first: that scoffers will come in the last days, walking according to their own lusts, 4 and saying, "Where is the promise of His coming [παρουσια]? For since the fathers fell asleep, all things continue as they were from the beginning of creation." ...*
> *8 But, beloved, do not forget this one thing, that **with the Lord one day is as a thousand years, and a thousand years as one day**. 9 The Lord is not slack concerning His promise, as some count slackness, but is longsuffering toward us, not willing that any should perish but that all should come to repentance. 10 But the day of the Lord will come as a thief in the night..."*

Note that Peter reminded his readers of something they already knew – *"do not forget this one thing."* He wanted them to recall the previous oral apostolic teaching about Psalm 90:4, and its application to Christ's return, explaining the delay. Thus Peter and his readers not only viewed the future reign of Christ over the nations as a millennial "Day," but they also categorized the time preceding Christ's return in millennial "Days" as well.

Peter began this chapter saying that his purpose was to remind his readers of *"the words which were spoken before by the holy prophets, and of the commandment of us, the apostles of the Lord and Savior"*[167] (the apostolic preaching). The word *"commandment"* (Greek – "εντολη") was just used only three verses earlier to refer to the totality of the apostolic preaching.

The second epistle of Peter strongly suggests chiliasm's millennial week. Peter referred to the Apostles' vision of Christ's Kingdom on the Mount of Transfiguration as occurring *"after six days,"*[168] (after the six days of the week, on the Sabbath). He referred to the dawn of *"that Day,"* using the word "Day" in reference to Christ's coming Kingdom. Peter's apostolic preaching and testimony about Christ's second coming was based on this event which confirmed the Old Testament prophecies. And he explained the delay in the coming of Christ's Kingdom in terms of millennial Days, referring his readers to David's Psalm that a day in God's reckoning is a millennium.

---

[167] 2 Peter 3:2

[168] I say Peter referred to the transfiguration being after six days because it is contained in Mark's account. Mark was written as the recollections of Peter's preaching according to Eusebius' Church history (Bk II, ch. xv). That the preview of Christ's Kingdom took place "after six days" was therefore a part of Peter's apostolic preaching, about which he reminded his readers.

Peter did not attempt to explain the full apostolic teaching on this subject in his epistle. Rather, he said that his purpose was only to offer a brief reminder of the previous apostolic preaching which provided confirmation and explanation of the prophets. All of this strongly suggests that Peter taught the millennial week chronology. Virtually all of the necessary components are there. The only thing lacking is specific mention of the total number of millennial Days, the direct connection to the seven days of the week. Yet, that this occurred "after six days" already implies this. There would be no reason to do this if Peter merely meant to remind them of previous apostolic teaching. It is apparent that Peter's last recorded words, what he wished to stress to the early churches, concerned the affirmation of what the prophets taught about the coming of Christ's Kingdom, that Jesus had provided proof and confirmation to His Apostles, and that the remaining time until it would come is to be measured in millennial Days.

Finally, notice that Peter also reminded his readers of Jesus' parable of the "thief in the night" in the same passage.

> *2 Peter 3:8-10a*
> *8 But, beloved, do not forget this one thing, that with the Lord one day is as a thousand years, and a thousand years as one day. 9 The Lord is not slack concerning His promise, as some count slackness, but is longsuffering toward us, not willing that any should perish but that all should come to repentance.*
> *10 But **the day of the Lord will come as a thief in the night**, ...*

It has been almost two "Days" since Jesus ascended to heaven. As will be shown in a later chapter, the prophets told us how many millennial "Days" would intervene between Jesus' ascension and Israel's healing and restoration at Christ's return.

The Millennial Week According to Paul

Hebrews was one of Paul's last epistles. In chapters 3-4, he expounded upon two Old Testament texts which refer to Christ's coming Kingdom as *"the seventh day,"* the *"Sabbath,"* and *"God's Rest."* He stated plainly that the creation week in Genesis refers to God's future Sabbath Rest in which believers will share. His two prophetic texts were Psalm 95:8-11 and Genesis 2:2-3. The two passages that Paul had before him when writing Hebrews 3-4 were as follows:

> *Psalm 95:8-11 LXX (My translation)*
> 8*"This day, if you hear His voice, you should not harden your hearts as in the provocation, as in the day of testing in the wilderness 9 where your fathers tried me, they tested Me and saw My works. 10 Forty years I was disgusted with that generation. And I said, 'They are always straying in their heart and they do not know my ways,' 11 as I swore in My anger whether they shall enter into My rest."*

> *Genesis 2:2-3 LXX*
> *2 And God finished on the sixth day his works which he made, and he ceased on the seventh day from all his works which he made. 3 And God blessed the seventh day and sanctified it, because in it he ceased from all his works which God began to do.*

Psalm 95 was an exhortation by David to Israel not to follow the example of their forefathers "this day," when God's people would be given a second opportunity to inherit the Promised Land. David understood that Israel had failed to realize the promise to Abraham of the eternal land inheritance. He foresaw the ultimate fulfillment of the permanent Abrahamic land inheritance as future.[169] David warned against repeating the Kadesh Barnea "rebellion" when Israel wandered in the wilderness for forty years until that whole generation died off. Only their children went into the land that God promised to Abraham. And even then, they did not attain under Joshua the permanent rest and possession of the land God promised to Abraham and his Seed. Israel was ejected from the land during the Babylonian captivity and again in AD 70.

In Hebrews 3-4, Paul turned to Psalm 95 and Genesis 2:2-3, using these two texts to repeat and emphasize David's warning. Like David, he reminded his readers of the future promise of the eternal land inheritance, which he called the *"Sabbath Rest,"* and the *"seventh day."*

> *Hebrews 3:5 – 4:11 (My translation)*
> *5 And Moses was indeed faithful in all his household as a servant, as a witness of what would be spoken later. 6 But Christ is as a Son over His own household, of whose household we are if we clutch the confidence and rejoicing of*

---

[169] cf. Gen. 13:15, 17:8 & Psalm 37

the confirmed hope[170] unto the consummation,[171] 7 according to which[172] the Holy Spirit says:

> *[Quoting Psalm 95] "This day, if you hear His voice, 8 you should not harden your hearts as in the provocation, as in the day of testing in the wilderness 9 where your fathers tried me, they tested Me and saw My works. 10 Forty years I was disgusted with that generation. And I said, 'They are always straying in their heart and they do not know my ways,' 11 as I swore in My anger whether they shall enter into My Rest."[173]*

12 Beware brothers, if at that time[174] a wicked heart of unbelief shall[175] be found in any of you, in apostatizing from the living God. 13 But encourage one another each day until[176] that [day] which is called 'This day,' so that none from among you may be hardened by the seduction of sin. 14 For we have become partakers of the Christ[177] if we should

---

[170] "The confirmed hope" is the permanent land inheritance of the Abrahamic Covenant. It was confirmed by God's oath to Abraham (Heb. 6:13-20). It was taken hold of and proclaimed by Jesus Christ, and confirmed by the Apostles' testimony (Heb. 2:3). It was further confirmed by supernatural signs of the Holy Spirit accompanying the Apostles (Heb. 2:4). It was fully confirmed to the Apostles Peter, James, and John on the Mount of Transfiguration. It was confirmed to Paul's readers by the eyewitness testimony of these Apostles.

[171] The end of the age (Matt. 10:22; Matt. 24:6,13,14; 1 Cor. 1:8; Rev. 2:26)

[172] Psalm 95 is a prophecy about the "consummation."

[173] at the "consummation," when Psalm 95:7-11 will be proclaimed

[174] μηποτε – referring to the "consummation" to which *"this day …"* refers.

[175] future tense, referring again to the consummation.

[176] Most translations incorrectly render this, "while it is called Today."

[177] sharers in the inheritance of the "Son" in Psalm 2.

clutch the original confirmed foundation unto the consummation, 15 when it is to be proclaimed:[178]

> [Quoting again from Psalm 95] *"This day, if you hear His voice, you should not harden your hearts as in the provocation."*

16 For some having heard, provoked [God], but not all who came out of Egypt by Moses. 17 Yet with whom was He disgusted forty years? Was it not the ones sinning, whose corpses fell in the wilderness? 18 And to whom did He swear would not enter His Rest, except those who were unconvinced? 19 And we see that they were unable to enter because of disbelief.

4:1 We should fear then, if at that time[179] *any of you might appear to have fallen short of the remaining promise*[180] *to enter into His Rest. 2 For we also have been told the good message as they were (but the message heard [by them] had no benefit, not having been mixed with faith in the hearers).*[181] *3. For we — the ones who believed — are entering*[182] *the Rest, (just as He said:*

---

[178] The exhortation in Psalm 95, *"This day..."* is to be proclaimed at the consummation of the age.

[179] μηποτε – "if at that time" refers to the future 'Kadesh Barnea' when the believer's faith in God's promise of the inheritance (Rest) will be put to the test in the time of great tribulation.

[180] The "remaining promise" is the future fulfillment of the promise of entering His rest implied in the quotation of Psalm 95. (Psalm 37 shows that David had the same understanding).

[181] The "good news" was preached to the Israelites at Kadesh Barnea by Joshua and Caleb, but they rejected it, (Num. 13:30; 14:6-9). *"And all the congregation said to stone them with stones."* (Num. 14:10)

[182] Paul was still speaking from the perspective of the future Kadesh Barnea (the time of testing just before Christ's Kingdom arrives) which he introduced in verse 1 with the words, "at such time." This is why he used the present tense "we ... are entering," and the aorist tense "the ones who believed," just as in verse 1 he used

[Quoting again Psalm 95] *"As I swore in My anger, whether they shall come into My Rest,"*)[183] *although the labors have been performed*[184] *since the founding of the world.*[185]

4 For He has declared somewhere **concerning the seventh [day] thus**:

[Quoting Gen. 2:2] *"And God ceased in* **the seventh day** *from all His works."*

5 And thus again:

[Quoting again from Psalm 95] *"whether they shall come into* **My Rest**.*"*[186]

6 Since then it remains for some to enter into it, and those to whom it was previously announced did not enter because of stubbornness, He specifies another set day – 'This day.'

7 After such a long time[187] *He says in [the Psalm of] David, according as was previously proclaimed,*[188]

[Quoting again from Psalm 95] *"This day if you hear His voice, you should not harden your hearts."*[189]

---

the perfect tense "appear to have fallen short." His verb tenses in verses 1-3 are from the perspective of the consummation of the age.

[183] Psalm 95:11 LXX

[184] Some translations read "finished." But the Greek word means to occur, to come to be, to be performed.

[185] Contrasting the future "Rest" of Psalm 95 with the labor of mankind under the curse since the "foundation of the world." It is the same contrasting relationship that the 6 days of creation had to the Creator's Sabbath rest, and the 6 day work week has to the Sabbath day.

[186] Psalm 95:11 LXX

[187] Such a long time after the rebellion in the wilderness David wrote this Psalm which placed the opportunity to realize God's Rest in the future.

[188] Joshua and Caleb (Num. 14:6-9) and Moses (Deut. 1:29) previously pleaded with the Israelites at Kadesh Barnea to trust God and go into the Land.

[189] Psalm 95:8 LXX

*8 For if Joshua [had provided] them the Rest, He[190] would not have been speaking of another day after those. 9 **Consequently, a Sabbatical[191] awaits the people of God**.*

10 For the one entering into His Rest, he has also ceased from his own labors[192] just as God did from His.

*11 Therefore, we should be diligent to enter into **that Rest**, so that none fall into the same pattern of stubbornness.*

Paul understood the term, "this day," in Psalm 95 to refer to the end times, when another opportunity to enter the Promised Land would be given to God's people. In chapter 4, he went on to draw a most interesting conclusion from this Psalm regarding the future hope of believers. *"We should fear then, if at that time any of you might appear to have fallen short of the remaining promise to enter into His Rest."* Paul inferred a second opportunity to enter "His rest" from this prophetic Psalm: *"This day if you hear His voice, you should not harden your hearts. ... whether they shall enter My rest."* He then explained what the "Rest" was in Psalm 95. *"'As I swore in My anger, whether they shall come into My Rest,' although the labors have been performed since the founding of the world."* Since God was speaking in this Psalm, "My Rest" refers to God's rest. And this refers to the seventh day of creation when God rested from all His labor. The next clause, *"although the labors have been performed since the founding of the world"* refers to man's

---

[190] God through David in Psalm 95

[191] A Sabbath to be kept (a Sabbath awaits). Paul called the Kingdom age the "Sabbath."

[192] When the faithful believer enters God's rest (the 7th Millennium, the "Sabbatical"), he has reached the end of his own labors, just like God did at the very end of His creation labor.

toiling under the curse for the last six millennia which precede God's Rest.

Paul then unmistakably stated that our future hope, the promise of entering into God's Rest, is the "seventh day." *"For He has declared somewhere* __concerning the seventh [day]__ __thus__*: 'And God ceased in* __the seventh day__ *from all His works'* [quoting Genesis 2], *And thus again: 'whether they shall come into* __My Rest__*'"* [quoting Psalm 95]. Thus both of these passages speak of "the seventh day" according to Paul. In the latter passage it is "My Rest" which Paul calls "the seventh day." And since it is that same "rest" in Psalm 95 which Paul refers to the future Kingdom and hope of believers, it is therefore clear that the future Kingdom is "the seventh Day," which he also calls our "Sabbatical."

If the future hope of believers – the Kingdom of Messiah – is the "seventh Day," the "Sabbath," and God's "Rest" (which in the creation account occurred on the seventh day), six previous "Days" are logically required. Otherwise, the "Rest" for which we wait would not be the "seventh" Day.

Granted, Paul did not define this seventh-day Sabbath rest as a millennium here. However, Peter did define the previous "Days," during which we are waiting for Christ's return, as millennia,[193] referring to Psalm 90:4. Therefore, a week of six millennia under the curse, followed by the Sabbath Day millennium, was most definitely part of the later apostolic preaching. The early Christian writers we quoted previously

---

[193] 2 Pet. 3:8-9

did not make this up. It was the teaching of the Apostles in their last letters, just before the deaths of Peter and Paul.

The Millennial Week According to John

John was the only one of the three Apostles who had seen the great vision on the Mount of Transfiguration to outlive the destruction of Jerusalem in AD 70. His contribution to apostolic chiliasm comes from the twentieth chapter of Revelation. There he spoke of Christ's and the saints' rule over the nations as being one millennium. Of course, John did not mention this millennium as being preceded by six others. However, when adding his account to the information already provided by Peter and Paul, we have all of the components of chiliasm's millennial week chronology explicitly taught in the New Testament.

- God's millennial "Days" in Psalm 90:4 are applied to the duration of our living under the curse prior to Christ's coming to establish His Kingdom. (Peter)
- The Kingdom is also referred to as a "Day" in the context of David's statement about God's millennial days. (Peter)
- Christ's future Kingdom is called the "seventh day," "Sabbatical," and God's "Rest" – connecting it to the creation week (Paul)
- Christ's reign over the nations is clearly defined as a millennium. (John)

That the early Christians claimed the creation account was both history and prophecy should not come as a surprise given all of this evidence from the New Testament. Yet, there is one more reason to suppose they were right.

> *Isaiah 46:9-10 LXX*
> *9 "I am God, and there is none like Me, __declaring the end from the beginning__."*

The creation account describes "the beginning" – *"in the beginning God created the heaven and the earth."* God has been prophesying the "end" from the creation account. God has been declaring the "end" since Genesis chapter one.

Based on this accumulated Scriptural evidence, and the fact that the disciples of the Apostles unanimously held this view, it is reasonable to conclude that Christ's reign over the nations will begin six thousand years from the day of Adam's sin and expulsion from Eden. Chiliasm is not some quirky theory that the early Christians borrowed from the Jews. It is explicitly taught in Scripture.

We are very near to God's fulfilling His promise to His Son. *"I will declare the decree: The LORD said to Me, 'You are My Son, Today I have begotten You. Ask of Me, and I will give You the nations for Your inheritance, And the ends of the Land for Your possession. You shall shepherd them with a rod of iron. You shall shatter them like a potter's vessel.'"*[194]

---

[194] Psalm 2:7-9 LXX My translation

Chapter 4
The EVOLUTION of ESCHATOLOGY

Within a century after John's Patmos visions, some philosophically minded Greek Christians began to resist chiliasm. It was not the millennial week timeframe of six thousand years plus the Sabbath Rest that annoyed them, but rather the implications of a resurrected material body and the Land inheritance within the restored material creation.

Such a Jewish "earthly" hope clashed with the lofty philosophical ideas of the Greeks to which gentile Christians were accustomed. Receiving the renovated Promised Land from the Nile to the Euphrates Rivers as an everlasting inheritance did not sit well with many of them. In a way, they were similar to modern amillennialists and dispensationalists who see God's promise to Abraham and his Seed as being beneath them. They had a more "heavenly" mindset, to which they attempted to make the Scriptures conform.

The Greek mindset, derived from Plato and fully developed in Gnosticism which flourished in those days, held that physical matter was itself corrupt. Consequently, anything consisting of physical matter was inherently corrupt by its very nature. Greeks did not aspire to a resurrected material body because it would merely be continued entrapment within corrupt matter. Jerusalem had recently been destroyed by the Romans, and these philosophical Greek Christians did not desire an eternal city on earth as the capitol of Christ's Kingdom on a renovated earth. This too was continued entrapment within a physical world consisting of corrupt matter. Salvation in the Greek mind involved escape from the material creation and ascending into the heavens in a purely "spiritual" state of eternal bliss.

Pagans had long before pioneered the idea that the soul of man ascends into the heavens to join the gods. The Egyptians built solar ships which they buried with their departed rulers to escort their souls through the heavens to the stars. Plato envisioned a series of heavenly spheres, through which one must pass in order to reach his ultimate destiny in the heavens. The Greek-pagan mindset of the afterlife was entirely bound up in the idea of escaping the earth and ascending to a supposed heavenly destiny.

The Jews knew no such hope. There is absolutely nothing in the Old Testament Scriptures to suggest such a thing. The Jewish hope was horizontal, awaiting the Messiah who would arrive at the end of the age to restore Jerusalem, Israel, and the whole earth.

The entrance of Jewish-Christian apostolic eschatology into this Greek world was bound to spawn a clash of ideas, followed by a synthesis of contrary world views. The intention of the Apostles was to overthrow the philosophical speculations of the Greek mind with the power of the Gospel of Jesus Christ and the simple hope of resurrection and the eternal inheritance. The message of Christ was cast against the backdrop of the promises to the Patriarchs and the prophecies of the Old Testament, understood literally.

When pristine apostolic Christianity arrived in the Greek pagan culture, the presuppositions of the Greek mind did not immediately disappear. Some Greek Christians did not readily accept a completely new way of thinking. Instead, they read Scripture through a Greek philosophical lens, seeing in the biblical text the concepts of Plato and his transmigration of souls, and interpreting the text using Greek methods which depended heavily on allegory and mysticism. This created serious problems for the Apostles.

Both Paul and John had to grapple with Greek philosophical presuppositions being imposed on Christian theology. Paul devoted the entire fifteenth chapter of 1 Corinthians to defending the very concept of the resurrection of the body of flesh, which many of the Corinthian Christians had already dismissed because of their taste for Greek philosophy.

> *1 Corinthians 15:12-15*
> *12 Now if Christ is preached that He has been raised from the dead, how do some among you say that there is no resurrection of the dead? 13 But if there is no resurrection of the dead, then Christ is not risen. 14 And if Christ is not risen, then our preaching is empty and your faith is also empty. 15 Yes, and we are found false witnesses of God, because we have testified of God that He raised up Christ, whom He did not raise up — if in fact the dead do not rise.*

Such thinking is not really surprising given that Corinth was just a stone's throw from Athens, the center of Greek philosophy. It was the Greeks in Athens who mocked Paul when he began to speak of the resurrection of the dead.[195] And all Christians who received the Apostles' witness about Christ's resurrection and the future hope of our resurrection received the same kind of ridicule from the intellectuals in Greek society. This public scorn for apostolic Christianity, which arose from a taste for Platonic philosophical principles, was downright embarrassing to many early Christians who wished their new Faith to be viewed as intellectually acceptable and even superior to the philosophies of the Greeks.

The error of the Corinthians gives us our first glimpse into the corruption of apostolic eschatology by the intrusion of Greek philosophy. After Paul's martyrdom, the same thinking quickly led to the rise of Gnosticism within some of the churches founded by Paul.

Gnosticism was the result of blending the Greek philosophy, that matter was inherently corrupt, with the Jewish and Christian Scriptures. The Gnostic doctrines were more extreme than merely the denial of the resurrection and inheritance on a restored earth. They also claimed that the Creator was not the supreme God, but a lesser god. This was a natural result of their aversion to physical matter, which the Creator had made. If matter was corrupt by its very nature, then the One who created matter must be in some way corrupt. Therefore, many Gnostics claimed that the Creator

---

[195] Acts 17:32

was not the "Father" Jesus proclaimed, but a lesser god. Some went so far as to claim that the "Christ" was pure spirit (not consisting of matter), and the man Jesus was a totally separate person (consisting of matter). The two could not be the same person in Gnostic thinking because Jesus' fleshly humanity would mean He was corrupt. So, they invented a myth that the "Christ" Spirit descended on Jesus at His baptism, and left Him at the crucifixion. Gnostics denied the body and blood of Jesus Christ provided atonement because such flesh would also be corrupt, consisting of matter. Thus, salvation in Gnosticism was not atonement, but the gaining of philosophical knowledge which eventually allowed the Gnostic Christian to escape the bondage of the material body and this creation and to ascend through heavenly spheres into eventual union with the unseen God. This dichotomy between substance and spirit was pressed to extremes of heresy.

John set out to directly confront the developing Gnostic thinking in his Epistles and the prologue to his Gospel. He sought to root out this heresy from the churches. This is why he drew a line in the sand, writing that those who do not confess that *"Jesus the Christ has come in the flesh"* are of the spirit of Antichrist. Gnosticism was poison to pristine Christianity; it was of the spirit of Antichrist.

Within a century after Paul first corrected the Corinthian's error, many Christians again began to cave under the cultural pressure, and to succumb to the same thinking as the Corinthians.

Justin gives us an early peak at the rising dissent among those calling themselves "Christians" in his Dialogue with a Jew named Trypho. Justin described himself and others like him as *"right-minded Christians on all points."* Yet, he acknowledged others as true Christians who questioned whether Jerusalem would be rebuilt. However, those who denied the resurrection of the flesh body and taught that believers are taken to heaven, Justin called "heretics."

> *"And Trypho to this replied, '... But tell me, do you really admit that this place, Jerusalem, shall be rebuilt; and do you expect your people to be gathered together, and made joyful with Christ and the patriarchs, and the prophets, both the men of our nation, and other proselytes who joined them before your Christ came?'"*[196]

The question posed to Justin by this unbelieving Jewish man concerned only the rebuilding of Jerusalem which had recently been destroyed by the Romans, and whether Messiah would gather gentile Christians together with faithful Jews in this restored Jerusalem. Justin's answer shows a divided opinion among Christians on this point in his day, only a few decades after John wrote Revelation.

> *"Then I answered, 'I am not so miserable a fellow, Trypho, as to say one thing and think another. I admitted to you formerly, that I and many others are of this opinion, and [believe] that such will take place, as you assuredly are aware; but, on the other hand, I signified to you that many*

---

[196] AD 150 – Justin Martyr, Dialogue with Trypho (a Jew), chapter lxxx

who belong to the pure and pious faith, and are true Christians, think otherwise."[197]

The eschatological division among Christians *"who belong to the pure and pious Faith, and are true Christians"* at this early date concerned only whether the city of Jerusalem (destroyed by the Romans) would be restored and then become the location of the gathering of Christ's followers. Justin described many who agreed with him, but also many who did not agree.

Those whom Justin said *"belong to the pure and pious faith, and are true Christians,"* were still chiliasts. They still believed in a future millennium of Christ's reign upon the earth. The disagreement concerned whether Jerusalem would be rebuilt, and whether the prophecies which spoke of its restoration in Isaiah and Ezekiel ought to be interpreted literally. Tertullian is an example of one who held the contrary view to Justin's which was emerging.

> *"As for the restoration of Judaea, however, which even the Jews themselves, induced by the names of places and countries, hope for **just as it is described** [literally], it would be tedious to state at length how **the figurative interpretation is spiritually applicable to Christ and His church**, and to the character and fruits thereof."* [198]

Tertullian did not accept the literal interpretation of the restoration of Israel and Jerusalem recorded in Isaiah and

---

[197] Ibid.

[198] Tertullian, Against Marcion, Book III, Ch. xxv

Ezekiel. He thought that Jerusalem in the Kingdom would be replaced (not rebuilt) by the city John described as the "New Jerusalem" descending out of heaven to the earth. Tertullian continues:

> *"But we do confess that a kingdom is promised to us upon the earth, although before heaven, only in another state of existence; inasmuch as it will be after the resurrection for a thousand years **in the divinely-built city of Jerusalem, "let down from heaven**," which the apostle also calls "our mother from above;" and, while declaring that our πολιτευμα, or citizenship, is in heaven, he predicates of it that it is really a city in heaven. This both Ezekiel had knowledge of and the Apostle John beheld."*[199]

Tertullian and other chiliasts like him[200] allegorized the prophecies in Isaiah and Ezekiel which speak of Jerusalem's restoration. They did this in order to accommodate a literal interpretation of the New Jerusalem in Revelation 21 coming down from God out of heaven, thinking this was to take place at the beginning of the Millennium.

Justin, on the other hand, took the prophecies of Isaiah and Ezekiel literally,[201] claiming that the present city of Jerusalem which had been destroyed by the Romans would be rebuilt by the Messiah at His coming. In this regard, his eschatology agreed with the Jewish expectation of his opponent, Trypho. Justin and others who agreed with him understood the New

---

[199] ibid
[200] Commodianus, Christian Discipline, XLIV
[201] Isa. 52; Isa. 62; Isa. 65:17-25; Isa. 66; Ezekiel 40-44

Jerusalem in Revelation, descending down from God out of heaven, to be a figurative way of expressing the divinely rebuilt city of Jerusalem as described in Isaiah and Ezekiel.[202]

A third view among chiliasts regarding the holy city was held by Irenaeus, who, like modern premillennialists, accepted the rebuilding of Jerusalem during the Millennium after the "pattern" of the New Jerusalem in heaven, followed by the descent of the celestial city from heaven after the Millennium.[203]

All of these men were still chiliasts, despite their differences regarding the rebuilding of Jerusalem and the New Jerusalem in Revelation. They all believed that Christ would reign on the earth after His second coming for a thousand years. They differed only regarding the interpretation of the prophecies in Isaiah and Ezekiel which describe the restoration of the city at Christ's return, and how these Old Testament prophecies relate to John's description of the "New Jerusalem" in the closing chapters of Revelation (whether they were the same city or different cities, and if different, whether the New Jerusalem in Revelation would descend at the beginning or end of the Millennium).

While including among the orthodox those who disagreed with him over the future of the ruins of Jerusalem, Justin denounced in the strongest terms all those who called themselves Christians but held an eschatology which denied

---

[202] Lactantius, Divine Institutes, Bk. VII, ch. xxiv; Lactantius, Epitome of Divine Institutes, ch. lxxii.
[203] Irenaeus, Against Heresies, Bk. V, xxxv

the future Kingdom on earth, and substituted a heavenly destiny. Because these so-called "Christians" had an aversion to all things consisting of matter, they also denied that the same flesh corpse which was placed in the grave would be raised again to live within this creation.

> *"Moreover, I pointed out to you that some who are called Christians, but are godless, impious heretics, teach doctrines that are in every way blasphemous, atheistical, and foolish. But that you may know that I do not say this before you alone, I shall draw up a statement, so far as I can, of all the arguments which have passed between us; in which I shall record myself as admitting the very same things which I admit to you. For I choose to follow not men or men's doctrines, but God and the doctrines [delivered] by Him. For if you have fallen in with some who are called Christians, but who do not admit this [truth], and venture to blaspheme the God of Abraham, and the God of Isaac, and the God of Jacob; who say there is no resurrection of the dead, and that their souls, when they die, are taken to heaven; do not imagine that they are Christians."[204]*

Notice in Justin's opinion, those who denied the hope of the resurrection of the flesh body in order to participate in the Land inheritance *"blaspheme the God of Abraham, and the God of Isaac, and the God of Jacob."* Why did Justin say this? Why not just *"they blaspheme God"* or *"they blaspheme the God of Abraham?"* Why include Abraham, Isaac, and Jacob? It is because the hope of God's promise to Abraham, that the Land in which he lived as a pilgrim and foreigner would one day

---

[204] Justin Martyr, Dialogue with Trypho, chapter lxxx

belong to him and his Seed permanently,[205] was also repeated by God in person to Isaac,[206] and then in person again to Jacob.[207] The promised permanent Land inheritance was not only to Abraham's descendants, but to Abraham himself,[208] to Isaac himself, to Jacob himself, and Abraham's Seed, whom Paul indicated was Christ[209] and all who have been baptized into Him.[210]

Stephen pointed out that Abraham never received one foot of this land while he was still alive,[211] and Hebrews states that Joshua did not provide Israel with the fulfillment of this promise.[212] This is why Justin and Irenaeus, when defending the hope of chiliasm, anchored it squarely in the Abrahamic Covenant.[213]

The only way for Abraham, Isaac, Jacob, and Abraham's Seed (Christ and those baptized into Him) to inherit the Land was by means of the resurrection of their flesh bodies. The denial of this Land inheritance hope was also a denial of the means of achieving it through the resurrection of the flesh. Thus, Justin considered it blasphemy against the God of Abraham, Isaac, and Jacob to flatly deny His promise to the patriarchs

---

[205] Gen. 17:8

[206] Gen. 26:1-5

[207] Gen. 28:13-15

[208] Gen. 13:15-17

[209] Gal. 3:16

[210] Gal. 3:26-29

[211] Acts 7:2-5

[212] Heb. 4:8

[213] Irenaeus, Against Heresies, Bk. V, ch. xxxii, quoted at the beginning of this chapter

and all believers who are the *"heirs according to the promise."*[214] Justin then went on to describe the true apostolic eschatology.

> *"But I and others, who are right-minded Christians on all points, are assured that there will be a resurrection of the dead, and a thousand years in Jerusalem, which will then be built, adorned, and enlarged, [as] the prophets Ezekiel and Isaiah and others declare."*[215]

Justin drew a clear line of demarcation. Christians who held to chiliasm, with its resurrection of the flesh and restoration of Jerusalem and the Promised Land (according to the literal interpretation of the prophecies of Isaiah and Ezekiel) were *"right minded Christians on all points,"* following the doctrines of God declared by the prophets. Those who rejected the restoration of the city of Jerusalem destroyed by the Romans were in error by Justin's standards, but still Christians. However, those who followed *"men or men's doctrines,"* denying the future Land inheritance promised to Abraham and the resurrection of our flesh bodies to live within this creation, who adopted the philosophy and hope of Plato and Gnosticism with its ascent into the heavens, these were not to be considered Christians, but heretics. That Justin's Dialogue was widely published and highly regarded in the middle of the second century shows that his assessment was the opinion of most Christians only three or four decades after John's death.

---

[214] Gal. 3:29

[215] Justin Martyr, Dialogue with Trypho, chapter lxxx

In another work devoted to defending the resurrection of the flesh, Justin described the philosophical basis the heretics used for rejecting the resurrection of the body of flesh.

> *"They who maintain the wrong opinion say that there is no resurrection of the flesh; giving as their reason that it is impossible that what is corrupted and dissolved should be restored to the same as it had been. And besides the impossibility, they say that the salvation of the flesh is disadvantageous; and they abuse the flesh, adducing its infirmities, and declare that it only is the cause of our sins, so that if the flesh, say they, rise again, our infirmities also rise with it."[216]*

Since salvation to the Platonic Greek mind involved escaping the matter of the physical creation, resurrection would not be beneficial but counterproductive because the soul would remain trapped within physical substance and continue to be corrupted by it. Likewise, living within a physical, restored creation for a thousand years would also be corrupting to the soul. This aversion to physical substance was why the Greeks of Athens mocked Paul's preaching about the resurrection, and why the Corinthian church was in danger of abandoning the apostolic Faith. And it is why chiliasm was eventually discarded and replaced with amillennialism, after the defenders of the apostolic Faith passed on.

From Conflict to Synthesis

As the second century droned on, Greek thinking continued its intrusion into Christian theology. Justin and Irenaeus were

---

[216] Justin, On the Resurrection, II

quite alarmed by this. They strenuously argued that Greek philosophical arguments held by some Christians needed to be expunged entirely from Christian thinking. These great apologists for the *"Faith once for all delivered to the saints"* pushed back against the tide with all their might until their lives were snuffed out in martyrdom.

> *"Considering, therefore, even such arguments as are suited to this world, and finding that, even according to them, it is not impossible that the flesh be regenerated; and seeing that, besides all these proofs, the Savior in the whole Gospel shows that there is salvation for the flesh, why do we any longer endure those unbelieving and dangerous arguments, and fail to see that we are retrograding when we listen to such an argument as this: that the soul is immortal, but the body mortal, and incapable of being revived? For this we used to hear from Pythagoras and Plato, even before we learned the truth."* [217]

In Justin's opinion, Christianity was "retrograding" by entertaining *"such arguments as are suited to this world,"* those of the Greek philosophers. The arguments Justin was here refuting were those of Christians who increasingly interpreted the Scriptures through the lens of the Greek philosophers.

> *"If therefore the great God showed future things by Daniel, and confirmed them by His Son; and if Christ is the stone which is cut out without hands, who shall destroy temporal kingdoms, and introduce an eternal one, which is the resurrection of the just; as he declares, 'The God of heaven*

---

[217] Justin, On the Resurrection, X

*shall raise up a kingdom which shall never be destroyed,' —
let those thus confuted come to their senses."*[218]

Towards the end of the second century, Irenaeus shows that this thinking was gaining a considerable foothold within the churches through the influence of the philosophical writings.

"Since, again, some who are reckoned among the orthodox go beyond the prearranged plan for the exaltation of the just, and are ignorant of the methods by which they are disciplined beforehand for incorruption, they thus entertain heretical opinions. For the [Gnostic] *heretics, despising the handiwork of God, and not admitting the salvation of their flesh, while they also treat the promise of God contemptuously, and pass beyond God altogether in the sentiments they form, affirm that immediately upon their death they shall pass above the heavens and the Demiurge, and go to the Mother (Achamoth) or to that Father whom they have feigned. Those persons, therefore, who disallow a resurrection affecting the whole man, and as far as in them lies remove it from the midst [of the Christian scheme], how can they be wondered at, if again they know nothing as to the plan of the resurrection?"*[219]

Irenaeus bemoaned Christians *"who are reckoned among the orthodox"* yet were not satisfied with the destiny of the redeemed as revealed through the Abrahamic Covenant. Instead, they *"entertain heretical opinions"* of the Gnostics. He then described what the "heretics" (Gnostics) taught – an

---

[218] Irenaeus, Book V, ch. xxvi, 2
[219] Irenaeus, Against Heresies, Book V, xxxi

ascension into heaven and the rejection of the resurrection of the flesh. Consequently, these otherwise "orthodox" Christians, in adopting any of the Gnostic thinking, were themselves in danger of joining the ranks of "heretics" outside the Christian Faith. The heretics had removed some of the essential tenets of the apostolic Faith from the body of received doctrines.

Irenaeus continued, pinpointing the source of the poison – the "heretical discourses" of the Greeks which these Christians insisted on consuming.

"Inasmuch, therefore, as the opinions of certain [orthodox persons] are derived from heretical discourses, they are both ignorant of God's dispensations, and of the mystery of the resurrection of the just, and of the [earthly] kingdom which is the commencement of incorruption, by means of which kingdom those who shall be worthy are accustomed gradually to partake of the divine nature; and it is necessary to tell them respecting those things, that it behooves the righteous first to receive the promise of the inheritance which God promised to the fathers, and to reign in it, when they rise again to behold God in this creation which is renovated, and that the judgment should take place afterwards. For it is just that in that very creation in which they toiled or were afflicted, being proved in every way by suffering, they should receive the reward of their suffering; and that in the creation in which they were slain because of their love to God, in that they should be revived again; and that in the creation in which they endured servitude, in that they should reign. For God is rich in all things, and all things are His. It is fitting,

therefore, that the creation itself, being restored to its primeval condition, should without restraint be under the dominion of the righteous; and the Apostle has made this plain in the Epistle to the Romans, when he thus speaks: "For the expectation of the creation waiteth for the manifestation of the sons of God. For the creation has been subjected to vanity, not willingly, but by reason of him who hath subjected the same in hope; since the creation itself shall also be delivered from the bondage of corruption into the glorious liberty of the sons of God."[220]

The restoration of the creation at the end of six millennia, the resurrection of the flesh at Christ's coming, and Jesus' own bodily resurrection as the prototype for ours, were viewed by the early orthodox church leaders as a consistent and indivisible body of apostolic truth. The main cause for deviation from this truth was pressure from Greek philosophy and its mixture with Christianity as the Gospel spread throughout the Hellenized world. Christian consumption of the "heretical discourses" was poison as far as the earliest Christian apologists were concerned.

A Rising Conflict over the Eternal State

The early chiliasts were not totally immune from viewing Scripture through a Greek philosophical lens. As we begin to move beyond those who had close connections to the Jewish Apostles, there was a greater tendency to use allegory to interpret the Old Testament prophets.

---

[220] Irenaeus, Against Heresies, Book V, xxxii

The earliest chiliasts interpreted the prophecies of Messiah's Kingdom on earth literally. The prophets were plain that this Kingdom would have no end.

Isaiah 9:6-7

6 For unto us a Child is born, Unto us a Son is given; And the government will be upon His shoulder. And His name will be called Wonderful, Counselor, Mighty God, Everlasting Father, Prince of Peace.

7 Of the increase of His government and peace **There will be no end, Upon the throne of David and over His kingdom, To order it and establish it with judgment and justice From that time forward, even forever.** *The zeal of the Lord of hosts will perform this.*

Dan. 7:13-14, 27

13 "I was watching in the night visions, And behold, One like the Son of Man, Coming with the clouds of heaven! He came to the Ancient of Days, And they brought Him near before Him. 14 **Then to Him was given dominion and glory and a kingdom, That all peoples, nations, and languages should serve Him. His dominion is an everlasting dominion, Which shall not pass away, And His kingdom the one Which shall not be destroyed.** *...*

27 Then the kingdom and dominion, And the greatness of the kingdoms under the whole heaven, Shall be given to the people, the saints of the Most High. **His kingdom is an everlasting kingdom,** *And all dominions shall serve and obey Him.'*

Justin and Irenaeus agreed that the Kingdom would continue on earth after the end of the Millennium, and the final judgment.

> *"If therefore the great God showed future things by Daniel, and confirmed them by His Son; and if Christ is the stone which is cut out without hands, who shall destroy temporal kingdoms,* **and introduce an eternal one,** *which is the resurrection of the just; as he declares,* '**The God of heaven shall raise up a kingdom which shall never be destroyed**,' — *let those thus confuted come to their senses."*[221]

However, some chiliasts continued making concessions to the allegorizing tendencies of the Gnostics and their heavenly destiny expectations. These chiliasts abandoned the idea that Christ's Kingdom on earth was eternal. Instead, they saw the Kingdom as a temporary state lasting only a thousand years. This would be followed by the destruction of the earth and an eternity in heaven. This became Tertullian's view towards the end of the second century.

> *"After its thousand years are over, within which period is completed the resurrection of the saints, who rise sooner or later according to their deserts there will ensue the destruction of the world and the conflagration of all things at the judgment: we shall then be changed in a moment into the substance of angels, even by the investiture of an incorruptible nature, and so be removed to that kingdom in*

---

[221] Irenaeus, Book V, ch. xxvi, 2. See also Justin, Dialogue with Trypho, chs. xxxi – xxxix.

heaven of which we have now been treating, ... What appears to be probable to you, when Abraham's seed, after the primal promise of being like the sand of the sea for multitude, is destined likewise to an equality with the stars of heaven — are not these the indications both of an earthly and a heavenly dispensation?[222]

Tertullian's justification for two Kingdoms, one terrestrial followed by one celestial, was an allegorical interpretation of God's promise to Abraham. God promised that Abraham's seed would be "as the sand of the seashore," which Tertullian interpreted as referring to the Millennium of Christ's reign on Earth. God also said that Abraham's seed would be "as the stars of heaven," which he interpreted as referring to a Kingdom in heaven after the Millennium.

The Rising Hatred of All Things Jewish

As Christianity spread among the Hellenized world, many Christian circles began to show signs of a rising sense of superiority over the Jews. For one thing, the Jews had been very antagonistic to Christ and His Apostles, as recorded in the Gospels. The Scriptures do not paint a pretty picture of the Jewish nation in the Torah,[223] the Prophets,[224] or the New Testament.[225] The recent destruction of Jerusalem by the

---

[222] Tertullian, Against Marcion, Book III, Ch. xxv

[223] Israel's constant complaining in the wilderness and rebellion at Kadesh Barnea

[224] The prophets used terms like "adulterous wife" to refer to Israel's worship of idols during the time of the Kings.

[225] Jesus' charge against the Scribes and Pharisees as "hypocrites"; His referring to them as being "of your father the devil," and "of the synagogue of Satan"; Stephen's charge against the Sanhedrin, *"You stiff-necked and uncircumcised in heart and ears! You always resist the Holy Spirit; as your fathers did, so do you. Which of the prophets did your fathers not persecute? And they killed those who foretold the coming of*

Romans in AD 70, and Jesus' accurate prediction of God's judgment upon them forty years earlier,[226] was seen as proof of Christianity's triumph over Judaism.

At the same time, the Jews were feverishly trying to counter the early Christians' very successful use of the Septuagint[227] against the Jewish interpretations of the prophecies about Christ. Christian evangelism not only proclaimed Jesus as Messiah, but also proclaimed the Jews as His murderers. The more Christianity spread among the Greek speaking world, the more the Jews were pronounced guilty and disparaged by Christians. Jewish rabbis filled the need to develop alternate explanations about various prophecies of Christ. Justin even charged them with altering the text of some copies of the Old Testament itself, and provided specific examples of their attempt to expunge support for Jesus' being the Messiah[228] in order to justify His execution on grounds of blasphemy.

Unfortunately, Paul's compassionate attitude towards his erring Jewish brothers[229] became quite rare in Christian circles because of the continued and rising tension between the two groups. His prophetic command not to boast against the natural branches[230] was largely ignored. Greek Christians' scorn for the Jews began to translate into scorn for all things

---

the Just One, of whom you now have become the betrayers and murderers, who have received the law by the direction of angels and have not kept it."

[226] Matt. 23:32-39; Luke 19:41-44; Luke 21:5,20-24

[227] The Septuagint (LXX) is the Greek translation of the Old Testament made by 70 Jewish scholars about 250 years before the birth of Jesus Christ. It was the Bible of the Jews of the Diaspora, as well as the early Christians.

[228] Justin Martyr, Dialogue with Trypho, ch. lxxi - lxxiii

[229] Rom. 9:1-5

[230] Rom. 11:11-36

Jewish. And that translated into denouncing the Sabbath and all of the Jewish festivals.

Since chiliasm saw the six days of the work week as prophetic of the six millennia of man's struggle under the curse, and the Sabbath as prophetic of the Millennial Rest, and since it was the Jews who were honoring the Sabbath consistently, many Christians began to distance themselves from chiliasm as they attempted to distance themselves from Judaism, Jews, and all things Jewish.

Christians living at this time were under tremendous pressure to be seen as separate from the Jews, and to be seen as intellectuals who could hold their own in any philosophical discussion with the Greeks. These combined pressures proved too much for the early churches to withstand as the familiarity with the Apostles receded into antiquity.

Chapter 5
The RISE of the THEOLOGIANS

The early apologists whom we have quoted in support of chiliasm were mostly ordained bishops (pastors) entrusted with the care of local churches. They had direct or indirect linkage to the Apostles. These men considered it their sacred duty to preserve apostolic tradition as best they understood it, as it was handed down within the churches founded by the Apostles. And many of them paid for their dedication with their own blood.

However, as the men who knew the Apostles or their disciples finished their courses in victory, a new breed of Christian leaders began to emerge around the end of the second century. These men were not bishops (pastors / elders) of local churches where spiritual instruction was carried out by ordained and approved elders. They were not sworn to faithfully uphold and defend the traditions handed down by the Apostles. They were intellectuals and accomplished writers operating outside the local church. They established schools of Christian philosophy and theology patterned after the Greek philosophical schools. Enter the age of the theologian and the seminary.

The most famous such school was in Alexandria, Egypt. Alexandria had come to rival Athens as the center of Greek philosophy and learning. The Alexandrian school and its theologians, Clement and Origen, sought to interact with the

123

arguments presented in the "heretical discourses," and to mold Christianity into a religion acceptable to the Greek intellectual without the kind of ridicule Paul encountered at Athens being heaped upon it or upon them.

Clement of Alexandria

Clement was called "the ethical philosopher of Christians" by the editor of his works.[231] His extensive work, *Stromata*, begins by answering the anticipated objection to the plethora of quotations of Greek philosophers included in his work, and his strong defense of Greek philosophy as being good and beneficial to the Christian.

> *"In reference to these commentaries, which contain ... the Hellenic opinions, I say thus much to those who are fond of finding fault. First, even if philosophy were useless, if the demonstration of its uselessness does good, it is yet useful. Then those cannot condemn the Greeks, who have only a mere hearsay knowledge of their opinions, and have not entered into a minute investigation in each department, in order to acquaintance with them."*

Clement disarmed his critics' objections with the same arguments that are often used today to defend unholy practices in the churches. Even if Greek philosophy is useless, it is beneficial for the Christian to study it so he can refute it. Those who have not studied Greek philosophy in great detail have no right to condemn it according to Clement of Alexandria. This argument is not much different than one

---

[231] Ante Nicene Fathers, Roberts and Donaldson, Vol. II, preface to Clement's Works

used by certain Gnostics groups, that Christians needed to indulge in every excess of the flesh so they could gain knowledge by experience. Such is the foolishness of this reasoning. Clement continues:

> "... [He] who sets forth the most essential doctrines so as to produce persuasion in his hearers, engendering admiration in those who are taught, and leads them to the truth. And such persuasion is convincing, by which those that love learning admit the truth; so that **philosophy** does not ruin life by being the originator of false practices and base deeds, although some have calumniated it, **though it be the clear image of truth, a divine gift to the Greeks**; nor does it drag us away from the faith, as if we were bewitched by some delusive art, but rather, so to speak, by the use of an ampler circuit, obtains a common exercise demonstrative of the faith. Further, the juxtaposition of doctrines, by comparison, saves the truth, from which follows knowledge."[232]

Clement's gratuitous praise of Greek philosophy demonstrates that he was going against the natural instincts of Christians, as well as the precedent set by the earlier apologists. By making the claim, *"nor does it drag us away from the faith, as if we were bewitched by some delusive art,"* he implicitly shows that many Christians believed it to be just that. And why would Christians have this opinion? It was because the Apostle Paul had clearly marked Greek philosophy as the road to apostasy. *"O Timothy! Guard what was committed to your trust, avoiding the profane and idle babblings and contradictions of what is falsely called 'knowledge' —*

---

[232] Clement of Alexandria, Book I, ch. ii

by professing it some have strayed concerning the faith."[233] Note the two-pronged defense that Paul prescribed for his protégé against slipping into heresy:

- Guard the apostolic tradition
- Avoid Greek philosophy

This was precisely the stated agenda of the earlier apologists and martyrs who unanimously held to chiliasm.[234] Yet, Clement prescribed exactly the opposite. He disregarded the apostolic warning and apostolic tradition, placing Greek philosophy on a par with the Jewish Scriptures.

> *"Philosophy came into existence, not on its own account, but for the advantages reaped by us from knowledge, we receiving a firm persuasion of true perception, through the knowledge of things comprehended by the mind."*[235]

Philosophy is speculation, the judgment of things by human intellect. Yet, *"the heart is deceitful above all things, and desperately wicked; Who can know it?"*[236] Impure motives of the heart corrupt the mind so that it cannot be objective.

---

[233] 1 Tim 6:20-21. Irenaeus took the title for his 5 Volume massive work from this verse. It is usually abbreviated as "Against Heresies." But Irenaeus' original title was, *"A Refutation and Overthrow of What is Falsely called Knowledge."* The stark contrast between Irenaeus as an apologist for the apostolic Faith, and Clement as an apologist for Plato, could not be more evident.

[234] http://www.pfrs.org/foundation/Tertullian.pdf,
http://www.pfrs.org/foundation/Irenaeus.pdf

[235] Clement of Alexandria, Stromata, Book I, ch. ii

[236] Jer. 17:9

Paul's view of Greek philosophy, expressed to the Corinthians living just outside the world capitol of Greek philosophy, Athens, was precisely the opposite of Clement's.

1 Corinthians 2:6-16

6 "However, we speak wisdom among those who are mature, yet not the wisdom of this age, nor of the rulers of this age, who are coming to nothing. 7 But we speak the wisdom of God in a mystery, the hidden wisdom which God ordained before the ages for our glory, 8 which none of the rulers of this age knew; for had they known, they would not have crucified the Lord of glory.

9 But as it is written: "Eye has not seen, nor ear heard, Nor have entered into the heart of man The things which God has prepared for those who love Him."

10 But God has revealed them to us through His Spirit. For the Spirit searches all things, yes, the deep things of God. 11 For what man knows the things of a man except the spirit of the man which is in him? Even so no one knows the things of God except the Spirit of God. 12 Now we have received, not the spirit of the world, but the Spirit who is from God, that we might know the things that have been freely given to us by God.

13 These things we also speak, not in words which man's wisdom teaches but which the Holy Spirit teaches, comparing spiritual things with spiritual. 14 But the natural man does not receive the things of the Spirit of God, for they are foolishness to him; nor can he know them, because they are spiritually discerned. 15 But he who is spiritual judges all things, yet he himself is rightly judged by no one. 16 For "who has known the mind of the LORD that he may instruct Him?" But we have the mind of Christ."

In contrast, consider Clement's opinion of Greek philosophy.

"Accordingly, before the advent of the Lord, philosophy was necessary to the Greeks for righteousness. And now it becomes conducive to piety; being a kind of preparatory training to those who attain to faith through demonstration. "For thy foot," it is said, "will not stumble, if thou refer what is good, whether belonging to the Greeks or to us, to Providence." For God is the cause of all good things; but of some primarily, as of the Old and the New Testament; and of others by consequence, as philosophy. Perchance, too, philosophy was given to the Greeks directly and primarily, till the Lord should call the Greeks. For this was a schoolmaster to bring "the Hellenic mind," as the law, the Hebrews, "to Christ." Philosophy, therefore, was a preparation, paving the way for him who is perfected in Christ."[237]

The contradiction between Paul and Clement of Alexandria, head of the Alexandrian school, could not be more glaring. To Paul, Greek philosophy was *"the wisdom of this age,"* from *"the spirit of this world,"* and *"man's wisdom."* According to Paul, the Greek philosophers and their students could not comprehend God's truth because *"the natural man does not receive the things of the Spirit of God, for they are foolishness to him, nor can he know them because they are spiritually discerned."*

---

[237] Clement of Alexandria, Stromata, Bk. I, ch. v

Even Justin, who had studied the philosophers prior to his conversion, when proving to the Greeks that the philosophers were ignorant, wrote: *"I think we ought to examine the opinions even of these sages. For we shall see whether each of these does not manifestly contradict the other. But if we find that even they do not agree with each other, I think it is easy to see clearly that they too are ignorant."*[238] He then went on to prove that they all disagreed with each other on a multitude of crucial points, and thus were ignorant of divine truth.

Yet, Clement of Alexandria viewed the writings of these men as a fountain of truth, *"being a kind of preparatory training to those who attain to faith,"* on a par with the Law of Moses given by divine revelation. He even placed the writings of the philosophers on a par with the teachings of Christ, quoting both Jesus and Plato as fellow witnesses to the same truths.

> *"For there are with the Lord both rewards and '__many mansions__' corresponding to men's lives. 'Whosoever shall receive,' says He, 'a prophet in the name of a prophet, shall receive a prophet's reward; and whosoever shall receive a righteous man in the name of a righteous man, shall receive a righteous man's reward; and whoso shall receive one of the least of these my disciples, shall not lose his reward.' … They shall work, therefore, in accordance with* **the appropriate __mansions__ of which they have been deemed worthy as rewards**, *being fellow-workers in the ineffable administration and service. 'Those, then,' says* **__Plato__**, *'who seem called to a holy life, are those who, freed and __released from those earthly localities as from prisons, have__*

---

[238] Justin, Hortatory Address to the Greeks, Ch. V

*reached the pure dwelling-place on high.' In clearer
terms again he [Plato] expresses the same thing: 'Those who
by philosophy have been sufficiently purged from those
things, live without bodies entirely for all time. Although
they are enveloped in certain shapes; in the case of some, of
air, and others, of fire.' He adds further: '**And they reach
abodes fairer than those**, which it is not easy, nor is there
sufficient time now to describe.' Whence with reason, [Jesus
said] 'blessed are they that mourn: for they shall be
comforted'."[239]*

It is easy to see that Clement's treatment of Jesus' words were
not from the Jewish framework which the original hearers
possessed. He commented here on the "many mansions"
which Jesus promised to His disciples at the Last Supper.
Rather than interpreting this statement as Jesus' Jewish
disciples would certainly have, Clement instead saw Jesus as
affirming Plato's heavenly spheres and bodiless afterlife.

The Jewish disciples would have understood Jesus' statement
about *"My Father's House"* containing *"many mansions"* as
referring to the Temple in Jerusalem. When Jesus drove the
moneychangers from the Temple, He shouted, *"Make not **My
Father's House** a house of merchandise."* When the disciples saw
what Jesus did and heard His words they remembered Psalm
69:9, *"The zeal for your house has eaten me up."*[240] The house of
the Lord, what Jesus called, *"My Father's House,"* was clearly
the Temple in the minds of the disciples and everywhere in
Scripture. Solomon's Temple contained *"many mansions."*

---

[239] Clement of Alexandria, Stromata, Bk. IV, ch. vi
[240] John 2:16-17

They were three-story apartments attached to and surrounding the Temple structure. They served as hotel rooms for the priests to temporarily occupy while they fulfilled their week of service at the Temple.[241] Josephus described them in Herod's Temple,[242] the same priestly apartments the disciples would have seen. Ezekiel's prophecy of the Kingdom Temple also included these three-story hotel rooms for priests, which surrounded the Temple on the north, south, and west sides.[243]

If we consider Jesus' words from the perspective of His Jewish disciples and their familiarity with the Old Testament Scriptures and the current Temple, it is obvious that He was promising them a place of priestly service in the Kingdom Temple.

According to Luke's account of this discourse, Jesus promised them a place at His table in His Kingdom, judging the twelve tribes of Israel.[244] In the Law, the Temple priests served as the Supreme Court of Israel.[245] And in the prophecies of Christ's coming Kingdom in Jerusalem, believers were to be the new priesthood. *"But you shall be called priests of the Lord, the ministers of God: you shall eat the strength of nations, and shall be admired because of their wealth. Thus shall they inherit the land a second time, and everlasting joy shall be upon their head."*[246] Priests are those who intercede between God and men – in this case

---

[241] 1 Kings 6:5,10; 1 Chron. 9:33
[242] Josephus, Wars of the Jews, Bk. V, ch. v
[243] Ezek. 41:5-11
[244] Luke 22:28-30
[245] Deut. 17:8-13
[246] Isaiah 61:6-7 LXX

those who remain among the nations. Revelation confirms this prophecy and applies it to resurrected Christians: *"Blessed and holy is he who has part in the first resurrection. Over such the second death has no power, but* **they shall be priests** *of God and of Christ, and shall reign with Him a thousand years."*[247] This, of course, means that such ruling Priests would stay in this three-story hotel during their week of service at the Temple, just as the priests did under the Law of Moses.

Clement of Alexandria did not consider how Jesus' statement would have been understood by His Jewish disciples to whom He was speaking, within their setting, culture, and background. Instead, Clement took Jesus' words in John 14 to His disciples as affirming Plato's heavenly spheres! This is an astounding perversion of Jesus' teaching. Instead of showing that Jesus affirmed the Hebrew prophets, Clement put Plato in the place of the prophets as the forerunner of Christ! Jesus was affirming Plato. What blasphemy! Yet this connection between John 14 and Plato's heavenly spheres is the primary cause of the heavenly destiny beliefs of most Christians today, holding either to amillennialism or dispensationalism.[248]

It was the influence of the Alexandrian school, its method of interpreting Scripture through the presuppositions of Greek

---

[247] Rev 20:6

[248] Chiliasts were not entirely immune to the lure of the heavenly destiny of Greek philosophy. Some believed that the most faithful Christians – those who endured martyrdom – would enjoy a higher existence after the Millennium in the presence of the Father in heaven, while all other Christians would enjoy paradise and the New Jerusalem on Earth forever. (Martyrdom of Justin Martyr, Ch. iv; Irenaeus, Book V, ch. xxxvi). In this way they elevated martyrdom, seeing it as something to be sought after. This idea no doubt originated from Rev. 6:9-11, which seems to mention a special place of honor for martyrs.

philosophy, and employing the allegorical interpretation methods of the Gnostics to deny the plain sense of the text,[249] which led to the demise of chiliasm and the development of its replacement, amillennialism. The tools used to overthrow the apostolic Faith were these:

- elevating Greek philosophy on a par with Scripture
- viewing Scripture through a philosophical lens
- denying the plain sense of Scripture in favor of allegorical interpretations

It was through the Alexandrian school's influence that chiliasm was eventually expunged from Christian theology. The chiliastic hope rooted in the Land promise of the Abrahamic Covenant, and the resurrection of the flesh in order to dwell in the restored Promised Land, was tossed out. It was replaced with Plato's heavenly spheres, and a denial of the resurrection of the body of flesh. All of this can be traced to the misinterpretation of the "many mansions" statement in John 14:1-3 being used as a Trojan horse to flood the early churches with Greek philosophy.

---

[249] One might argue that the early apologists who were chiliasts also occasionally used allegorical interpretation. The fact is, the Bible does use allegory and non-literal speech sometimes. However, when it does, it can be easily recognized. There is a vast difference between the use of non-literal language, such as parables, figures of speech, and the recognition of prophetic types in Scripture (something widely used by the early chiliasts), and denying the plain sense of the text. The early apologists did not deny the plain sense of the text, but only augmented the literal reading of Scripture with prophetic types. The methodology of the Alexandrian school, however, was the wholesale denial of the plain sense of Scripture in favor of an alternative mystical interpretation which they claimed arose from a "spiritual" understanding of the text. They claimed that the literal reading was "carnal," meant to mislead those uninitiated in their "mysteries."

The resurrection was not overtly denied by the Alexandrian school, because it was a tenet of the Apostles' Creed which candidates for baptism had acknowledged for a very long time: *"I believe … in the resurrection of the flesh."* Rather, like the Gnostics, the Alexandrian school began to redefine biblical terms. They claimed that the "resurrection" was spiritual, not physical.

Origen

Clement's successor as head of the Alexandrian school was Origen. He followed in the footsteps of his predecessor. His fascination with Greek philosophy led him to propose many doctrines that are clearly heretical. For example, he was the father of universalism, the idea that all of God's creatures will be saved, including fallen angels and the devil himself.[250] He taught that the heavenly bodies, sun, moon, stars, planets, were living creatures with a free will, and that they possessed life and reason.[251]

Origen further developed Clement's adaption of Plato's heavenly spheres. Rather than seeing the heavenly spheres (Jesus' many mansions) as merely rewards, Origen viewed them as a series of heavenly classrooms. When departing this world, a Christian would begin a staged ascent into the heavens, graduating from one learning sphere (mansion) and ascending to the next until he at last reached the presence of God. Being in God's presence was only for those who had sufficiently learned philosophy, according to Origen.

---

[250] Origen, De Principis, Bk. I, ch. vi
[251] Origen, De Principis, Bk. 1, ch. vii

"'We shall be caught up in the clouds to meet Christ in the air, and so shall we ever be with the Lord.' We are therefore to suppose that the saints will remain there until they recognize the twofold mode of government in those things which are performed in the air. ...

I think, therefore, that all the saints who depart from this life will remain in some place situated on the earth, which holy Scripture calls paradise, as in some place of instruction, and, so to speak, class-room or school of souls, in which they are to be instructed regarding all the things which they had seen on earth. ... If anyone indeed be pure in heart, and holy in mind, and more practiced in perception, he will, by making more rapid progress, quickly ascend to a place in the air, and reach **the kingdom of heaven, through those _mansions_, so to speak, in the various places which the Greeks have termed spheres, i.e., globes, but which holy Scripture has called heavens;** *in each of which he will first see clearly what is done there, and in the second place, will discover the reason why things are so done: and thus he will, in order, pass through all gradations, following Him who hath passed into the heavens, Jesus the Son of God, who said, "I will that where I am, these may be also." And of this diversity of places He speaks, when He says,* **"In My Father's house are many mansions.**"[252]

Notice that the instruction given to believers after death, making them worthy of ascending to the next heavenly sphere, concerns knowledge of the mechanics of the creation. One remains in some spiritual "paradise" on earth after death until he is instructed by angelic beings and understands

---

[252] Origen, De Principis, Bk. II, ch. xi

biology, geology, botany, etc. Then, he ascends into the air where he remains and is instructed in climatology. He then ascends beyond the air into the next sphere where he is taught astronomy. He continues in this staged ascension through the "many mansions" (spheres) until he finally reaches the heaven of heavens.

Origen described Jesus as having ascended through this labyrinth of spheres. Like many amillennialists today,[253] he claimed that Jesus did not retain His resurrected body of flesh when He ascended into heaven.

> "He Himself is everywhere, and passes swiftly through all things; nor are we any longer to understand Him as existing in those narrow limits in which He was once confined for our sakes, i.e., not in that circumscribed body which He occupied on earth, when dwelling among men, according to which He might be considered as enclosed in some one place."[254]

The natural inference of Origen's scheme is that Christians follow in Jesus' footsteps, and also no longer possess a body of flesh as they ascend through these heavenly spheres.

> "When, then, the saints shall have reached __the celestial abodes__, they will clearly see the nature of the stars one by one, and will understand whether they are endued with life, or their condition, whatever it is. And they will comprehend also the other reasons for the works of God, which He

---

[253] See my debate with Norm Fields, amillennialist Church of Christ minister.
http://www.oasischristianchurch.org/air/debate_fields.html
[254] Origen, De Principis, Bk. II, ch. xi

136

Himself will reveal to them. For He will show to them, as to children, the causes of things and the power of His creation, and will explain why that star was placed in that particular quarter of the sky, and why it was separated from another by so great an intervening space; what, e.g., would have been the consequence if it had been nearer or more remote; or if that star had been larger than this, how the totality of things would not have remained the same, but all would have been transformed into a different condition of being. And so, when they have finished all those matters which are connected with the stars, and with the heavenly revolutions, they will come to those which are not seen, or to those whose names only we have heard, and to things which are invisible, which the Apostle Paul has informed us are numerous, although what they are, or what difference may exist among them, we cannot even conjecture by our feeble intellect. And thus the rational nature, growing by each individual step, not as it grew in this life in flesh, and body, and soul, but enlarged in understanding and in power of perception, is raised as a mind already perfect to perfect knowledge, no longer at all impeded by those carnal senses, but increased in intellectual growth; and ever gazing purely, and, so to speak, face to face, on the causes of things, it attains perfection."[255]

Origen did not derive such absurd ideas from the Scriptures, even though he used, or rather abused, the Scriptures to support them. They were derived from Greek philosophy. Origen provided a biblical basis for his ideas by employing the same interpretive methods as the Gnostics – allegorical interpretation. His use of allegory differed greatly from the

---

[255] Origen, De Principis, Bk. II, xi

early chiliast apologists. Origen was willing to completely discard the plain sense of the text, claiming that only the "mystical" hidden meaning was true. He applied this mystical interpretation to the historical books as well as the prophets.

> *"Being taught, then, by him that there is one Israel according to the flesh, and another according to the Spirit, when the Savior says, 'I am not sent but to the lost sheep of the house of Israel,' we do not understand these words as those do who savor of earthly things, … but we understand that there exists a race of souls which is termed "Israel," as is indicated by the interpretation of the name itself: for Israel is interpreted to mean a "mind," or "man seeing God." The apostle, again, makes a similar revelation respecting Jerusalem, saying, "The Jerusalem which is above is free, which is the mother of us all." And in another of his Epistles he says: "But ye are come unto mount Zion, and to the city of the living God, and to the heavenly Jerusalem, and to an innumerable company of angels, and to the Church of the first-born which is written in heaven." If, then, there are certain souls in this world who are called Israel, and a city in heaven which is called Jerusalem, it follows that those cities which are said to belong to the nation of Israel have the heavenly Jerusalem as their metropolis; and that, agreeably to this, we understand as referring to the whole of Judah (of which also we are of opinion that the prophets have spoken in certain mystical narratives), any predictions delivered either regarding Judea or Jerusalem, or invasions of any kind, which the sacred histories declare to have happened to Judea or Jerusalem. Whatever, then, is either narrated or predicted of Jerusalem, must, if we accept the words of Paul as those of*

Christ speaking in him, be understood as spoken in conformity with his opinion regarding that city which he calls the heavenly Jerusalem, and all those places or cities which are said to be cities of the holy land, of which Jerusalem is the metropolis. For we are to suppose that it is from these very cities that the Savior, wishing to raise us to a higher grade of intelligence, promises to those who have well managed the money entrusted to them by Himself, that they are to have power over ten or five cities. If, then, the prophecies delivered concerning Judea, and Jerusalem, and Judah, and Israel, and Jacob, not being understood by us in a carnal sense, signify certain divine mysteries, it certainly follows that those prophecies also which were delivered either concerning Egypt or the Egyptians, or Babylonia and the Babylonians, and Sidon and the Sidonians, are not to be understood as spoken of that Egypt which is situated on the earth, or of the earthly Babylon, Tyre, or Sidon. Nor can those predictions which the prophet Ezekiel delivered concerning Pharaoh king of Egypt, apply to any man who may seem to have reigned over Egypt, as the nature of the passage itself declares. In a similar manner also, what is spoken of the prince of Tyre cannot be understood of any man or king of Tyre. And how could we possibly accept, as spoken of a man, what is related in many passages of Scripture, and especially in Isaiah, regarding Nebuchadnezzar? ... But let us see whether it may not be understood more fittingly in the following manner: viz., that as there is a heavenly Jerusalem and Judea, and a nation undoubtedly which inhabits it, and is named Israel; so also it is possible that there are certain localities near to these which may seem to be called either Egypt, or Babylon, or Tyre, or

Sidon, and that the princes of these places, and the souls, if there be any, that inhabit them, are called Egyptians, Babylonians, Tyrians, and Sidonians. From whom also, according to the mode of life which they lead there, a sort of captivity would seem to result, in consequence of which they are said to have fallen from Judea into Babylonia or Egypt, from a higher and better condition, or to have been scattered into other countries.[256]

This is pure and unadulterated *unbelief*. Origen erected a mystical parallel universe in the heavens, with places having the same names as those on earth. He claimed that the histories and prophecies of the Old Testament Scriptures did not refer to the actual locations and events on earth, but to the mystical places and events in his parallel universe – Gnostic wonderland! Yes, this is the theology of the hero of amillennialism, the one who laid much of the groundwork for the rejection of chiliasm. This is the wisdom of man in flights of fantasy, when the mind is not anchored to divine revelation or guided by the Spirit of truth.

There were many Greek Christians, like Clement and Origen, who could not turn loose of Greek philosophy who were similarly infatuated with man's own intellect. Consequently, Origen was widely read in Christian circles and his school flourished because Origen's brand of Christianity could compete in the Greek culture enamored with *"nothing else but either to tell or to hear some new thing."*[257] His impact on early

---

[256] Origen, De Principis, Book IV, ch. i (20)
[257] Acts 17:21

Christian thinking was profound, and he churned out many disciples from his school, along with a great deal of literature.

However, not everyone was so easily persuaded by Clement's and Origen's philosophical arguments. There were still faithful men within the apostolic churches who would not allow the ancient apostolic beliefs to be overturned without a fight. Many bishops of local churches despised Origen and his philosophical school, even in his home town of Alexandria. Peter, bishop of the church in Alexandria, was quoted as saying in his last words just before his martyrdom, "... *Origen, that framer of a perverse dogma laid many temptations, who cast upon the Church a detestable schism, which to this day is throwing it into confusion.*"[258]

Other bishops of local churches strongly opposed Origen as well. Methodius was bishop of the churches of Olympus and Patara, in Lycia (Asia Minor). Like the early apologists and bishops, he too became a martyr. He is known best as the antagonist and nemesis of Origen. And he was as strong a chiliast as were the earlier apologists.

> "*For I cannot endure the trifling of some who shamelessly do violence to Scripture, in order that their opinion, that the resurrection is without flesh, may find support; supposing rational bones and flesh, and in different ways changing it backwards and forwards by allegorizing ... But it is evidently absurd to think that the body will not co-exist with the soul in the eternal state, because it is a bond and fetters; in order that, according to their view, we who are to live in*

---

[258] Peter of Alexandria, The Genuine Acts of Peter

the kingdom of light may not be forever condemned to be bondmen of corruption. For as the question has been sufficiently solved, and the statement refitted in which they defined the flesh to be the soul's chain, the argument also is destroyed, that the flesh will not rise again, lest, if we resume it, we be prisoners in the kingdom of light." [259]

"That Origen said that the body was given to the soul as a fetter after the fall, and that previously it lived without a body; but that this body which we wear is the cause of our sins; wherefore also he called it a fetter, as it can hinder the soul from good works."[260]

"That man, with respect to his nature, is most truly said to be neither soul without body, nor, on the other hand, body without soul; but a being composed out of the union of soul and body into one form of the beautiful. But Origen said that the soul alone is man, as did Plato."[261]

Methodius understood that Origen's errors did not merely affect eschatology. Wrong eschatology reaches into the very fundamentals of biblical doctrine, the cause of sin, the nature of man's existence, and consequently the nature of the incarnation of Christ and the value of the atoning sacrifice of His flesh. Origen (and many amillennialists today) saw man as an immaterial ghost, which they called the "soul," the body being only a temporary accessory. Chiliasts saw man as a living body.

---

[259] Methodius, Discourse on the Resurrection, Part I, ii-iii
[260] Methodius, Discourse on the Resurrection, Part III, ii
[261] Methodius, Discourse on the Resurrection, Part III, iii

The implications of Origen's heresy on the incarnation of Jesus Christ, as well as his death and resurrection, are profound. It is an entirely different "Christianity" that has the Son of God assuming a flesh suit (instead of becoming flesh), and then disposing of His flesh suit when He ascended into heaven, no longer needing flesh since He was free of this physical creation forever.

Peter indicated that Jesus' physical descent from David granted Him the right to the Throne of David, that His flesh body from David's seed would be raised to sit on David's throne. *"Therefore, being a prophet, and knowing that God had sworn with an oath to him that of the fruit of his body, according to the flesh, He would raise up the Christ to sit on his throne, he, foreseeing this, spoke concerning the resurrection of the Christ."*[262]

But the Jesus of Origen offered only His flesh-suit as a sacrifice for our sins. His body of flesh will never sit on David's Throne. It was discarded when He ascended into heaven.[263] His blood is not "precious" in this scheme, but something to be discarded. And how could Jesus Christ come in the flesh and remain sinless if human flesh is inherently corrupt and the real cause of sin? Origen's view was only one baby step away from full-blown Gnosticism.

Methodius continues in his condemnation of Origen:

---

[262] Acts 2:29-31

[263] See my debate with Norm Fields, amillennial Church of Christ minister. http://www.oasischristianchurch.org/air/debate_fields.html

"Origen, after having fabled many things concerning the eternity of the universe, adds this also: 'Nor yet from Adam, as some say, did man, previously not existing, first take his existence and come into the world. Nor again did the world begin to be made six days before the creation of Adam'."[264]

Like Jewish Cabalists and occultists, Origen denied that the flesh created from dust became a "living soul" when God breathed His "breath of life" into it.[265] He claimed instead that all "souls" (ghosts) existed in heaven prior to conception or birth of the child. Origen claimed that the preexistent ghost-soul enters into human flesh as a temporary experience for the purpose of instruction. In Origen's theology, every person existed before Adam's body was created. In this regard, he adopted Plato's "immortality of the soul."

In a feeble attempt at mocking chiliast eschatology, Origen took the chiliast claim – that the six days of creation are prophetic of six thousand years – and insisted that it required a 13,000 year scheme rather than a 7,000 years scheme as chiliasts believed. He argued that if the six days are prophetic of six millennial days (6,000 years), then God must have taken six thousand years to create everything, not six 24-hour days. Origen mocked chiliasts as "clever arithmeticians" because they understood the six days of creation literally as a true historical record, and prophetically as a pattern of millennia. Methodius first quotes Origen's sarcastic argument, and then heaps scorn on him for such a "trifling" insignificant argument.

---

[264] Methodius, Extracts from the Work On Things Created, IX
[265] Genesis 2:7

[Methodius, quoting Origen] *"'But if anyone should prefer to differ in these points, let him first say, whether a period of time be not easily reckoned from the creation of the world, according to the Book of Moses, to those who so receive it, the voice of prophecy here proclaiming: 'Thou art God from everlasting, and world without end.... For a thousand years in Thy sight are but as yesterday: seeing that is past as a watch in the night.' For when a thousand years are reckoned as one day in the sight of God, and from the creation of the world to His rest is six days, so also to our time, six days are defined, as those say who are clever arithmeticians* [here Origen mocks chiliasts as "clever arithmeticians"]. *Therefore, they say that an age of six thousand years extends from Adam to our time. For they say that the judgment will come on the seventh day, that is in the seventh thousand years. Therefore, all the days from our time to that which was in the beginning, in which God created the heaven and the earth, are computed to be thirteen days; before which God, because he had as yet created nothing according to their folly, is stripped of His name of Father and Almighty.'*

'But if there are thirteen days in the sight of God from the creation of the world, how can Wisdom say, in the Book of the Son of Sirach: "Who can number the sand of the sea, and the drops of rain, and the days of eternity?"'

This is what Origen says seriously, and mark how he trifles."[266]

---

[266] Methodius, Extracts from the Work On Things Created, IX

The bitter struggle over eschatology was between the bishops of local churches (like Methodius) who defended the pristine Faith and the theologians who insisted on synthesizing Christianity with Greek philosophy. It continued to fester until after the conversion of the emperor Constantine.

Chapter 6
ROME EMBRACES PLATO

T he Emperor Constantine's alleged conversion in AD 312 brought radical changes to Christianity. The persecution of Christians by the state suddenly stopped. Yet, the price of outward tranquility was the emperor's inserting himself into Christian theology.

Constantine's goal was to unite his empire. Any division could lead to serious political problems and revolts. Adopting Christianity, which had grown enormously during the persecutions, was seen as having the potential to unite the fracturing empire.

Under Constantine, the formerly persecuted churches were suddenly granted the favor of the emperor. Yet, the underlying doctrinal divisions that were still simmering were seen by Constantine as a threat to his power. This is why Constantine convened the Council of Nicaea, to resolve doctrinal conflicts within Christianity. The primary conflict was between the Arians and Trinitarians. But the issue of eschatology was also addressed. The emperor was present at the proceedings, and personally oversaw the work of the bishops, imposing his long shadow over them.

In his opening address to the Christian bishops whom he had summoned, Constantine let his views be known regarding the chiliasm controversy, siding with Plato and his Alexandrian

147

devotees, Clement and Origen, and against the earlier apologists and martyrs.

> *"Plato ... plainly declares that a rational soul is the breath of God, and divides all things into two classes, intellectual and sensible: consisting of bodily structure; the one comprehended by the intellect alone, the other estimated by the judgment and the senses. The former class, therefore, which partakes of the divine spirit, and is uncompounded and immaterial, is eternal, and inherits everlasting life; but the latter, being entirely resolved into the elements of which it is composed, has no share in everlasting life. He [Plato] farther teaches the admirable doctrine, that those who have passed a life of virtue, that is, the spirits of good and holy men, are enshrined, after their separation from the body, in the fairest mansions of heaven. A doctrine not merely to be admired, but profitable too. For who can believe in such a statement, and aspire to such a happy lot, without desiring to practice righteousness and temperance, and to turn aside from vice?"[267]*

> *"If indeed we in any sense aspire to blessedness like that of God, our duty is to lead a life according to his commandments: so shall we, having finished a course consistent with the laws which he has prescribed, dwell forever superior to the power of fate, in eternal and undecaying mansions. ... raising our affections above the things of earth, and directing our thoughts, as far as we may, to high and heavenly objects: for from such endeavors, it is*

---

[267] Eusebius, Oration of Constantine, ch. ix

said, a victory accrues to us more valuable than many blessings."[268]

Not a few bishops were dazzled by Constantine, including Eusebius, the church historian. Pleasing the Christian emperor became a very high priority among many church leaders. His royal favor was a great incentive to set apart their doctrinal differences, and for some, even overpowering the incentive to please Christ. And Constantine lavished church leaders with honor and wealth when they pleased him and assisted him in achieving his goals.

Constantine set out to enforce unity of the Christian religion with the use of law and force against all "schismatics," those who would not submit to the state-approved Roman Catholic Church and its official doctrines. He put everyone who would not go along on notice.

"Forasmuch, then, as it is no longer possible to bear with your pernicious errors, we give warning by this present statute that none of you henceforth presume to assemble yourselves together. We have directed, accordingly, that you be deprived of all the houses in which you are accustomed to hold your assemblies: and our care in this respect extends so far as to forbid the holding of your superstitious and senseless meetings, not in public merely, but in any private house or place whatsoever. Let those of you, therefore, who are desirous of embracing the true and pure religion, take the far better course of entering the catholic Church, and uniting with it in holy fellowship, whereby you will be enabled to

---

[268] Eusebius, Oration of Constantine, ch. xiv

arrive at the knowledge of the truth. In any case, the delusions of your perverted understandings must entirely cease to mingle with and mar the felicity of our present times: I mean the impious and wretched double-mindedness of heretics and schismatics. ... And in order that this remedy may be applied with effectual power, we have commanded, as before said, that you be positively deprived of every gathering point for your superstitious meetings, I mean all the houses of prayer, if such be worthy of the name, which belong to heretics, and that these be made over without delay to the catholic Church; that any other places be confiscated to the public service, and no facility whatever be left for any future gathering; in order that from this day forward none of your unlawful assemblies may presume to appear in any public or private place. Let this edict be made public."

Eusebius then recounted the effect of the emperor's edict on all "heretics and schismatics."

"Thus the members of the entire body became united, and compacted in one harmonious whole; and the one catholic Church, at unity with itself, shone with full luster, while no heretical or schismatic body anywhere continued to exist. And the credit of having achieved this mighty work our Heaven-protected emperor alone, of all who had gone before him, was able to attribute to himself."[269]

It is true that the victors get to write the history books. And the chosen vessel for writing the history of the Christian

---

[269] Eusebius, Constantine, Bk. III, ch. lxvi

Church under the emperor Constantine was Eusebius, bishop of Caesarea, Constantine's lap dog.

Eusebius' speech on the festival honoring Constantine clearly demonstrates that the emperor was the real authority for Christian doctrine in this new Roman Catholic Church – State.

> *"He who is the pre-existent Word, the Preserver of all things, imparts to his disciples the seeds of true wisdom and salvation, and at once enlightens and gives them understanding in the knowledge of his Father's kingdom. Our emperor, his friend, acting as interpreter to the Word of God, aims at recalling the whole human race to the knowledge of God; proclaiming clearly in the ears of all, and declaring with powerful voice the laws of truth and godliness to all who dwell on the earth."*[270]

Eusebius fully supported the Platonic – Christian eschatology, as is quite apparent in this same speech.

> *"[T]he Word of God, … by his Divine teaching, inviting the souls of men to prepare for those mansions which are above the heavens."*[271]

> *"Who, like him, has persuaded multitudes throughout the world to pursue the principles of Divine wisdom, to fix their hope on heaven itself, and look forward to the mansions there reserved for them that love God?"*[272]

---

[270] Eusebius, Oration, ch. ii
[271] Eusebius, Oration, ch. xiv
[272] Eubius, Oration, ch. xvii

The writings of Clement of Alexandria and Origen were abundant and popular in Eusebius' day. In fact, Eusebius had high praise for Origen. Yet, the much older chiliast writings of the earliest Christian apologists still remained in circulation, and were an embarrassment to the Roman Church – State. Chiliasm needed to be suppressed by more than just the emperor's praise of the new Platonic – Christian eschatology.

Revisionism to Defeat Chiliasm

Eusebius was chosen to write a history of Christianity as Josephus had done for Judaism, also under the emperor's supervision. Eusebius' History of the Christian Church is clearly biased, resorting to historical revisionism when convenient, being heavily skewed against the early chiliasts. Eusebius essentially charged the earliest bishop-apologist-martyrs with conveying heresy.

Some chiliast works were also revised by later editors to expunge their chiliasm. This is evident in the surviving works of Victorinus, bishop and martyr of Poetovio (Ptui, Slovenia), who wrote commentaries on Genesis and Revelation in about AD 258. His Genesis commentary shows plainly that he was a chiliast, and that he expected Christ and the saints to reign on earth in the seventh millennium.

> *"And in Matthew we read, that it is written Isaiah also and the rest of his colleagues broke the Sabbath — that that true and just Sabbath should be observed in the seventh millenary of years. Wherefore to those seven days the Lord attributed to each a thousand years; for thus went the warning: 'In Thine eyes, O Lord, a thousand years are as one day.' Therefore in*

the eyes of the Lord each thousand of years is ordained, for I find that the Lord's eyes are seven. Wherefore, as I have narrated, that true Sabbath will be in the seventh millenary of years, when Christ with His elect shall reign."[273]

Yet, his commentary on the twentieth chapter of Revelation contained in the Ante Nicene Fathers has clearly been edited, making Victorinus contradict himself. The edited portion retains the six millennia of chiliasm, but interprets the "first resurrection" as referring to salvation in the present age (like amillennialists). It places the reign of Christ and the saints during the sixth millennium (which the editor thought was present), rather than in the seventh (future) millennium, as in Victorinus' commentary on creation. The net effect is to retain the Millennial Week idea of chiliasm, but claim that the Kingdom of Christ and Satan's being bound were present (6th millennium), and the seventh millennium referred to a heavenly abode.

"Those years wherein Satan is bound are in the first advent of Christ, even to the end of the age; and they are called a thousand, according to that mode of speaking, wherein a part is signified by the whole, … Moreover, that he says that he is bound and shut up, that he may not seduce the nations, the nations signify the Church, seeing that of them it itself is formed, and which being seduced, he previously held until, he says, the thousand years should be completed, that is, what is left of the sixth day, to wit, of the sixth age, which subsists for a thousand years; after this he must be loosed for a little season. The little season signifies three years and six

---

[273] Victorinus, On the Creation of the World

months, in which with all his power the devil will avenge himself trader Antichrist against the Church."[274]

Thus in the edited commentary of Victorinus we have a blend of chiliasm and amillennialism. The seventh millennium in this scheme would be the heavenly hope envisioned by the amillennialists. That the intention of the editor was to expunge the concept of a future "earthly" Kingdom at Christ's return is quite clear from the statement added at the very end of the work, which has no connection to the context in which it is found.

> *"Therefore they are not to be heard who assure themselves that there is to be an earthly reign of a thousand years; who think, that is to say, with the heretic Cerinthus. For the kingdom of Christ is now eternal in the saints, although the glory of the saints shall be manifested after the resurrection."*[275]

Who was the mysterious editor of Victorinus' commentary?

> *"Jerome is responsible for an extensive revision of Victorinus' commentary, dated to 398, which he particularly undertook at the request of a friend to adjust Victorinus' commentary in those verses and passages displaying interpretations which were taken to be chiliastic / millennialistic, a theological opinion which had since been rejected by the Church at large ... . Consequently, essentially two versions of Victorinus' commentary have come down to*

---

[274] Victorinus, Commentary on the Apocalypse, Ch. xx
[275] Victorinus, Commentary on the Apocalypse, Ch. 22

us: his original and the Hieronymian edition. I have undertaken to translate Victorinus' original and only Jerome's letter to Anatolius (which serves as a prologue to Jerome's version) and Jerome's ending of the work (which replaces Victorinus' commentary on chapters 20 and 21 of the Apocalypse). A relatively poor translation of Jerome's version is included in the Nicene-Post Nicene Fathers collection." [276]

Jerome's letter to Anatolius describes his process of purging chiliasm from this ancient commentary on the Apocalypse.

"Those crossing over the perilous seas find different dangers. If a storm of winds has become violent, it is a terror; if the moderate air has calmed the back of the elements, lying calm, they fear traps. Thus is seen in this book which you have sent to me, which is seen to contain the explanation of the Apocalypse by Victorinus. Also, it is dangerous, and opens to the barkings of detractors, to judge the short works of eminent men. For even earlier Papias, the bishop of Hierapolis, and Nepos, the bishop of parts of Egypt, perceived of the kingdom of the thousand years just as Victorinus. And because you are in your letters entreating me, I do not want to delay, but nor do I want to scorn praying. I immediately unwound the books of the greats, and what I found in their commentaries about the kingdom of the thousand years, I added to the little work of Victorinus, erasing from there those things which he perceived according to the letter.

---

[276] Edgecomb, Kevin P., St Victorinus of Poetovio: Commentary on the Apocalypse, http://www.bombaxo.com/victapoc.html

"From the beginning of the book to the sign of the cross, we have corrected things which are the corruptions of inexperience of scribes. Know that from there to the end of the book is added. Now it is yours to judge, and to confirm what pleases. If our life will be made longer and the Lord will give health, for you, our most capable genius will sweat over this book, dearest Anatolius."[277]

Jerome was a contemporary and friend of Augustine, the theologian who systematized and popularized the Amillennial view, and invented what later became Calvinism. Jerome's replacement ending to Victorinus' commentary contains a direct quote from Augustine's commentary on Revelation 20 in his amillennial treatise, The City of God.

"Now the thousand years may be understood in two ways, so far as occurs to me: either because these things happen in the sixth thousand of years or sixth millennium (the latter part of which is now passing), as if during the sixth day, which is to be followed by a Sabbath which has no evening, the endless rest of the saints, so that, speaking of a part under the name of the whole, he calls the last part of the millennium — the part, that is, which had yet to expire before the end of the world — a thousand years; ...

"For it is not said 'that he should not seduce any man,' but 'that he should not seduce the nations' — meaning, no doubt, those among which the Church exists — 'till the thousand years should be fulfilled,' — i.e., either what

---

[277] Jerome to Anatolius, translated by Kevin P. Edgecomb, http://www.bombaxo.com/victapoc.html

remains of the sixth day which consists of a thousand years,..."[278]

Compare to the edited commentary of Victorinus:

*"Moreover, that he says that he is bound and shut up, that he may not seduce the nations, the nations signify the Church, seeing that of them it itself is formed, and which being seduced, he previously held until, he says, **the thousand years should be completed, that is, what is left of the sixth day, to wit, of the sixth age, which subsists for a thousand years;...**"*

Jerome and Augustine lived two centuries after Victorinus. Yet, the blending of the Millennial Week of chiliasm with the new amillennialism, identifying the "millennium" of Christ's reign in Revelation 20 with the 6th millennium then thought to be present, was something Augustine had pioneered, as is evident in the quotes from The City of God.

Fortunately, Victorinus' commentary on the Apocalypse has also survived unedited to testify against Jerome's revisionism. It was translated from the original Latin into French by Martine Dulaey,[279] and from this text it has been translated into English by Kevin P. Edgecomb.[280] In the unaltered commentary on Revelation 20, Victorinus' chiliasm is plain.

---

[278] Augustine, City of God, Bk. 20, ch. 7
[279] Martine Dulaey, Victorin de Poetovio. Sur l'Apocalypse et autres écrits (Source Chrétiennes 423. Paris: Les Éditions du Cerf, 1997).
[280] http://www.bombaxo.com/victapoc.html

"And the scarlet devil is imprisoned and all his fugitive angels in the Tartarus of Gehenna at the coming of the Lord; no one is ignorant of this. And after the thousand years he is released, because of the nations which will have served Antichrist: so that they alone might perish, as they deserved. Then is the general judgment.

"Therefore he says: 'And they lived,' he says, 'the dead who were written in the book of life, and they reigned with Christ a thousand years. This is the first resurrection. Blessed and holy is he who has a part in the first resurrection: toward this one the second death has no power.' Of this resurrection, he says: 'And I saw the Lamb standing, and with him 144 thousands,' that is, standing with Christ, namely those of the Jews in the last time who become believers through the preaching of Elijah, those who, the Spirit bears witness, are virgins not only in body, but also in language. Therefore, as he reminds above, the 24 elder-aged said: 'Grace we bring to You, O Lord God who has reigned; and the nations are angry.'

"At this same first resurrection will also appear the City and the splendid things expressed through this Scripture. Of this first resurrection Paul also spoke to the Macedonian church, thus: 'For as we have thus said to you,' he says, 'by the Word of God, that at the trumpet of God, the Lord Himself will descend from heaven for raising up; and the dead in Christ will stand first, then we who are living, as we will be taken up with Him in the clouds to meet the Lord in the air; and thus we will always be with the Lord.' We have heard the trumpet spoken of; it is observed that in another place the Apostle names another trumpet. Therefore he says to the

Corinthians: 'At the last trumpet, the dead will rise, will become immortal, and we will be changed.' He says the dead will be raised immortal for bearing punishments, but it is shown that we are to be changed and to be covered in glory. Therefore where we hear 'the last trumpet,' we must understand also a first, for these are two resurrections. Therefore, however many were not previously to rise in the first resurrection and to reign with Christ over the world, over all nations, will rise at the last trumpet, after the thousand years, that is, in the last resurrection, among the impious and sinners and perpetrators of various kinds. He rightly adds, saying: Blessed and holy is he who has a part in the first anastasis: toward this one the second death has no power. For the second death is being thrown into hell."[281]

It was bad enough that Jerome truncated the oldest known commentary on Revelation and added his own commentary on chapter 20, plagiarized from Augustine. Yet, the sinister nature of his crime is fully exposed by his attributing chiliasm to the heretic Cerinthus. *"Therefore they are not to be heard who assure themselves that there is to be an earthly reign of a thousand years; who think, that is to say, with the heretic Cerinthus. For the kingdom of Christ is now eternal in the saints, although the glory of the saints shall be manifested after the resurrection."*[282]

Jerome's false charge against chiliasm was borrowed from Eusebius' recent "History of the Christian Church." The

---

[281] Victorinus' Commentary on the Apocalypse, unedited version, translated by Edgecomb, Kevin P., http://www.bombaxo.com/victapoc.html

[282] Jerome's edited ending to Victorinus' Commentary

connection to Cerinthus was made by Eusebius citing two of Origen disciples as sources, Caius and Dionysius.

> *"WE have understood that at this time Cerinthus, the author of another heresy, made his appearance. Caius, whose words we quoted above, in the Disputation which is ascribed to him, writes as follows concerning this man:*
> *'But Cerinthus also, by means of revelations which he pretends were written by a great apostle, brings before us marvelous things which he falsely claims were shown him by angels; and he says that after the resurrection the kingdom of Christ will be set up on earth, and that the flesh dwelling in Jerusalem will again be subject to desires and pleasures. And being an enemy of the Scriptures of God, he asserts, with the purpose of deceiving men, that there is to be a period of a thousand years for marriage festivals.'*
> *And Dionysius, who was bishop of the parish of Alexandria in our day, in the second book of his work On the Promises, where he says some things concerning the Apocalypse of John which he draws from tradition, mentions this same man in the following words:*
> *'But (they say that) Cerinthus, who founded the sect which was called, after him, the Cerinthian, desiring reputable authority for his fiction, prefixed the name. For the doctrine which he taught was this: that the kingdom of Christ will be an earthly one. And as he was himself devoted to the pleasures of the body and altogether sensual in his nature, he dreamed that that kingdom would consist in those things which he desired, namely, in the delights of the belly and of sexual passion, that is to say, in eating and drinking and marrying, and in festivals and sacrifices and the slaying of*

victims, under the guise of which he thought he could indulge his appetites with a better grace.'
These are the words of Dionysius." [283]

It is curious that Eusebius used such recent sources in his attempt to link chiliasm with the heretic, Cerinthus, since neither source could have had any firsthand information about the subject, living more than a century after Cerinthus.

Eusebius' first source, Caius, not only attributed chiliasm to the heretic Cerinthus, but also the authorship of the book of Revelation![284] No doubt his attributing Revelation to Cerinthus was because of the twentieth chapter which describes the Millennium on earth after the first resurrection. Caius was vehemently opposed to chiliasm, making him an extremely unreliable source.

Eusebius second source, Dionysius, was a student of Origen, and succeeded him as head of the Alexandrian school. Since the Alexandrian school was the primary enemy of chiliasm, Eusebius' use of such sources to link chiliasm to the heretic Cerinthus is invalid. That Eusebius quoted these sources who lived very near his own day, who could not possibly have had any personal knowledge of Cerinthus, gives the appearance that he was merely packaging his own historical revisionism in the words of others, none of which give his statements any real historical credibility.

---

[283] Eusebius, Church History, Book III, ch. xxviii
[284] Catholic Encyclopedia, Caius, http://www.newadvent.org/cathen/03144a.htm

The charge that the early apologists adopted chiliasm from Cerinthus is patently absurd. Cerinthus was a Gnostic who blended elements of Christianity, Judaism, and Gnosticism. He was the contemporary and nemesis of John the Apostle in his later years. It is believed by many that John wrote the prologue to His Gospel and his three epistles to counter the influence of Cerinthus. Yet, we learn of this heretic and John's distain for him from Irenaeus, a chiliast.

> *"But Polycarp also was not only instructed by apostles, and conversed with many who had seen Christ, but was also, by Apostles in Asia, appointed bishop of the Church in Smyrna, whom I also saw in my early youth, for he tarried [on earth] a very long time, and, when a very old man, gloriously and most nobly suffering martyrdom, departed this life, having always taught the things which he had learned from the Apostles, and which the Church has handed down, and which alone are true. To these things all the Asiatic Churches testify, as do also those men who have succeeded Polycarp down to the present time, — a man who was of much greater weight, and a more steadfast witness of truth, than Valentinus, and Marcion, and the rest of the heretics. He it was who, coming to Rome in the time of Anicetus caused many to turn away from the aforesaid heretics to the Church of God, proclaiming that he had received this one and sole truth from the Apostles, — that, namely, which is handed down by the Church. There are also those who heard from him that John, the disciple of the Lord, going to bathe at Ephesus, and perceiving Cerinthus within, rushed out of the bath-house without bathing, exclaiming, 'Let us fly, lest even the bath-house fall down, because Cerinthus, the enemy of*

> *the truth, is within.' And Polycarp himself replied to Marcion, who met him on one occasion, and said, 'Dost thou know me?' 'I do know thee, the first-born of Satan.' Such was the horror which the Apostles and their disciples had against holding even verbal communication with any corrupters of the truth.*"[285]

This is the same Irenaeus who attributed chiliasm, the Kingdom of Christ on the earth in the seventh millennium, to the same Polycarp and those like him who were acquainted with the Apostles. *"The presbyters, the disciples of the Apostles, affirm that this is the gradation and arrangement of those who are saved."*[286] The *"presbyters, the disciples of the Apostles"* were all chiliasts as far as we can tell, including Polycarp, Ignatius, and Papias (all taught personally by John). It is absurd to suggest that the early apologists who vehemently opposed the Gnostic heretics, including Cerinthus, derived their belief in chiliasm from the very Gnostics they refuted as heretics! That Cerinthus held to some of the tenets of chiliasm only shows that he had mixed some of the apostolic teachings with his own perverted blend of Christianity, Judaism, and Gnosticism.

Cerinthus did not teach chiliasm, which places the resurrection of believers at Christ's coming before the millennium. Rather, he was the first post-millennialist. *"Cerinthus believed in a happy millennium which would be realized here on earth previous to the resurrection and the spiritual kingdom*

---

[285] Irenaeus, Against Heresies, Bk. III, ch. iii, 4
[286] Irenaeus, Against Heresies, Bk. V, ch. xxxvi

of God in heaven."[287] Thus, Cerinthus' eschatology had more in common with Amillennialism than with chiliasm, placing both the resurrection and the Kingdom of Christ after the "millennium," and claiming that the destiny of believers is heaven. The only thing he had in common with chiliasts is taking the millennium in Revelation 20 as a literal thousand years. Cerinthus taught that Christ would not return until 1000 years after His ascension.

Chiliasm Existed Before Cerinthus

It is easy to show that essential tenets of chiliasm (which conflict with amillennialism) are to be found in the very earliest of writers who were intimate with the Apostles. The earliest of the Apostolic Fathers, Clement of Rome, whom Paul called his "fellow worker," was a chiliast. He viewed the Kingdom of Christ as entirely future, to commence at the future resurrection of the saints.

> *"All the generations from Adam even unto this day have passed away; but those who, through the grace of God, have been made perfect in love, now possess a place among the godly, and shall be made manifest at the revelation of the kingdom of Christ. For it is written, "Enter into thy secret chambers for a little time, until my wrath and fury pass away; and I will remember a propitious day, and will raise you up out of your graves."*[288]

---

[287] Catholic Encyclopedia, http://www.newadvent.org/cathen/03539a.htm
[288] Clement of Rome, Epistle to the Corinthians, ch. L

He also held out the future inheritance in the Promised Land, quoting the Land inheritance promises in Psalm 37 as the hope of Christians.

> *"Let us be kind one to another after the pattern of the tender mercy and benignity of our Creator. For it is written, 'The kind-hearted shall inhabit the Land, and the guiltless shall be left upon it, but transgressors shall be destroyed from off the face of it.' And again [the Scripture] saith, 'I saw the ungodly highly exalted, and lifted up like the cedars of Lebanon: I passed by, and, behold, he was not; and I diligently sought his place, and could not find it. Preserve innocence, and look on equity: for there shall be a remnant to the peaceful man'."*[289]

This Psalm states several times that the wicked will be cut off, but the righteous shall inherit the Land and dwell in it forever. That Clement pointed his readers to this Psalm as containing the Christian hope, being motivation for righteous living, implies that he held the chiliast hope based on the Abrahamic Covenant. The Corinthian church to which he was writing no doubt shared this hope also.

Clement of Rome was a presbyter of the church in Rome while Paul was still alive, before the heretic Cerinthus had any contact with the early Christians. How then could Clement of Rome borrow chiliasm from Cerinthus?

Like Polycarp, Ignatius was John's disciple. He was bishop of the church in Antioch (Paul's home church). He held the same

---

[289] Clement of Rome, Epistle to the Corinthians, ch. xiv

chiliast view as Clement of Rome and Polycarp, that the Kingdom of God was after the future resurrection.

> *"If any man follows him that makes a schism in the Church, he shall not inherit the kingdom of God."*[290]

Thus, the Church was not seen as being "the Kingdom of God" (as in amillennialism), but rather members of the Church saw "the Kingdom of God" as their destiny after the resurrection (as in chiliasm). On the way to his execution in Rome, Ignatius wrote to Polycarp, his fellow student of John's, (who would soon follow in martyrdom), encouraging him to press on to his inheritance in the Kingdom of God.

> *"Let not those who seem worthy of credit, but teach strange doctrines, fill thee with apprehension. Stand firm, as does an anvil which is beaten. It is the part of a noble athlete to be wounded, and yet to conquer. And especially we ought to bear all things for the sake of God, that He also may bear with us, and bring us into His kingdom. Add more and more to thy diligence; run thy race with increasing energy; weigh carefully the times. Whilst thou art here, be a conqueror; for here is the course, and there are the crowns."*[291]

The Epistle describing the martyrdom of Polycarp, written by the church in Smyrna where he was bishop, closes with a clear statement indicating belief in the same idea: the Kingdom of Christ is to be entered in the future at the resurrection of the just, rather than being present now as the later opponents of

---

[290] Ignatius, Epistle to the Philadelphians, Ch. iii
[291] Ignatius, Epistle to Polycarp, ch. iii

chiliasm claimed. The members of Polycarp's church in Smyrna would certainly reflect the views of their pastor. And since this was an encyclical letter to be passed on to all the churches of Asia Minor, it no doubt reflects the views of these churches which had fellowship with one another.

> *"When, therefore, ye have yourselves read this Epistle, be pleased to send it to the brethren at a greater distance, that they also may glorify the Lord, who makes such choice of His own servants. To Him who is able to bring us all by His grace and goodness into his everlasting[292] kingdom, through His only-begotten Son Jesus Christ, to Him be glory, and honor, and power, and majesty, forever. Amen. Salute all the saints. They that are with us salute you, and Evarestus, who wrote this Epistle, with all his house."*[293]

After attempting to link chiliasm to the heretic Cerinthus, by quoting the works of anti-chiliasts, Eusebius later contradicted himself, a telltale sign of lying and revisionism. He attributed chiliasm instead to Papias, bishop of Hierapolis, who was a fellow student of John's along with Polycarp, bishop of Smyrna, and Ignatius, bishop of Antioch.

> *"The same writer [Papias] gives also other accounts which he says came to him through unwritten tradition, certain strange parables and teachings of the Savior, and some other more mythical things. To these belong his statement that there will be a period of some thousand years after the*

---

[292] As in 2 Peter 1:11, the Greek reads, "αιωνιαν βασιλειαν" ("age enduring Kingdom" not "everlasting Kingdom" as in the English translation).
[293] Martyrdom of Polycarp, ch. xx

resurrection of the dead, and that the kingdom of Christ will be set up in material form on this very earth. I suppose he got these ideas through a misunderstanding of the apostolic accounts, not perceiving that the things said by them were spoken mystically in figures. For he appears to have been of very limited understanding, as one can see from his discourses. But it was due to him that so many of the Church Fathers after him adopted a like opinion, urging in their own support the antiquity of the man; as for instance Irenaeus and anyone else that may have proclaimed similar views. Papias gives also in his own work other accounts of the words of the Lord on the authority of Aristion who was mentioned above, and traditions as handed down by the presbyter John; to which we refer those who are fond of learning."[294]

Papias' works, according to both Irenaeus and Eusebius, contained many firsthand accounts of Papias' discussions with those who had heard Jesus and the Apostles teach. And these accounts gave many details about the future Kingdom of Christ and the saints reigning on the earth for a thousand years. Papias' five books have all perished long ago; the Catholic Encyclopedia explains why. *"The cause of the loss of this precious work of an Apostolic Father was the chiliastic view which he taught."*[295] In other words, his works were destroyed because the Church did not like his attributing chiliasm to Jesus and the Apostles based on eyewitness accounts.

---

[294] Eusebius, Church History, Bk. III, ch. xxxix
[295] Catholic Encyclopedia, Papias, http://www.newadvent.org/cathen/11457c.htm

Eusebius dismissed these many firsthand accounts as the results of Papias' *"very limited understanding"* and not realizing that the teaching of Jesus and the Apostles which the eyewitnesses reported to him were not meant to be taken literally, but allegorically. That is, not only is the literal reading of the Hebrew prophets to be discarded in favor of allegorical interpretation, but so also were the words of Jesus Christ and His Apostles to be discarded, and those who heard and reported them. And since Papias was such an unsophisticated, stupid man, taking these sayings of Jesus literally, he must have been the one who concocted chiliasm. And from him, all the other chiliasts were led astray, according to Eusebius.

Of course, this does not take into account the chiliasm of Clement of Rome, a companion of Paul, who served the church in Rome long before Papias was bishop in Hierapolis! Apparently Eusebius was doing his best to revise history in favor of the emperor's Platonic version of Christianity. But, revisionism always leaves a trail.

Historical Revisionism Continues

Modern day amillennialists frequently claim that chiliasm was borrowed from the Jews. It is true that Jewish eschatology involved the resurrection of the body and an inheritance in the restored Promised Land. One must remember that the Apostles were Jewish, as were all the prophets. Why wouldn't their eschatology have a Jewish flavor? The New Testament clearly points out the mistake made by the Jews. It was not the belief in a physical resurrection, or the restoration of Jerusalem and the Land. In fact, these things are affirmed in the New Testament.[296] Rather, the mistakes of the Jews are clearly described in the New Testament – failing to see *"that Christ must first suffer"* before entering into His glory,[297] that remission of sins through Christ must be preached to all nations before[298] His reign on earth would commence, and supposing that their physical descent from Abraham guaranteed the second, eternal Land inheritance to them.

Furthermore, pre-Christian Jewish eschatology did not include the Millennial Week theory, that God would instruct and discipline humanity for six millennia after which the Kingdom would come and Christ would reign for a thousand years over the nations. Some of the Jewish apocryphal works had various timetables for the coming of the Messiah.[299] Yet, none made the connection to the six days of creation or the Sabbath Rest being the reign of the Messiah, or that man would endure six thousand years of toil under the curse to be followed by a millennium of Messiah's rule over the nations.

The complete absence of the Millennial Week idea from pre-Christian Jewish eschatology is really rather surprising. If anyone would have invented such a concept on their own, surely it would have been the Jews who were commanded to work six days and rest on the Sabbath. Yet, the idea seems not to have occurred to them. Instead, it sprang to life during the age of the Apostles, and is found fully developed among those who knew the Apostles and who led apostolic churches.

---

[296] Acts 1:6-8; Acts 3:19-21; Acts 28:20; Rom. 8:16-25
[297] Luke 24:26
[298] Luke 24:46-49
[299] The Book of Enoch has a 10 "week" scheme, ch. xci - xciii

The fact that this idea only appeared in Jewish writings centuries after the Apostles strongly suggests that it was eventually borrowed from interaction with Christians. The Babylonian Talmud, written circa AD 300-500, is apparently the first clear mention of this theory in Jewish literature.

> *"R. Kattina said: Six thousand years shall the world exist, and one [thousand, the seventh], it shall be desolate, as it is written, And the Lord alone shall be exalted in that day. Abaye said: it will be desolate two [thousand], as it is said, After two days will he revive us: in the third day, he will raise us up, and we shall live in his sight.*
>
> *It has been taught in accordance with R. Kattina: Just as the seventh year is one year of release in seven, so is the world: one thousand years out of seven shall be fallow, as it is written, And the Lord alone shall be exalted in that day,' and it is further said, A Psalm and song for the Sabbath day, meaning the day that is altogether Sabbath — and it is also said, For a thousand years in thy sight are but as yesterday when it is past.*
>
> *The Tanna debe Eliyyahu teaches: The world is to exist six thousand years. In the first two thousand there was desolation; two thousand years the Torah flourished; and the next two thousand years is the Messianic era."*[300]

Jewish Cabbalists of the middle ages picked up the idea from the Babylonian Talmud and embellished it. The *Sefer Ha-Temunah*, a 13th century Cabbalist work, expands the

---

[300] Babylonian Talmud, Tractate Sanhedrin, Folio 97a

Millennial week into a complete Jubilee cycle of 49,000 years (7 x 7 millennia).[301]

The early Christian writers did not adopt Jewish mysticism. The apologists who strongly defended chiliasm held the contemporary Jewish interpretations of the rabbis in contempt. This is particularly evident in Justin's Dialogue with Trypho (a Jew). Justin was a converted philosopher, having studied under several schools of Greek philosophy. Yet, coming to Christ, he rejected these philosophies in favor of the Christian interpretation of the Jewish prophets. He also had nothing but contempt for the interpretations of the unbelieving Jews. In his discussion with Trypho (a Jew), he repeatedly pointed out the blindness of the Jewish teachers and rejected their interpretations of the prophets.

> "'I excuse and forgive you, my friend,' I said. 'For you know not what you say, but have been persuaded by teachers who do not understand the Scriptures...'"[302]

> "Then I answered, '... be not confounded, nay, rather remain still more zealous hearers and investigators, despising the tradition of your teachers, since they are convicted by the Holy Spirit of inability to perceive the truths taught by God, and of preferring to teach their own doctrines'."[303]

---

[301] Rabbi Nathan Slifkin, The Challenge of Creation: Judaism's Encounter with Science, Cosmology, and Evolution, 2006
[302] Justin, Dialogue with Trypho (A Jew), ch. ix
[303] Ibid. ch. xxxviii

"But I am far from putting reliance in your teachers, who refuse to admit that the interpretation made by the seventy elders [the Septuagint] who were with Ptolemy [king] of the Egyptians is a correct one; and they attempt to frame another."[304]

"He shall raise all men from the dead, and appoint some to be incorruptible, immortal, and free from sorrow in the everlasting and imperishable kingdom; but shall send others away to the everlasting punishment of fire. But as to you and your teachers deceiving yourselves when you interpret what the Scripture says as referring to those of your nation then in dispersion, and maintain that their prayers and sacrifices offered in every place are pure and well-pleasing, learn that you are speaking falsely, and trying by all means to cheat yourselves."[305]

"I quoted from the words of Jeremiah the prophet, and Esdras, and David; but from those which are even now admitted by you, which had your teachers comprehended, be well assured they would have deleted them, as they did those about the death of Isaiah, whom you sawed asunder with a wooden saw."[306]

"But they are cisterns broken, and holding no water, which your own teachers have digged, as the Scripture also expressly asserts, 'teaching for doctrines the commandments of men.' And besides, they beguile themselves and you,

---

[304] Ibid. ch. lxxi
[305] Ibid. ch. cxvii
[306] Ibid. ch. cxx

supposing that the everlasting kingdom will be assuredly given to those of the dispersion who are of Abraham after the flesh, although they be sinners, and faithless, and disobedient towards God, which the Scriptures have proved is not the case."[307]

Since the early Christian apologists rejected the Greek philosophies, Gnostics like Cerinthus, and the Jewish misinterpretations of Scripture, how can we account for the sudden spontaneous appearance of chiliasm among them unless it was indeed handed down by the Apostles?

The pressure from Justin's former philosophical pursuits would have led him towards amillennial tendencies, which are much more consistent with Greek philosophy. Yet, he argued against such. He also solidly refuted Trypho, a Jew, and explained the errors of the Jewish eschatology. It is not logical to suppose that Justin (or any of the other early apologists) would blindly follow a purely Jewish idea without clear apostolic precedent founded upon the Scriptures. Yet, no such theory existed among the Jews at this early date.

On the other hand, it is easy to see how an apostolic chiliasm could quickly degrade into proto-amillennialism as Greek believers refused to abandon their own worldview and presuppositions (like the Corinthians), preferring to view Scripture through a Greek philosophical lens. That the heretic Cerinthus adopted some chiliast ideas is no surprise, since his theology was a blend of Judaism, Christianity, and Gnosticism.

---

[307] Ibid. ch. cxl

Augustine eventually put the finishing touches on amillennialism, which provided the theological justification for Christianity's merger with the Roman state. The primitive eschatology of chiliasm, with its future return of Christ to overthrow the kingdoms of the world (including Rome) and establish a world Kingdom in Jerusalem, was not compatible with Rome's military pursuits. Augustine gave Rome the needed theological structure. The Roman Empire, in their thinking, became the Kingdom of God on earth. The emperor and bishop of Rome became partners in this new Christian kingdom. The bishop of Rome would declare the emperor to be God's chosen agent, and the emperor used the sword to enforce the unity of this Roman State – Church, and in so doing attempted to unify the empire. The emperor used the Church, and the Church used the emperor.

Augustine's development of amillennialism can easily be traced to the influence of Origen, and his own preoccupation with the philosophies of Plato. Even the Catholic Encyclopedia acknowledges that Augustine's views were a blend of Christianity and Platonism.

> *"Augustine gradually became acquainted with Christian doctrine, and in his mind the fusion of Platonic philosophy with revealed dogmas was taking place. ... It is now easy to appreciate at its true value the influence of neo-Platonism upon the mind of the great African Doctor. It would be impossible for anyone who has read the works of St. Augustine to deny the existence of this influence. ... But the method was a dangerous one; in thus seeking harmony*

between the two doctrines he thought too easily to find Christianity in Plato, or Platonism in the Gospel."[308]

An honest evaluation of the historical evidence weighs heavily in favor of chiliasm being the apostolic teaching. All deviations from this eschatology can easily be accounted for by the pressures of Greek philosophy corrupting the apostolic teaching. Chiliasm was the view of the earliest Christians who had direct or indirect association with the Apostles. The men who defended it were traditionalists, insisting on preserving the Faith exactly as it was handed down. Its defenders were mostly bishops of local churches whose job it was to faithfully transmit the Apostles' teaching to the next generation. These men were antagonistic toward the Jewish interpretations of Scripture, and would not have adopted them in opposition to the Apostles' doctrine. Nor would they have adopted the opinions of the Gnostic heretic, Cerinthus, whom they vehemently opposed and denounced. The Millennial Week theory was not Jewish, and it was certainly not Gnostic. That leaves only one possibility, that it was Apostolic.

The amillennial view, which arose gradually along with the rejection of chiliasm, was based on Christians adopting "heretical discourses" of the Greeks, and philosophical speculations of men who thought more of their own reasoning powers than of preserved apostolic tradition. Its "proof text" was Jesus' statement about *"many mansions"* in *"My Father's house"* which was blended with Plato's heavenly spheres theory.

---

[308] Catholic Encyclopedia, St. Augustine

The Alexandrian school laid the groundwork for Christianity's acceptance within the intellectual arena, not by proving its superiority over Greek philosophical foolishness, as Justin and Irenaeus had done, but by transforming the mystery of God into just another Greek myth. The merger between Church and state after the conversion of Constantine sealed the demise of ancient chiliasm. Apostolic Christianity was dead, and a new Platonic Christianity had taken its place with the backing of the new "Christian" Emperor. What Satan could not destroy through persecution he destroyed through patronizing and flattery.

Chapter 7
DEMISE of the MILLENNIAL WEEK

No doubt many readers of this book are wondering how the early Christians could hold to a Millennial Week chronology, which would put the second coming of Christ almost two millennia in the future. Some of the New Testament's earlier books seem to indicate an expectancy of Christ's return in the lifetimes of the first century Christians. For example, Paul's statement that *"we who are alive and remain"*[309] at the coming of the Lord could imply that he expected to see Christ's return.

We must not lose sight of the fact that the Apostles themselves were progressively learning from the Holy Spirit throughout their entire ministries. For example, the early chapters of Acts illustrate clearly that the Apostles were not initially prepared to receive gentiles as their equals and fellow heirs of the promises in the Abrahamic Covenant. This is strikingly apparent in Peter's defense to the Jerusalem church for preaching to and baptizing Cornelius' household. He said rather defensively, *"Who was I that I could withstand God?"*[310] The progressive development of theology among the Apostles is also evident in the Jerusalem Council, when the Apostles and elders deliberated Paul's ministry,[311] many being at first unwilling to give their blessing.

---

[309] 1 Thess. 4:15
[310] Acts 11:1-18
[311] Acts 15

179

Even at the close of John's ministry, decades after the other Apostles were dead, John had to finally put to rest the rumor that he would live to see Jesus' second coming, based on a common misunderstanding of Jesus.[312] *"Jesus said to him, 'If I will that he remain till I come, what is that to you? You follow Me.' Then this saying went out among the brethren that this disciple would not die. Yet Jesus did not say to him that he would not die, but, 'If I will that he remain till I come, what is that to you?'"*[313] If this saying was popular among the early Christians, and if John only corrected it after the other Apostles had died, then we can assume that the Apostles had not previously quashed this rumor. Yet, it was clearly a false expectation, as John pointed out. It was based on a misunderstanding of Jesus' statement.

John did not receive the last installment of apostolic revelation until his exile on Patmos, several decades after Peter's and Paul's deaths at Rome. Thus, none of the other Apostles were familiar with the things in the book of Revelation. All these things show that the Apostles did not have full and complete knowledge from the very beginning of their ministries. They learned progressively from the Spirit, just as the prophets before them, and just as they had done during Jesus' public ministry. God saw fit to keep John alive until the entire body of Christian teaching was complete and had been entrusted to the next generation of faithful men.

In the earlier epistles, Paul tended to write as though he expected Jesus' return to be very soon, although he never

---

[312] John 21:19-25
[313] John 21:22-23

stated that it would. Yet, in his later Epistles, he wrote as though it was quite some distance away. This is apparent in his instructions to Timothy, describing the conditions in the future. *"For the time will come when they will not endure sound doctrine, but according to their own desires, because they have itching ears, they will heap up for themselves teachers; and they will turn their ears away from the truth, and be turned aside to fables."*[314] This was new revelation given to Paul towards the end of his ministry. The Spirit indicated to Paul that a considerable period of time would elapse before Jesus' return, and that a massive state of apostasy would occur among the Christian churches in those days. Peter implied the same thing in his last epistle, written at about the same time (the mid-sixties): *"… knowing this first: that scoffers will come in the last days, walking according to their own lusts, and saying, 'Where is the promise of His coming?'"*[315] This is when Peter also reminded them that God's "days" are measured in millennia,[316] implying his knowledge of the Millennial Week.

The progressive nature of the Apostles' own learning, as reflected in the changing tone of their epistles regarding expectancy, strongly suggests that the Millennial Week concept was not known to the Apostles until shortly before Peter's and Paul's deaths around AD 66-67. It was noted in the third chapter that the New Testament books which support chiliasm's Millennial Week are only those written shortly before the deaths of Peter and Paul – Hebrews and 2 Peter – and of course, Revelation. It is no coincidence that

---

[314] 2 Tim 4:3-4
[315] 2 Peter 3:3-4
[316] 2 Peter 3:8

these three books were later challenged by anti-chiliasts as not being part of the canon of New Testament Scriptures. The fact that the earlier epistles appear to suggest (but never state) that Christ's coming could be in their own lifetimes does not contradict later revelation of the Millennial Week at the end of their ministry. John would have been the one to popularize this later teaching after the other Apostles were dead. Perhaps this is why the "Millennium" is explicitly defined for us in Revelation 20. It is, therefore, not surprising that the Millennial Week idea was so strongly promoted by the early writers who had personal links to John and his oral tradition.

Expectancy in the Early Christian Writers

We also find a certain expectation of Jesus' return within the writings of the very men quoted earlier who promoted the Millennial Week idea. But this should not be mistaken for a belief that the end times were imminent. Irenaeus rebuked those who were trying to calculate the name of the Antichrist, using the numerical values of the Greek letters to add up to 666. His advice was to await the breakup of the Roman Empire and the arrival of the ten kings described in Daniel 2 and Revelation 17, all of which had to occur before the Antichrist could arise.[317] This was not seen as being imminent, since Rome was at its height during Irenaeus' day. Yet this did not diminish their enthusiasm about Christ's return.

Textual Variations in the Septuagint

There were several early Christian attempts to develop a chronology of the Bible in order to pinpoint where they were on the Millennial Week timeline. Yet, they all used the Greek

---

[317] Irenaeus, Book V, ch. xxvi - xxx

Septuagint for their chronological data, since the Hebrew text was not readily available to them, and they would have to rely on unbelieving Jews to explain it to them since they did not speak or read Hebrew.

Most of the chronological data is the same in the Hebrew text and the LXX for the periods of time after Abraham. However, the chronological data in the LXX was intentionally corrupted by the Jewish translators for the period from creation to Abraham. These genealogies were systematically lengthened by 100 years per generation in the Septuagint. For example, the Hebrew text states that Adam was 130 years old when Seth was born. But the LXX has 230 years. The Hebrew text says that Seth lived 105 years when Enos was born. The LXX has 205 years. About three-fourths of the generations from Adam to Abraham were lengthened by a century each in the LXX. This makes any chronology based on the Greek Old Testament about 1500 years too long! Consequently, the early Christians who attempted chronologies from the Septuagint concluded that the sixth millennium was almost completed in their day.

Theophilus of Antioch[318] is considered the originator of the study of biblical chronology among Christians. He was a contemporary of Justin and Irenaeus, and was a highly regarded pastor of the church of Antioch after the martyrdom of Ignatius. His chronology is typical, based entirely on the Septuagint.

---

[318] Theophilus lived from AD 115 to AD 181. (Ante Nicene Fathers, Vol. II, p. 171)

"Adam lived till he begat a son, 230 years. And his son Seth, 205. And his son Enos, 190. And his son Cainan, 170. And his son Mahaleel, 165. And his son Jared, 162. And his son Enoch, 165. And his son Methuselah, 167. And his son Lamech, 188. And Lamech's son was Noah, of whom we have spoken above, who begat Shem when 500 years old. During Noah's life, in his 600th year, the flood came. The total number of years, therefore, till the flood, was 2242. And immediately after the flood, Shem, who was 100 years old, begat Arphaxad. And Arphaxad, when 135 years old, begat Salah. And Salah begat a son when 130. And his son Eber, when 134. And from him the Hebrews name their race. And his son Phaleg begat a son when 130. And his son Reu, when 132 And his son Serug, when 130. And his son Nahor, when 75. And his son Terah, when 70. And his son Abraham, our patriarch, begat Isaac when he was 100 years old. Until Abraham, therefore, there are 3278 years."[319]

As will be demonstrated later, the Hebrew text places the birth of Abraham at 2000 years from creation. Theophilus' calculations are longer by 1278 years for this period alone. After further calculations of the period from Abraham to the sacking of Jerusalem by Nebuchadnezzar, Theophilus calculated the total as follows:

"And after these kings, the people, continuing in their sins, and not repenting, the king of Babylon, named Nebuchadnezzar, came up into Judaea, according to the prophecy of Jeremiah. He transferred the people of the Jews to Babylon, and destroyed the temple which Solomon had built.

---

[319] Theolophilus of Antioch, To Autolycus, Book III, ch. 24

And in the Babylonian banishment the people passed 70 years. Until the sojourning in the land of Babylon, there are therefore, in all, 4954 years 6 months and 10 days. And according as God had, by the prophet Jeremiah, foretold that the people should be led captive to Babylon, in like manner He signified beforehand that they should also return into their own land after 70 years. These 70 years then being accomplished, Cyrus becomes king of the Persians."[320]

Adding the 70 years of exile, from creation to the first year of Cyrus was 5024 years according to Theophilus' calculations. He then turned to the secular histories of the Greeks and Romans in an attempt to reconstruct the period from Cyrus to his day. His conclusion was as follows:

"And from the foundation of the world the whole time is thus traced, so far as its main epochs are concerned. From the creation of the world to the deluge were 2242 years. And from the deluge to the time when Abraham our forefather begat a son, 1036 years. And from Isaac, Abraham's son, to the time when the people dwelt with Moses in the desert, 660 years. And from the death of Moses and the rule of Joshua the son of Nun, to the death of the patriarch David, 498 years. And from the death of David and the reign of Solomon to the sojourning of the people in the land of Babylon, 518 years 6 months 10 days. And from the government of Cyrus to the death of the Emperor Aurelius Verus, 744 years. All the years from the creation of the world amount to a total of 5698 years, and the odd months and days."

---

[320] Theolophilus of Antioch, To Autolycus, Book III, ch. 25

The terminus ad quem was the death of the Roman emperor, Aurelius Versus (AD 180). Thus, using the chronology of Theophilus, the end of the sixth millennium would have been the year AD 482.

Theophilus made several important mistakes in his chronology. The most important was his reliance on the dates in the Septuagint. The second was his reliance on the secular histories of the Greeks and Romans for the period after Cyrus, instead of the prophecy of Daniel's 70 weeks.

Of course, one might legitimately ask whether the LXX genealogical data might actually be correct, and the Hebrew text we now have might have been shortened. This question is quickly resolved by the fact that other ancient pre-Christian evidence supports the readings in the Hebrew text against the LXX. This includes many of the genealogies in the Samaritan Pentateuch, which follow the Hebrew dates in Genesis 5, but agree with the Septuagint in some of the dates in chapter 11.[321]

Greek was not the only language into which the Old Testament Scriptures were translated in ancient times. It was also translated into Aramaic directly from the Hebrew, most likely by Jews not long after the time of Christ.[322] The early Aramaic translation became the Old Testament of the Aramaic-speaking churches of the east and is called the

---

[321] This shows that the Samaritan Pentateuch had some contact in its transmission history with both the Hebrew and the LXX, and that the shorter dates in the Hebrew text are at least as ancient as the dates in the LXX.

[322] Francis Crawford Burkitt, Early Eastern Christianity, 71 ff. 1904.

"Peshitta," meaning common or straight. The Peshitta agrees completely with the Hebrew dates in Genesis.

Likewise, the Old Testament of the Latin Vulgate, translated by Jerome in the fourth century, follows a very old Hebrew text. The dates in the Vulgate also agree with the modern Hebrew text.

Some pre-Christian Jewish non-canonical books show dependence on the shorter dates of the Hebrew text as well. The book of Jubilees gives the birth of Abraham around 1860 years after creation, very close to the total derived from the Hebrew text, and far shorter than the LXX.

The variant readings in the Septuagint are almost certainly the result of an intentional manipulation of the text. There is a distinct pattern to these changes proving that they are not the result of accidental scribal error, but intentional manipulation to fulfill some particular agenda. In most of the twenty generations, in Genesis 5 & 11, the age of the father when his son was born is exactly 100 years longer in the LXX. Yet, the time that he lived after his son was born is shortened by the same 100 years, so that the total life-spans still agree with the Hebrew text. For example, the Hebrew Bible states that Seth was born in Adam's 130th year. Then the text says Adam lived 800 years more, making a total of 930 years, within the Millennial Day in which God said Adam would die. The Septuagint adds exactly 100 years, claiming that Seth was born in Adam's 230th year. If this had been the only alteration to Adam's lifespan, then Adam would have lived 1030 years, beyond the Millennial Day in which God said he would die.

So, the LXX translators also subtracted exactly 100 years from Adam's remaining years after Seth was born, making it 700 instead of 800 as in the Hebrew text.

The systematic pattern of adding 100 years to each lifespan before a the son was born, followed by subtracting 100 years from the remaining years, continues for most of the generations listed in the Genesis genealogies in the Septuagint.

The net effect of these intentional alterations was to keep the total lifespans undisturbed, yet throw off any attempt at a continuous chronology. Chronologies follow the genealogical tree using only the portion of an individual's lifetime until the next son in the genealogy was born, adding up the ages of each father when his son was born.

It seems the Septuagint translators did not want to disturb the total life-spans of the patriarchs, having them live longer than one millennium. Yet, they clearly wanted to throw off anyone wishing to construct a chronology of the period. The Hebrew text gives a total for the period from Adam to Abraham as about 2000 years. Yet, the Septuagint gives a total of about 3400 years. Since this is the only real effect from this systematic alteration, it is logical to infer that the motive was to deny the reader a true chronology.

Why would the Jewish scribes who translated the Hebrew Scriptures into Greek intentionally alter the text? We should keep in mind that they were employed by Ptolemy, king of Egypt, to make this translation for his library in Alexandria.

188

Perhaps they wanted to throw off any attempt at a chronology by a non-Jew, or even by the common Jewish people. The Hebrew language was fast becoming a dead language, used only by the elite scribes and priests by the time of Christ. The common people spoke Greek. Obscuring the chronological data could have been their way of keeping the prophecies of the time when the Kingdom would arrive out of reach of the secular authorities. While the Jews apparently did not know of the Millennial Week concept until after it was introduced by Christians, they developed other sophisticated chronological schemes which attempted to predict the exact year of the coming of Messiah and His Kingdom.[323]

The early Christian chiliasts' reliance on the Greek Old Testament for their chronological data skewed their timelines by roughly 1400 years. And since most could not read Hebrew, but relied on the LXX exclusively, it is not surprising that their chronologies reflect the incorrect (longer) genealogies. So, they expected the end of the sixth millennium much closer to their own time.

Hippolytus interpreted the measurements of the Ark of the Covenant in an allegorical way to confirm the Christian chronology based on the Septuagint.

> *"In mentioning the "other," moreover, he specifies the seventh [Millennium], in which there is rest. But someone may be ready to say, How will you prove to me that the Savior was born in the year 5500? Learn that easily, O man; for the things that took place of old in the wilderness, under*

---

[323] Both the book of Enoch and Book of Jubilees contain such schemes.

Moses, in the case of the tabernacle, were constituted types and emblems of spiritual mysteries, in order that, when the truth came in Christ in these last days, you might be able to perceive that these things were fulfilled. For He says to him, "And thou shalt make the ark of imperishable wood, and shalt overlay it with pure gold within and without; and thou shalt make the length of it two cubits and a half, and the breadth thereof one cubit and a half, and a cubit and a half the height;" which measures, when summed up together, make five cubits and a half, so that the 5500 years might be signified thereby.

"At that time, then, the Savior appeared and showed His own body to the world, (born) of the Virgin, who was the "ark overlaid with pure gold," with the Word within and the Holy Spirit without; so that the truth is demonstrated, and the "ark" made manifest. From the birth of Christ, then, we must reckon the 500 years that remain to make up the 6000, and thus the end shall be."

Hippolytus lived from AD 170 – 236, writing only a few decades after Theophilus of Antioch. He expected the return of Christ in less than three centuries. After him, Cyprian demonstrated a similar expectation based on the same early Christian chronology. *"Six thousand years are now nearly completed since the devil first attacked man."*[324] Shortly thereafter, Lactantius[325] wrote, *"I have already shown above, that when six thousand years shall be completed this change must take place, and that the last day of the extreme conclusion is now drawing near."*[326]

---

[324] Cyprian, Treatise XI, 2
[325] AD 260-330
[326] Lactantius, Divine Institutes, Book VII, ch. 25

The rise of amillennialism did not immediately mean the demise of the Millennial Week chronology, or of predicting the approximate time of Christ's return based on this theory using the dates derived from the LXX. For a short time the Millennial Week idea was adapted to amillennialism. The amillennial writers simply placed the "Kingdom" age as being the remaining portion of the sixth millennium (not taking the 1000 years of Revelation 20 literally) instead of being the seventh millennium as in chiliasm.[327] In this hybrid form of amillennialism, the seventh millennium became the eternal state in heaven. It is apparent then that the new amillennialists were not opposed to the Millennial Week concept. Their objection was against chiliasm's resurrection of material bodies, the eternal destiny of the redeemed on a restored earth, and the futurity of Christ's reign on earth in the age to come.

The Millennial Week concept finally died with a whimper when the six millennia (based on LXX calculations) expired and Christ did not reappear. From the fifth century onward, the Millennial Week idea was largely abandoned by Christians. They supposed it was just some quaint aberration of the earliest Church fathers. It simply would not work anymore using the chronological data in the Septuagint.

About this time the Roman Catholic Church commissioned Jerome to translate the Hebrew Scriptures into Latin. Also the churches of the east were using the Peshitta Aramaic

---

[327] This is apparent from the edited version of Victorinus' Commentary on the Apocalypse, ch. xx and from Augustine's City of God from which this portion was borrowed.

translation. Both translations contained the correct chronological data in the Hebrew genealogies of the ancients. Yet, Christians from the fifth century onward using these translations would not be inclined to adopt the Millennial Week theory. Virtually all Christians have looked for the return of Christ to occur fairly soon. If they were to use the chronology based on the Hebrew text to calculate the end of the sixth millennium, Jesus' return would be 1500 years in the future – not a very attractive option to those longing for the blessed hope! Those who used the LXX were disappointed that six millennia had apparently already passed and Jesus had not come. And those who used an Old Testament based on the Hebrew text would have to conclude that Jesus' coming was so far into the future as to make it virtually irrelevant. Because of this, the Millennial Week theory fell out of favor and remained dormant until recent times, when chronology based on the Hebrew text once again puts the second coming very near.

After the Reformation, it became popular to understand Revelation from a historicist perspective, taking the 1260 days in Revelation as 1260 years of the Roman Catholic "Beast's" reign. Many interpreters began to set dates for the return of Christ near to their own time. All of them failed because of a faulty presupposition that the 1260 days are 1260 years. When it became apparent that the Roman Catholic "Beast" had reigned for more than 1260 years and Jesus had not returned, the "year-day" theory began to collapse of its own weight, just as the Millennial Week theory had using a chronology based on the Septuagint.

In modern times we have seen a brief revival of the Millennial Week chronology as we approached the year 2000. This was largely among dispensationalists who used Ussher's chronology, placing the creation around 4004 BC. There was a flurry of date-setting pointing to around the year 2000. Jack Van Impe made use of this theory for a while, making predictions which all failed. Another notable example was Edgar Whisenant's book, *88 Reasons Why the Rapture Could be in 1988*. In his reason #16, Whisenant used the Millennial Week (based on Ussher's chronology) to pinpoint the beginning of the seventh millennium in 1995 (4004 BC + 6000 years). He then subtracted seven years for the tribulation and arrived at 1988 for the supposed pretribulation rapture.

Aside from Whisenant's faulty pretribulation rapture view, his interpretation was doomed from the start because of his reliance on Ussher's chronology. Ussher and virtually all relatively modern Christian chronologists have made several critical errors, particularly regarding Daniel's 70-weeks prophecy. In part II of this book, a chronology which solves the problems Ussher was unable to solve will be provided. This chronology puts the 70th week and Jesus' return still several years in the future.

Chapter 8
The RISE of DISPENSATIONALISM

The early chiliasts had interpreted "Mystery Babylon, Mother of Harlots" of Revelation 17-18 as Rome, the murderer of the Apostles and a myriad of other Christian martyrs. In chiliasm, the Roman Empire was to eventually fall and be partitioned into ten regions ruled by ten kings. After the two witnesses of Revelation 11 prophesy for the first half of Daniel's 70th week, they would be killed and the ten kings would deliver the kingdom to Antichrist and raze the city of Rome to the ground. Antichrist would then engage in a reign of terror for the latter half of Daniel's 70th week. Rome was the enemy of Christ and Christianity according to chiliasts.

But with the conversion of the Emperor Constantine in the fourth century, suddenly Rome became benevolent to Christianity. This radical shift from Rome's persecution of Christians to being their benefactor gave rise to a new eschatology in the minds of many. They supposed that the Kingdom of God had arrived, a time of justice and peace, with Christianity ruling the world.

Augustine, a prominent theologian and former Gnostic, built on many of Origen's ideas in his massive work, "The City of God." Augustine provided the theological framework for the new "Kingdom now" theory of amillennialism. Rome became the capitol of Christ's Kingdom instead of Jerusalem, and the bishop of Rome became the Vicar of Christ. Thus, the Roman Church began its reign over the earth.

What many Christians first saw as the fulfillment of prophecy – the arrival of the Kingdom of God on earth – soon became a nightmare. It suddenly became fashionable and politically correct to be a "Christian," and people flocked into the churches in droves to become baptized "Christians," bringing all their paganism and wickedness with them. Being a "Christian" meant greater opportunity in society and favor with the Emperor. Thus, the Church of the martyrs quickly morphed into the Church of the opportunists.

Roman Catholicism became the vehicle for the Emperor to control the masses. The military might of the empire became the means to enforce Church dogma. The Emperor gave lip service to the Roman Church, providing great wealth and power for its leaders. The Church reciprocated by pronouncing the Emperor as God's chosen king, and making loyalty to the Emperor part of one's Christian duty.

Enforcing the Emperor's will on the people, including the murder of "heretics," was carried out under the guise of Christ's sword of justice. Unity in doctrine of all the Christian Churches was a top priority for Constantine and his successors. These emperors merely used Christianity towards their own political ends, to solidify their own power and silence opposing voices. The new state-Church became as oppressive as pagan Rome had been to Christians who would not go along with this marriage. Instead of Roman Christianity bringing enlightenment, it instead brought the dark ages, enforcing the political will of an elite class under penalty of death and eternal damnation. The marriage of the Roman Empire and Christianity did not bring peace on earth, or a reign of righteousness and justice, but more persecution and corruption. The pristine Christian Church, with its loyalty to Christ and long list of faithful martyrs, had morphed into a monster. The abandonment of chiliasm and adoption of amillennialism paved the way.

While the political Roman Empire began to suffer defeat in battle after battle, and was finally overrun by enemies, the monstrosity it had created in the Roman Church remained. Its control of the masses under penalty of eternal damnation remained. Thus Rome continued to rule the region by granting salvation through her sacraments to those whom it chose, and appointing to eternal damnation those who opposed her. Politics in the region was always interwoven with the Roman Church, and the corruption continued unabated as Rome trafficked in human souls to maintain her power.

The Protestant Reformation dealt a severe blow to the Roman Church's control of the masses. But, in order to effectively oust the oppressive monster, a new eschatology was needed. Rome insisted that she was Christ's Kingdom on earth, and the pope was Christ's Vicar. In order for the new Protestants to sway the masses to rebel against Rome, the Kingdom of God would have to be redefined.

A Protestant version of amillennialism was developed for this purpose, with the "Kingdom of God" being a heavenly kingdom. Christ and the martyrs were alleged to be reigning over the earth from heaven[328] through the Protestant Churches.

Yet, the most effective tool in swaying the masses against Rome was a newly developed view of Revelation called, "historicism." Protestants saw great similarities between "Babylon the Great, Mother of Harlots" in Revelation 17-18, and Roman Catholicism. Thus, the Roman Catholic Church became the "Mother of Harlots" and the pope, who claimed to be Christ's Vicar, was cast as the "Antichrist."

The problem with this view is immediately apparent, since the period of the reign of Antichrist is given in Revelation as 42 months, and his persecution of the true Church as 1260 days. So, a new theory was put into play to solve this problem. The 1260 days were reinterpreted to mean 1260 years. This is commonly called the "year – day theory."

As mentioned previously, this view lent itself to a flurry of date-setting among Protestants, calculating the 1260 years from the Roman Church's rise to supreme power under the Roman Emperors, until the second coming. The alleged conversion of Constantine around AD 312 was an obvious starting point. By adding 1260 years, one could predict the second coming in the year 1572. Many dates were offered using various starting points in the life of Constantine and his successors. Each failed to produce the return of Christ. As all

---

[328] Note that this concept requires a Platonic view of the soul as immortal. Also, the saints which Scripture says are "sleeping" were said to be actively reigning before the resurrection of their bodies.

of the predictions of the second coming by historicists failed to materialize, many Christians lost interest in eschatology in general and the second coming of Christ in particular.

Yet, towards the end of the eighteenth century, the chaos of the French Revolution drove many Christians back to their Bibles to reconsider the basic teachings of amillennialism and historicism. It was within the climate of change and reevaluation that dispensationalism arose.

Dispensationalism is a hybrid of amillennialism and chiliasm. Like chiliasm, it maintains a more literal interpretation of the Old Testament covenants and prophecies. Dispensationalism takes the Abrahamic Covenant literally, seeing the ultimate fulfillment of the Land inheritance at the second coming of Christ. The prophecies of Israel's and Jerusalem's restoration are also taken literally. However, unlike chiliasm, it assigns this inheritance to physical Jews only, not to Christians. In a sense, it interprets "Abraham's seed" like the Pharisees did, thinking that they had a right to the covenants and promises simply by birthright and circumcision.[329]

Like amillennialism, dispensationalism continued to hold to a heavenly destiny for the "Church" developed by Origen from Platonic concepts and systematized by Augustine. Thus, a hard dichotomy between "Israel" and the "Church" was necessary. Dispensationalists claimed that "Israel" is God's "earthly people" and the "Church" is God's "heavenly people."

---

[329] This is also why many modern dispensationalists are Zionists, supporting modern Israel's claim on the Holy Land even while they reject Jesus Christ.

"The dispensationalist believes that throughout the ages God is pursuing two distinct purposes: one related to the earth with earthly people and earthly objectives involved which is Judaism; while the other is related to heaven with heavenly people and heavenly objectives involved, which is Christianity... Israel is an eternal nation, heir to an eternal land, with an eternal kingdom, on which David rules from an eternal throne' so that in eternity ...never the twain, Israel and church, shall meet."[330]

In order to maintain this dichotomy between Israel and the Church, the Bible itself was partitioned by dispensationalists. Everything that was pre-Pentecost related to "the Gospel of the Kingdom" and God's earthly program for Israel (including the Gospels).[331] The "mystery" of the "Gospel of Grace" was for the "Church" with its "heavenly destiny," and was revealed through Paul alone.[332]

These cardinal tenets of dispensationalism were not unprecedented, however. Marcion, a Gnostic heretic of the second century, had pioneered similar ideas and was soundly refuted by the early chiliasts. The premise which drove Marcion's theology was the typical Platonic – Gnostic idea that matter was inherently corrupt. So, the heavenly destiny concept was a big part of his teaching. Marcion claimed that the God of Israel was not the same God Jesus proclaimed, but a lesser god. He had a sharp dichotomy between Israel (to which belong the Abrahamic Covenant, the Law, and the

---

[330] Chafer, Lewis Sperry, Dispensationalism, p. 107 (Dallas, Seminary Press, 1936)
[331] Stam, Cornelius R., The Fundamentals of Dispensationalism, p. 55
[332] Stam, Cornelius R., The Fundamentals of Dispensationalism, p. 79

prophets) and the Church which had its own Scriptures, revealing a hidden mystery.[333] Marcion alleged that Paul alone was the conduit of this hidden body of doctrine, as Irenaeus explained:

> *"With regard to those (the Marcionites) who allege that Paul alone knew the truth, and that to him the mystery was manifested by revelation, let Paul himself convict them, when he says, that one and the same God wrought in Peter for the apostolate of the circumcision, and in himself for the Gentiles. Peter, therefore, was an apostle of that very God whose was also Paul; and Him whom Peter preached as God among those of the circumcision, and likewise the Son of God, did Paul [declare] also among the Gentiles. For our Lord never came to save Paul alone, nor is God so limited in means, that He should have but one apostle who knew the dispensation of His Son."[334]*

Like all of the early Gnostics, Marcion's theology was intended to deny the physical resurrection of the body and material inheritance within the restored creation. The dichotomy between the God of the Jews (with His earthly program) and the God Paul preached (with His "heavenly" program) drove Marcion's system. Dispensationalists ought to seriously contemplate the fact that they share much of this Gnostic heretic's ideas as the foundation of their system.

Dispensationalism is the supporting structure for the concept of a pretribulation rapture. According to dispensationalists,

---

[333] Irenaeus, Against Heresies, Bk. I, Ch. xxvii, 2
[334] Irenaeus, Against Heresies, Book III, ch. xiii

God promised, through the Abrahamic Covenant and the Prophets, an eternal Kingdom in Jerusalem for Israel. Because the Jews rejected their King and His Kingdom, God suspended His promises of the Kingdom. They allege that God then began a new "mystery" program for the Church which was nowhere prophesied in the Old Testament. This Church program has a heavenly people and destiny. In dispensationalism, Daniel's 70th week (the tribulation) concerns only God's interaction with Israel, His "earthly people." Thus, dispensationalists infer a pretribulation rapture of the Church to heaven so that God's "Church program" does not overlap the resumption of His program for Israel. Dispensationalists frequently spoke of the Church age as a "parenthesis" in God's dealing with the nation of Israel, as a postponement of the Kingdom age. The strong dichotomy between Israel (earthly) and the Church (heavenly) made it impossible for God to deal with the nation of Israel and the Church simultaneously. Thus a pretribulation rapture was inferred from this alleged dichotomy.

Key Players in the Development of Dispensationalism

John Nelson Darby, one of the founders of the Plymouth Brethren, is usually credited with the development of dispensationalism. Yet, a careful examination of the historical record shows that Darby borrowed his ideas from a newly-formed Charismatic cult. The story of the rise of dispensationalism and its accompanying pretribulation rapture begins in the late eighteenth century.

Manuel de Lacunza

Manuel de Lacunza was a Roman Catholic Jesuit priest. He was born in Chili in 1731 and sent to Spain at the age of fifteen to become a Jesuit priest. When the Jesuits were expelled from Spain in 1767, Lacunza moved to Imolo, Italy. He became a recluse, saturating himself with books including those banned by Rome. In 1790, he wrote a book on prophecy, called *The Coming of Messiah in Glory and Majesty*. Lacunza died shortly after completing his manuscript. In 1812, his book was published posthumously in Spain under the pen name, "Juan Josafat Ben-Ezra (a converted Jew)," allegedly to avoid detection since his ideas were contrary to Roman Catholic views. *"In 1816, a complete edition of his work was published in London, in four volumes, octavo, by the diplomatic agent of the republic of Buenos Ayres."*[335]

Lacunza's book promoted a return to the literal interpretation of Old Testament prophecy and the primitive futurist view of Revelation. His ideas were essentially those of the early chiliasts. He rejected the "year-day theory" of the historicists, where the tribulation was extended for 1260 years.[336] Instead of the Protestant "Antichrist" being the whole papal system (the whole succession of popes), Lacunza saw the Antichrist as a single individual who would reign for 1260 literal days (3.5 years). Immediately after the tribulation, Christ would return to destroy this man, raise the dead believers, restore

---

[335] Irving, Edward, Preliminary Discourse, p. 16-17, in The Coming of Messiah in Glory and Majesty, by Juan Josafat Ben-Ezra, A Converted Jew, Published by L. B. Seeley & Son, Fleet St., London, 1827

[336] Irving, Edward, Preliminary Discourse, pp. 20-25, 27

Jerusalem and the Temple, and reign over the earth from Jerusalem.

Edward Irving & the Proto-Charismatics

Edward Irving was a staunch Calvinist,[337] the pastor of a Church of Scotland (Presbyterian) congregation in London in the 1820s. Irving became aware of Lacunza's book, and was so impressed with it, he took it upon himself to translate it into English, adding a lengthy Preliminary Discourse of his own. Irving's English translation was published in 1827.

Irving was convinced by Lacunza's book of the premillennial return of Christ to reign in Jerusalem. But he was not willing to abandon the Protestant historicist view (that 1260 days equals 1260 years of the Roman Catholic Beast's rule).[338] Instead, Irving mixed the Protestant view with his own developing form of dispensationalism. While Lacunza held essentially the same view as the early chiliasts regarding Israel and the Church, Irving developed a much stronger dichotomy between them. His budding dispensationalism can be seen in his Preliminary Discourse, which includes most of the key elements of dispensationalism that later showed up in Darby's writings.

> *"When the Lord shall have finished the taking of witness against the Gentiles, and summed up the present dispensation of testimony in this great verdict of judgment, and while the execution is proceeding, he will begin to prepare another ark of testimony, or rather to make the whole*

---

[337] Irving, Edward, Preliminary Discourse, pp. 6-8
[338] Irving, Edward, Preliminary Discourse, pp. 20-25, 27

earth an ark of testimony; and to that end he will turn his Holy Spirit unto his ancient people the Jews, and bring unto them those days of refreshing spoken of by all the holy prophets since the world began."[339]

"I sought very diligently to define from the scriptures what was the precise place and purpose of the present spiritual dispensation, which God hath interposed between a dispensation of a local and typical character upon the one hand, and a dispensation yet to be, of a universal and real character upon the other; both centering in and radiating out from the Jewish people."[340]

"This idea being clearly demonstrated to my mind as the root and germ of the dispensations both Jew and Gentile, or of "earthly things" as distinguished from "heavenly things," or the things of the kingdom, (John iii) it was a very easy matter to derive and set forth the wisdom and adaption of those particular forms which the purpose assumed, under the one and the other of these great prepatory institutions of God."[341]

The primary driving force in Irving's developing dispensationalism was his initial unwillingness to abandon the Protestant "historicist" interpretation of Revelation. Irving began to entertain the idea that perhaps the historicist and futurist views of Revelation were both correct. He speculated that Revelation had a dual meaning. The first "spiritual" interpretation of Protestant historicism was to be played out

---

[339] Irving, Edward, Preliminary Discourse, pp. 4-5
[340] ibid, p. 9
[341] ibid, p. 10

over 1260 years of a papal Antichrist. A latter "literal" interpretation of a tribulation of 1260 days and a personal Antichrist was to be played out in the few years before Jesus returns.[342]

Part of the historicist view of Revelation included taking the seven letters in Revelation chapters two and three as representing seven consecutive periods of Church history. Irving retained this view,[343] and as we shall see, it became a key component in his dispensationalism and his later development of the pretribulation rapture.

Irving indicated that he had been teaching these things to his congregation beginning in Christmas 1825.[344] This was several years before Darby embraced any dispensational ideas. Yet, at this point, Irving's dispensationalism had not yet driven him to imagine a pretribulation rapture.[345]

Irving's theological musings were not confined to eschatology. He strongly denounced the apostasy of the Christian denominations in his preaching, ruffling the feathers of many, including those in his own denomination. Irving began proclaiming that God was about to restore Apostles, prophets, and all the supernatural spiritual gifts to the Church, and that a great Pentecostal outpouring would come just before the soon return of Jesus Christ. Right on schedule, rumors of ecstatic tongues, prophecies, visions and

---

[342] ibid, p. 23-25
[343] ibid, p. 25
[344] ibid, p. 4
[345] ibid, p. 38

other manifestations began circulating in Port Glasgow, Scotland, from the home of James and George MacDonald and their sister Margaret. People came from England, Ireland, and Scotland to observe the strange manifestations in the prayer meetings held by the MacDonalds.

The new Charismatic "revival" quickly spread to Irving's church with tongues, prophecy, and other alleged manifestations breaking out. Irving's new Pentecostalism became the talk of the British Isles. He was excoriated for his new eschatology and the Charismatic excesses occurring in his congregation. Finally, Irving went too far in his views on the person of Christ, claiming that Jesus had a fallen human nature. That was the last straw, and Irving was defrocked by the Church of Scotland.

But Irving was not to be deterred. He moved his congregation to a rented hall, forming the *Catholic Apostolic Church*. The ecstatic tongues and prophesies occurring in Irving's congregation continued to increase. Many such prophecies focused on the end-times and the coming of the Lord.

In March or April of 1830, after being ill and bedridden for about eighteen months, Margaret MacDonald claimed to have seen a series of visions. She wrote down some of these visions in a series of letters and sent copies to Edward Irving. A month later (June 1830), Irving claimed in a private letter, that Margaret's visions had a huge impact on him: "[T]he substance *of Mary Campbell's and Margaret MacDonald's visions or revelations, given in their papers, carry to me a spiritual conviction and a spiritual reproof which I cannot express."*[346]

Margaret's visions concerned a partial pretribulation rapture of the newly "Spirit-filled" (Charismatic) Christians, but the majority of the Church would be left behind to be purged by fire in the great tribulation. The "Spirit-filled" Christians would see a secret coming of Christ "in the air" which could not be seen by the natural eye. Only Christians who had received special spiritual "sight" through the new Pentecostal outpouring would be raptured to heaven at Jesus' secret, invisible coming "in the air." According to Margaret, these were represented by the "wise virgins" in Jesus' parable, in Matthew 25, who had extra oil for their lamps. The "foolish virgins," who had no oil (the Charismatic manifestations), represented the rest of Christianity which rejected the new Charismatic outpouring. These needed to be purged and purified by suffering at the hands of the Antichrist until they were fit to receive the outpouring of the Spirit. They would be gathered at the second coming after the tribulation when "every eye shall see Him." Margaret wrote:

> *"... Now there is distress of nations, with perplexity, the seas and the waves roaring, men's hearts failing them for fear - now look out for the sign of the Son of man. Here I was made to stop and cry out, Oh it is not known what the sign of the Son of man is; the people of God think they are waiting, but they know not what it is. I felt this needed to be revealed, and that there was great darkness and error about*

---

[346] Mrs. Oliphant, The Life of Edward Irving, Hurst and Blackett, London, publisher, 1865.

it; but suddenly what it was burst upon me with a glorious light I saw it was just the Lord himself descending from Heaven with a shout, just the glorified man. even Jesus; but that all must, as Stephen was, be filled with the Holy Ghost, that they might look up, and see the brightness of the Father's glory. I saw the error to be, that men think that it will be something seen by the natural eye; but 'tis spiritual discernment that is needed, the eye of God in his people. Many passages were revealed, in a light in which I had not before seen them. I repeated, 'Now is the kingdom of Heaven like unto ten virgins, who went forth to meet the Bridegroom, five wise and five foolish; they that were foolish took their lamps, but took no oil with them; but they that were wise took oil in their vessels with their lamps.' 'But be ye not unwise, but understanding what the will of the Lord is; and be not drunk with wine wherein is excess, but be filled with the Spirit.' This was the oil the wise virgins took in their vessels - this is the light to be kept burning - the light of God - that we may discern that which cometh not with observation to the natural eye. Only those who have the light of God within them will see the sign of his appearance. No need to follow them who say, see here, or see there, for his day shall be as the lightning to those in whom the living Christ is. 'Tis Christ in us that will lift us up - he is the light - 'tis only those that are alive in him that will be caught up to meet him in the air. I saw that we must be in the Spirit, that we might see spiritual things. John was in the Spirit, when he saw a throne set in Heaven. - But I saw that the glory of the ministration of the Spirit had not been known. I repeated frequently, but the spiritual temple must and shall be reared, and the fullness of Christ be poured into his body, *and then shall we be caught up to meet him. ... I felt that those who were filled with the spirit could see spiritual things, and feel walking in the midst of them, while those who had not the Spirit could see nothing - so that two shall be in one bed, the one taken and the other left, because the one has the light of God within while the other cannot see the Kingdom of Heaven. I saw the people of God in an awfully dangerous situation, surrounded by nets and entanglements, about to be tried, and many about to be deceived and fall. Now will THE WICKED be revealed, with all power and signs and lying wonders, so that if it were possible the very elect will be deceived. - This is the fiery trial which is to try us. ... The trial of the Church is from Antichrist. It is by being filled with the Spirit that we shall be kept. ... This is what we are at present made to pray much for, that speedily we may all be made ready to meet our Lord in the air - and it will be."* [347]

Margaret's visions of a pretribulation rapture struck a chord with Edward Irving who had already been developing his dispensationalist ideas. A marriage of these two concepts was inevitable.

Within less than six months of Irving's receiving Margaret MacDonald's letters, Irving's official quarterly publication, *The Morning Watch*, began publishing the concept of a secret pretribulation rapture of "Spirit-filled" believers. It had

---

[347] MacDonald, Margaret, as reproduced by Robert Norton in *The Restoration of Apostles and Prophets in the Catholic Apostolic Church* (1861), pp. 15ff. This letter represented only one of her many visions. Norton himself, who knew Margaret personally and had read all of her letters and conversed with her, represented her visions as the first time a pretribulation rapture had been was suggested.

previously promoted a posttribulation second coming through mid-1830. But, the September 1830 issue featured an article by *Fidus*, extrapolating a partial pretribulation rapture from the historicist theory that the seven letters in Revelation describe seven consecutive "Church Ages." Fidus saw the Philadelphian Church as the "Spirit-filled" believers, to be raptured to heaven prior to the tribulation. The Laodicean Church representing the rest of Christianity which would be purged in the tribulation.

"The most useful, although not perhaps the most accurate, course will be to state at the outset those conclusions which our subsequent investigations will be seen to warrant, regarding the allocation of the seven epistles. They are as follow:

1. The Ephesian church carries us down to the commencement of the great persecution by Nero, in A.D. 64.
2. That of Smyrna represents the church purified by trial at the hands of Rome, till the accession of Constantine, in 324.
3. The church at Pergamos sets forth the interval between the elevation of Constantine and the rise of the little horn, at the commencement of the 1260 years.
4. The church at Thyatira expresses the testimony of the church against the Papacy during the 1260 years.
5. That of Sardis indicates the state of the church from the end of the 1260 years, until the preparation for the coming of the Lord.
*6. The Philadelphian church expresses the period of that preparation, **until the Lord come to the air, and be met by his saints changed and risen**.*

7. The Laodicean church (the only one yet entirely future) is our sad monitor concerning the history of the church on earth __during that period of great tribulation which shall intervene between the coming of the Lord to the air and the establishment of his throne and rest in Zion__. ..."

"Philadelphia expresses brotherly love, whether between those who had or between those who had not been previously brethren. Accordingly, it represents that era, so often spoken of throughout the epistles, when they that look for the Lord shall, in the midst of the strife and selfishness of the last days, be knit together, by their common faith and hope, in the bonds of his mystical body, in the unity of the Holy Ghost; ... And what is very remarkable, [Philadelphia] now bears the name Allah Shehr, The City of God. Now its antitype is the church in that period which succeeds the great earthquake of the French Revolution (Rev. xi. 13); which is characterized by the earnest yet patient expectation of the Lord; which receives the answer of its faith __in being caught up to meet him; which is thus kept from the hour of temptation__; and which so becomes, not Laodecea chastised in love, but the victorious ministerer of great tribulation (Rev. ii.24,26; iii.10; Luke xxi.36; Heb. xi.5)."[348]

The ideas presented here are precisely the ideas first pioneered by Margaret MacDonald in her ecstatic visions only six months earlier. The Morning Watch was quickly becoming

---

[348] The Morning Watch, Quarterly Publication of the Catholic Apostolic Church (Irvingites), September 1830, pp. 510-514

the vehicle for providing a theological framework for Margaret MacDonald's pretribulation rapture of "Spirit filled" Christians.

In the June 1831 issue of The Morning Watch, Edward Irving made his pretribulationism crystal clear. His biblical support for the elite "Spirit-filled" believers being raptured before the tribulation was the catching up of the "man-child" in Revelation 12. Irving argued that the body of Christ has been *"united to Him by regeneration of the Holy Ghost, 'born of God, sons of God,' (Rev. ii. 27; xii. 5). And therefore __we with him are called Christ__ (1 Cor. xii. 12)."* Irving went on to say that, *"with this key* [that Spirit-filled Christians are also "Christ," and that the catching up of the "man child" refers to the rapture of Spirit-filled believers] *the Old Testament prophecies which speak of Christ must be interpreted, ... and especially those prophecies which speak of the pregnant woman: to all which an explicit key is given to us in the xiith chapter of Revelation; where, **though the child is spoken of as one** (ver. 5), **it is also described as many** (ver. 11), who overcame the accuser; and when that number is accomplished, there are still a remnant of her seed, whom the dragon doth persecute and seek to destroy (ver. 17). **This two-fold company – __the one gathered before__, and __the other after__ the travailing woman is cast out into the wilderness, ... – do together constitute the New Jerusalem, the bride of the Lamb**, which cometh down from heaven."*[349]

An anonymous writer in the December 1832 issue of The Morning Watch likely referred to Margaret MacDonald's letters (and probably her friend Mary Campbell & Emily

---

[349] The Morning Watch, June 1831 Issue, pp. 301-302.

Cardale of London) with the following words; *"The Spirit of God has caused several young women, in different parts of Great Britain, to condense into a few broken sentences more and deeper theology than ever Vaughan, Chalmers, or Irving uttered in their longest sermons; and therefore more than all the rest of the Evangelical pulpits ever put forth in the whole course of their existence."*[350] Thus, we see that credit for the new theory was publically acknowledged by the Irvingites to have originated with ecstatic trances of a few women.

British Lawyer, Robert Baxter, was an early member of the Irvingite Charismatics. Baxter adopted the pretribulation rapture views of Irving. He, along with several other "prophets" of the Catholic Apostolic Church, gave many prophecies, all of which failed. He later became disillusioned with the whole movement and abandoned Irvingism and pretribulationism. Upon his departure from the movement, he wrote an expose of Irvingism which documented Irving's early pretribulation teachings.

> *"An opinion had been advanced in some of Mr. Irving's writings, that before the second coming of Christ, and before the setting in upon the world of the day of vengeance, emphatically so called in the Scriptures, the saints would be caught up to heaven like Enoch and Elijah; and would be thus saved from the destruction of this world, as Noah was saved in the ark, and Lot was saved from Sodom."*[351]

---

[350] The Morning Watch, December 1832 issue, p. 249
[351] Baxter, Robert, Narrative of Facts, Characterizing the Supernatural Manifestations in Members of Mr. Irving's Congregation (1833)

Baxter wrote that Irving had borrowed the pretribulation rapture concept from a Scottish source, no doubt a reference to the MacDonalds of Port Glasgow, Scotland.

> *"[T]he delusion first appeared in Scotland ... it was not until adopted and upheld by Mr. Irving, that it began to challenge much attention..." "An opinion had been advanced in some of Mr. Irvings writings, that before the second coming of Christ, and before ... the day of vengeance[352] ... the saints would be caught up to heaven..."[353]*

Baxter, who had been himself one of the early Irvingite "prophets," described the utter failure of all the prophetic utterances of this movement. He did not deny that the ecstatic utterances were supernatural, but he denied that the Holy Spirit was the source. He concluded that they had all been deceived by lying spirits pretending to be the Holy Spirit.

> *"[Because of the] successive failures of prophecy and contradictions of utterance ... I was convinced it must be a work of Satan ... [W]e had all been speaking by a lying spirit, and not by the Spirit of the Lord."[354]*

> *"[T]he whole work is mimicry of the gifts of the Spirit."[355]*

> *"... the continual use which was made of the doctrine of the second advent of our Lord. This was the leading theme of our*

---

[352] Baxter later explained that the "day of vengeance" would begin with the arrival of "the Man of Sin." (p. 31)

[353] ibid, p. 17

[354] ibid, p. 118

[355] ibid, p. 135

utterances. ... [T]here must have been much error in our view of the manner and circumstances of the coming of the Lord, or we could not have been so deceived."[356]

Robert Norton was personally familiar with Margaret MacDonald and the Irvingite movement. He wrote a book on the Irvingite movement called, The Restoration of Apostles and Prophets in the Catholic Apostolic Church (1861). Norton took a favorable view of the Irvingites, writing in the preface that his book was offered *"as proofs or illustrations of its heavenly origin and character."* Norton named Margaret MacDonald was the first to proclaim the "new doctrine" of a pretribulation rapture, which was picked up by Irving.

> *"Marvelous light was shed upon Scripture, and especially on the doctrine of the second advent, by the revived spirit of prophecy. In the following account by Miss M.M---, of an evening during which the power of the Holy Ghost rested upon her for several successive hours, in mingled prophecy and visions, we have an instance;* <u>***for here we first see the distinction between the final stage of the Lord's coming, where every eye shall see him, and His prior appearing in glory to them that look for Him***</u>.

> *"She writes: --- 'I felt this needed to be revealed, that there was great darkness and error about it; but suddenly what it was burst upon me with a glorious light. I saw it was the Lord Himself descending from heaven with a shout - the*

---

[356] ibid, pp. 142,143

glorified Man - even Jesus; but that all must be, as Stephen was, filled with the Holy Ghost,...'[357]

The Plymouth Brethren

Samuel P. Tregelles was the most eminent Plymouth Brethren scholar of the 19th century with first-hand knowledge of the Irvingites. In an 1855 article in *The Christian Annotator*, Tregelles wrote that the true Christian hope is the final *"advent"* and *"not some secret advent, or secret rapture to the Lord, as Judaizers supposed might be the case..."*[358] (A later Plymouth Brethren writer, William Kelly, also identified the Irvingites as the "Judaizers" to whom Tregelles referred).[359] Nine years later, Tregelles published *"The Hope of Christ's Second Coming,"* in which he wrote:

> *"But when the theory of a secret coming of Christ was first brought forward (about the year 1832), it was adopted with eagerness: ... I am not aware that there was any definite teaching that there would be <u>**a secret rapture of the Church at a secret coming, until this was given forth as an "utterance" in Mr. Irving's Church, from what was there received as being the voice of the Spirit**</u>. But whether anyone ever asserted such a thing or not, <u>**it was from that supposed revelation that the modern doctrine and the modern phraseology respecting it arose. It came not from Holy Scripture, but from that**</u>*

---

[357] Norton, Robert, The Restoration of Apostles and Prophets in the Catholic Apostolic Church (1861), p. 15

[358] Tregelles, Samuel P., Premillennial Advent (The Christian Annotator, June 16, 1855), p. 190.

[359] Kelly, William, The Catholic Apostolic Body, or Irvingites (The Bible Treasury, Dec. 1890), p. 191.

> _which falsely pretended to be the Spirit of God_, _while_
> _not owning the true doctrine of our Lord's incarnation in the_
> _same flesh and blood as His brethren, but without taint of_
> _sin._"[360]

The last statement, _"not owning the true doctrine of our Lord's_
incarnation ... without taint of sin," referred to the Irvingite
Charismatic cult's view of the person of Christ – that He had a
sin nature.

Irish lawyer, John Nelson Darby, one of the founders of the
Plymouth Brethren, is typically credited by pretribulationists
as the man who developed dispensational pretribulationism.
Yet, Darby was a latecomer to pretribulationism which
originated among the Irvingites. Darby wrote his first
prophecy paper in 1829.[361] In this paper, he did not have
dispensationalist or pretribulationist views. Darby argued
that unfulfilled Old Testament prophecy concerning the
restoration of Israel should be applied to the Church, the
typical historicist – amillennial point of view. He also placed
the Church on earth until Armageddon, showing he was still
a posttribulationist. By this time, dispensationalist ideas were
already well-developed in Irving's 1826 Preliminary
Discourse. Darby was familiar with Irving and his ideas. On
pages 6-10 & 19-21, Darby referred to Irving, Lacunza, The
Morning Watch, and even quoted some of Irving's works
including his Preliminary Discourse! So, while dispensational
concepts may have eventually taken root in Darby's mind,

---

[360] Tregelles, Samuel P., The Hope of Christ's Second Coming (Ambassadors for
Christ, n.d. 1864), pp. 34,35.
[361] Darby, J. N., Reflections (1829), Prophetic No. 1, pp. 1-31.

they were not developed by him! He borrowed them from the Irvingite Charismatics.

In 1830, Darby was still defending historicism against futurism three months after the pretribulational "Fidus" article appeared in The Morning Watch. In the December 1830 issue of The Christian Herald, Darby published an article entitled, "On Days Signifying Years in Prophetic Language."[362] Darby defended the standard historicist view, that the 1260 day tribulation meant 1260 years. Consequently, he saw the tribulation as largely past, and could not possibly have been expecting a pretribulation rapture, which requires a futurist viewpoint.

In 1830, Darby also visited the MacDonald's in Port Glasgow, and observed the strange manifestations in their prayer meetings, as he later recalled. Darby described the sequence of events — who prayed, who spoke in tongues, etc.[363] But, while he noted Margaret's speaking, he failed to mention the subject of her prophesying. However, John Cardale, who was also present at these meetings, wrote that Margaret *"commenced also speaking ... **gave testimony to the judgments coming on the earth; but also directed the church to the coming of the Lord as her hope of deliverance**,"* and was heard speaking in a loud voice *"denouncing the coming judgments."*[364] Therefore, we can conclude that Darby was fully aware that the pretribulation rapture was a subject of the prophecies

---

[362] Darby, J. N., The Collected Writings of J. N. Darby, Prophetic No. 1, p. 40.
[363] Darby, J. N., The Irrationalism of Infidelity (London: 1853), pp. 283-285.
[364] Cardale, John B., On the Extraordinary Manifestations in Port Glasgow (The Morning Watch, Dec. 1830) p. 870, 871, 873.

among the MacDonalds and the Irvingite Charismatics. It was nine more years before Darby clearly espoused a pretribulation rapture in his published works.

While Irving himself was already developing dispensational ideas in 1825, his pretribulationism was not the direct outgrowth of the implications of his dispensational leanings. Rather, the secret rapture first appeared in the visions of Margaret MacDonald, followed by the ecstatic prophecies among Irving's congregation. Irving, having been already predisposed to dispensational ideas, simply adapted these supposed revelations into his budding dispensationalism.

It is clear that Darby was fully aware of the alleged prophecies and visions among the MacDonalds and Irvingites, Irving's dispensational ideas, and the published articles in The Morning Watch. Darby seems to have given the whole theory a facelift, disposing of the Charismatic connections, and developing Irving's partial pretribulation rapture into the full blown dispensational pretribulationism proclaimed today. As a respectable lawyer and clergyman, Darby was able to sell the new eschatology to the public who would naturally be skeptical of the excesses of the Irvingites.

Darby had great success in bringing the new eschatology to America where it was popularized by his disciples. Cyrus Scofield made dispensational pretribulationism the cornerstone of his new Scofield Reference Bible. Darby's disciples also founded several seminaries, such as Dallas Theological Seminary. A long series of "prophetic conferences" were held in America promoting dispensational pretribulationism. All of this had a profound effect on American Christianity. And this view still dominates Evangelical Christianity today.

I am heavily indebted to Dave MacPherson whose years of research uncovered the many out of print works cited in this chapter, and who graciously provided me with hundreds of pages of photocopies of these works for my own analysis.

PART II

A COMPLETE CHRONOLOGY FROM CREATION TO THE SECOND COMING OF CHRIST

Chapter 9
The 120 JUBILEE YEAR CALENDAR

The previous chapters have laid out for the reader the earliest Christian eschatology and how it evolved into the two common views held today, amillennialism and dispensationalism. The earliest Christian apologists and martyrs were chiliasts, firmly believing that God has limited His struggle with man under the curse to six millennia. After this Christ will return and establish His Kingdom on the earth. All those baptized into Jesus Christ are "Abraham's Seed" and will receive their inheritance on the earth along with Abraham, Isaac, and Jacob.

A few early chiliasts made attempts to develop a complete chronology to pinpoint the time when the Kingdom would arrive. Yet, they all failed because of their reliance on the Greek Old Testament which does not contain the accurate chronological data.

We now turn our attention to establishing a complete chronology from the Hebrew Bible alone. If this chronology is accurate, and if we can link it with the modern Gregorian calendar, it will pinpoint the year of Christ's return.

The Law of Moses established a very important principle which is relevant for our study of chronology, *"... by the mouth of two or three witnesses the matter shall be established."*[365] If

---

[365] Deut. 19:15

God was going to give us the exact length of time from creation to the coming of Messiah to establish His reign on earth, we would expect Him to provide two independent witnesses which would confirm each other. And indeed, that is precisely what He did. Not only does the Millennial Week chronology give us a total of 6000 years from Adam to the second coming of Christ, but there is a second parallel calendar which delivers precisely the same time-span of six millennia.

Moses recorded a very curious statement by God in Genesis 6:3. *"And the LORD said, 'My Spirit shall not strive with man forever, for he is indeed flesh; yet his days shall be one hundred and twenty years'."* The period of 120 years in this passage has usually been interpreted one of two ways.

Many suppose that God was limiting the life-spans of humans to 120 years. Yet, after the flood many people lived to well beyond this age. Human life-spans did decline over time, but not until many years after the flood, and they did not settle to around 120 years, but to around 70-80.[366]

Others think God was speaking of the duration of time until He would destroy the earth with a flood. Yet, the context indicates that God made this statement after Noah reached 500 years old.[367] It was therefore less than 100 years until the flood which came in Noah's 600th year.[368] Some commentators have suggested that God originally designated 120 years, but

[366] Psalm 90:10
[367] Gen. 5:32
[368] Gen. 7:6

shortened it because of man's wickedness.[369] Others claim that the narrative is out of sequence, God making this statement before the events recorded in the previous chapter.[370] Yet, none of these explanations seem adequate or natural. Instead, a third solution solves the difficulty and presents us with a golden nugget – the key to unlocking the entire chronology of the Bible.

In both the Hebrew text and the Septuagint, "man" has the definite article. The Hebrew literally reads, *"My Spirit shall not remain among the adam forever."* "Adam" was both the name of the first man and also the whole human race. Obviously, this statement does not refer to the man, Adam. The other possible interpretation, that it refers to the whole human race, would limit the Spirit's struggle with the whole human race to 120 years. This cannot refer to the flood, because the human race survived the flood. God's Spirit continued to struggle with the human race after the flood. Also, the flood occurred in less than 100 years from when God said this. Obviously, then, the period of 120 years cannot refer to normal solar years.

The Sabbatical and Jubilee Year Calendar

In Leviticus 25, we learn of God's Jubilee calendar of 50-year cycles[371] which God commanded Israel to observe. God

---

[369] John Gill's Commentary on Gen. 6:3

[370] Albert Barnes Commentary on Gen. 6:3

[371] Some claim that these cycles are actually 49 years. However, the Sedar Olam Rabbah, the ancient 2nd century Jewish chronology and the oldest word on the subject, states plainly that the cycles were 50 years. (Sedar Olam Rabbah, ch. 11, translated by Ken Johnson, PhD., p. 61). There is an example in Scripture of a Sabbatical year being followed by a Jubilee year (15th and 16th years of Hezekiah), which requires a 50 year cycle (Isaiah 37:30).

commanded Israel to farm their land for six years, and then allow the land to rest on the seventh year. This represents a "week" of years complete with its "Sabbath" year. This was to be repeated for seven "weeks" of years, totaling 49 years. Then, an extra year, the Jubilee year, was intercalated. The 50th year was called the "year of release" or "year of liberty" because all land reverted back to its original owner and all debts were cancelled. It was a very special kind of year that occurred only once every fifty years.

> *Leviticus 25:1-13*
>
> *1 And the LORD spoke to Moses on Mount Sinai, saying, 2 "Speak to the children of Israel, and say to them: 'When you come into the land which I give you, then the land shall keep a sabbath to the LORD. 3 Six years you shall sow your field, and six years you shall prune your vineyard, and gather its fruit; 4 but in the seventh year there shall be a sabbath of solemn rest for the land, a sabbath to the LORD. You shall neither sow your field nor prune your vineyard. 5 What grows of its own accord of your harvest you shall not reap, nor gather the grapes of your untended vine, for it is a year of rest for the land. 6 And the sabbath produce of the land shall be food for you: for you, your male and female servants, your hired man, and the stranger who dwells with you, 7 for your livestock and the beasts that are in your land — all its produce shall be for food.*
>
> *8 'And you shall count seven sabbaths of years for yourself, seven times seven years; and the time of the seven sabbaths of years shall be to you forty-nine years. 9 **Then you shall cause the trumpet of the Jubilee to sound** on the tenth day of the seventh month; on the Day of Atonement you*

*shall make the trumpet to sound throughout all your land.
10 And **you shall consecrate the fiftieth year**, and
proclaim liberty throughout all the land to all its
inhabitants. It shall be a Jubilee for you; and each of you shall
return to his possession, and each of you shall return to his
family. 11 That fiftieth year shall be a Jubilee to you; in it
you shall neither sow nor reap what grows of its own accord,
nor gather the grapes of your untended vine. 12 For it is the
Jubilee; it shall be holy to you; you shall eat its produce from
the field. 13 'In this Year of Jubilee, each of you shall return
to his possession.'"*

The special Jubilee year was announced by blowing a very
special trumpet. As will be shown later, the year in which
God announced to Noah that He was limiting His Spirit's
struggle with the whole human race to 120 "years" was itself
a Jubilee year – the 31st Jubilee year from creation. If the 120
"years" in Genesis 6 refers to these special Jubilee years,
which occur every 50th regular year, then God has limited the
Holy Spirit's struggle with humanity to exactly six millennia,
(120x50=6000). Consequently, a chronology based on the
biblical data which precisely fits such a Jubilee calendar
would be another significant proof of chiliasm's millennial
week.

The word "year" does not necessarily refer to a 365.25 day
solar year. It can refer to different time periods as well. There
are various kinds of years, each referring to the completion of
a certain cycle. The "solar year" (or tropical year) is the length
of time it takes to complete all four seasons. The "sidereal
year" is the length of time it takes for the sun to pass through

the entire zodiac. The "lunar year" is the time it takes for the moon to complete 12 cycles. Astronomers also have what they call the "Great Year," which is the estimated length of time it would take to complete one precession cycle of earth, roughly 26,000 solar years.

The Hebrew word for "year" is "shannah," which literally means to "duplicate," to complete a cycle until you begin to repeat it again. Since the Jubilee cycle is the longest cycle on the Jewish calendar which God appointed for Israel, and in the 51st year duplication begins, the Hebrew term "year" can literally refer to this 50-year cycle. If Genesis 6:3 refers to 120 special "Jubilee years" (which occur every 50th year), or to 120 Jubilee cycles (of 50 regular years), either way the total is the same, 6000 regular years. If the statement limiting God's struggle with mankind to 120 years refers to Jubilee years, the cycle of Jubilee years must be counted from the year of creation. God's struggle with humanity began on the day Adam sinned and was expelled from Eden.

The idea that the Jubilee calendar may be more than just something that the Jews began to use under Joshua is evident from an ancient Jewish book written shortly after the Babylonian captivity, called "The Book of Jubilees." This book purports to be a record of oral tradition from Moses. It claims that the Jubilee cycle was revealed to Moses as a continuous calendar counting down from Creation to the coming of Messiah to reign, using Sabbatical and Jubilee years. For example: *"And in the third week in the second jubilee she gave birth to Cain, and in the fourth she gave birth to Abel, and in the fifth she gave birth to her daughter Awan. And in the first (year) of the third jubilee, Cain slew Abel because (God) accepted the sacrifice of Abel, and did not accept the offering of Cain. And he slew him in the field: and his blood cried from the ground to heaven...* "[372] Thus, the concept that the Sabbatical and Jubilee calendar is God's calendar, beginning at creation, was a well-established concept in Judaism long before Christ. And since some of the early Christians referenced this book and sometimes quoted from it,[373] it is apparent that they were also familiar with this concept.

Ussher and other chronologists have identified the fall of man as occurring on the Tuesday following creation week. Man was created on the 6th day of creation (Friday) and fell into sin on the 10th day of creation. This was inferred by Ussher from the festival of Yom Kippur (Day of Atonement), which marks the anniversary of the fall of man on the 10th day of the first month[374] (on the Jewish civil calendar).[375] Ussher's claim is strongly supported by the symbolism of this festival.

---

[372] Book of Jubilees, ch. iv

[373] R.H. Charles, English translator of the Book of Jubilees, stated in his introduction that early Christian writers quoted from it, including Justin Martyr.

[374] Lev. 23:26

[375] The civil calendar is the original calendar used by Moses to date the genealogies. It begins on the new moon in September (Tishri). This was the only calendar in use until God commanded Moses to add a second calendar for tracking the festivals. This festival calendar began on the first day of the month (Nisan) in which God led the Israelites out of Egypt, in the spring. From the time of the exodus onward, the Jews have kept both calendars 6 months apart. The civil (original) calendar (fall to fall) was used to calculate the sabbatical weeks of years for planting and harvesting, and for the year of Jubilee. The festival calendar was used for everything else. Consequently, the Day of Atonement is on the 10th day of the 1st month on the civil calendar, and on the 10th day of the 7th month on the festival calendar.

The two goats symbolized the fall of man and his expulsion from Eden and the restoration of the creation.[376] Each year, on Yom Kippur, one of the goats was sacrificed for man's sins and its blood sprinkled on the Ark of the Covenant by the high priest. Hebrews states that this act symbolized man's need for the atonement of Jesus Christ.[377] The other goat was the scape-goat. The high priest laid his hands on the head of this goat, symbolically transferring the sins of the people to the scape-goat.[378] It was then turned loose into the wilderness, illustrating Adam's expulsion from Eden carrying his guilt with him. Since the Day of Atonement occurs on the 10th day following the first day of the first month, which is Rosh Hashanah (meaning "head of the year," marking the first day of creation), we can date the fall of Adam to Tuesday, Tishri 10, of year 1.

It is no coincidence that the Jubilee trumpet is sounded, marking the beginning of the year of Jubilee (50th year), on Yom Kippur, the 10th day of the first month (on the civil calendar).[379] Therefore the Jubilee year is offset from the regular civil years by 10 days, beginning 10 days later than regular years.

Some of the early Christians also recognized the connection of the Jewish feasts and Jubilee year with the arrival of Christ's Kingdom.

---

[376] Lev. 16:7-10
[377] Heb. 10:1-4
[378] Lev. 16:21
[379] Lev. 25:8-12

"For since in six days God made the heaven and the earth, and finished the whole world, and rested on the seventh day from all His works which He had made, and blessed the seventh day and sanctified it, so by a figure in the seventh month, when the fruits of the earth have been gathered in, we are commanded to keep the feast to the Lord, which signifies that, when this world shall be terminated at the seventh thousand years, when God shall have completed the world, He shall rejoice in us. ... Then, when the appointed times shall have been accomplished, and God shall have ceased to form this creation, __in the seventh month,__[380] __the great resurrection-day__, it is commanded that the Feast of our Tabernacles shall be celebrated to the Lord, of which the things said in Leviticus are symbols and figures."[381]

"For this is a symbol of the great assembly that is reserved for future times. Of which times there was a shadow in the land of Israel in the year called among the Hebrews "Jobel" (Jubilee), which is the fiftieth year in number, and brings with it liberty for the slave, and release from debt, and the like."[382]

"And if we read that every Hebrew keeps the same Passover, and that in the seventh year every prisoner is set free, and that at Jubilee, that is the fiftieth year, every possession returns to its owner, all this refers not to the present, but to the future; for being in bondage during the six days of this

---

[380] The seventh month on the festival calendar was the first month on the calendar beginning at creation.
[381] Methodius, Banquet of the Ten Virgins, IX, i
[382] Hippolytus, On the Psalms, I, 3

world, on the seventh day, the true and eternal Sabbath, we shall be free."[383]

Here we have a clear example of the earliest Christians associating the Millennial Week with the Jubilee cycle, as both predicting the coming of Christ's Kingdom.

If we count exactly 120 Jubilee years from the fall of man on Tishri 10th of year 1, the return of Christ must also be on Yom Kippur six thousand years later in order to fulfill the 120 Jubilee years to the very day.

Isaiah indicated that the second coming of Christ will occur at the beginning of a Jubilee year.

> *Isaiah 61:1-7 LXX*
> *1 The Spirit of the Lord is upon me, because he has anointed me; he has sent me to preach glad tidings to the poor, to heal the broken in heart, to **proclaim liberty** to the captives, and recovery of sight to the blind; 2 **to declare the acceptable year of the Lord**, and **the day** of recompence; to comfort all that mourn; 3 that there should be given to them that mourn in Sion glory instead of ashes, the oil of joy to the mourners, the garment of glory for the spirit of heaviness: and they shall be called generations of righteousness, the planting of the Lord for glory.*
> *4 And they shall build the old waste places, they shall raise up those that were before made desolate, and shall renew the desert cities, even those that had been desolate for many generations. 5 And strangers shall come and feed thy flocks,*

---

[383] Jerome, Against Jovinainus, Bk. II, xxv

and aliens shall be thy ploughmen and vine-dressers. 6 But ye shall be called priests of the Lord, the ministers of God: ye shall eat the strength of nations, and shall be admired because of their wealth. 7 Thus shall they inherit the land a second time, and everlasting joy shall be upon their head."

Compare this passage with the following instructions for the Jubilee year:

> *Lev. 25:8-11*
> *8 "And you shall count seven sabbaths of years for yourself, seven times seven years; and the time of the seven sabbaths of years shall be to you forty-nine years. 9 Then you shall cause the trumpet of the Jubilee to sound on the **tenth day** of the seventh month; on the Day of Atonement you shall make the trumpet to sound throughout all your land. 10 And you shall consecrate **the fiftieth year**, and **proclaim liberty** throughout all the land to all its inhabitants. It shall be a Jubilee for you; and each of you shall return to his possession, and each of you shall return to his family.*

The proclamation of "Liberty" throughout all the land was only done on the Jubliee year. Jesus read from Isaiah 61 in the synagogue of Nazareth, applying to himself the statements about preaching the glad tidings to the poor and proclaiming the year of liberty (Jubilee). Did Jesus preach about the year of Jubilee? Yes, if this refers to His second coming to establish His Kingdom on the earth. Jesus proclaimed *"the Gospel of the Kingdom,"*[384] and had a great deal to say about His second coming and the Kingdom.

---

[384] Matt. 4:23

It is evident therefore that Jesus will return on the 120[385]th Jubilee, on Yom Kippur, when He will personally sound the *"trumpet of the Jubilee."*[385] This corresponds to the *"trumpet of God"*[386] which *"the Lord Himself"* will blow.[387] He will blow the Jubilee trumpet *"immediately after the tribulation."*[388] This Jubilee trumpet is the *"last trumpet"* which Paul associated with the coming of Christ and the resurrection.[389] It is the *"last trumpet"* because it is the 120th Jubilee trumpet!

Significant Proofs from Internal Consistency

This proposed calendar of 120 Jubilee years from creation to the second coming can be objectively tested and verified. The following points, which demonstrate remarkable internal consistency, will all be shown from biblical data.

1. God told Noah, on a Jubilee year, that He was limiting the Spirit's struggle with the human race to 120 years.

2. Noah died and Abraham was born in the year 2,000 from creation, which was the 40th Jubilee year.

3. Isaac was born in the 41st Jubilee year.

---

[385] Lev. 25:9
[386] 1 Thess. 4:16
[387] Zech. 9:14
[388] Matt. 24:29-31
[389] 1 Cor. 15:52

4. The year of the exodus from Egypt, which was above all else the "year of release"[390] for Israel from slavery, falls exactly on the 50th Jubilee year from creation, the year 2,500. If every 50th regular year is a Jubilee year, the 50th Jubilee year (50x50) would be a Jubilee of Jubilees! It cannot be mere coincidence that the *year of release* from Egypt, the *year of liberty*[391] from slavery, was the 50th Jubilee year, the Jubilee of Jubilees!

5. The Sabbatical and Jubilee cycles on Joshua's Jubilee calendar, which he instituted when Israel had conquered their enemies in Canaan, synchronize perfectly with the Jubilee years on this calendar.

6. God gave David the Davidic Covenant, the promise of the Messiah from his loins, on the 59th Jubilee year!

7. The decree of Cyrus, setting the Jews at liberty, falls on the 70th Jubilee. Jeremiah prophesied that the captivity would end after 70 regular years.[392] And sure enough, it lasted exactly 70 years. However, the year of their release from captivity was also the 70th Jubilee year from creation, a kind of double fulfillment of Jeremiah's prophecy!

8. The 70-weeks prophecy in Daniel 9 begins on the 70th Jubilee year. The "weeks" of years are the Sabbatical periods of seven years on the same Jubilee calendar. The "70th week" of Daniel (the seven-year tribulation) ends on the day before

---

[390] Lev. 25:10 LXX *"And ye shall sanctify the year, the fiftieth year, and ye shall proclaim a release upon the land to all that inhabit it; it shall be given a year of release, a jubilee for you; and each one shall depart to his possession, and ye shall go each to his family."*
[391] Ezekiel 46:17 calls the Jubilee *"the year of liberty."*
[392] 2 Chron. 36:21; Jer. 29:10, Daniel 9:1-2

the 120th Jubilee year begins, at sundown on Tishri 9th, exactly 6,000 years from Adam's expulsion from Eden! The trumpet announcing the 120th Jubilee will sound the next day.

The following chapters lay out a complete chronology from creation to the second coming of Christ using biblical data alone. If the above claims can be proven from the biblical data, the evidence becomes overwhelming that this calendar is indeed correct. These are the things that make this theory credible and worthy to be believed even though it does not always align with all of the dates derived from secular historical sources. The clear patterns and internal consistency are powerful evidence of a Divine designer of human history. It is staggering proof that God is in control of human history, and He will complete what He started exactly when He said He would.

Chapter 10
A BIBLICAL CHRONOLOGY

B oth Christians and Jews have attempted to date the creation and the major historical events recorded in the Hebrew Bible. When apparently conflicting data is found in Scripture, a variety of solutions have been offered and incorporated into these chronologies. No two chronologies agree, although generally they place the creation somewhere between 3760 BC – 4004 BC.

The Problem of Dating the Persian Kings

All of these chronologies have used a combination of biblical and secular data. Even chronologists who claim to base their work on biblical data alone fill in supposed missing biblical data using secular data. For example, Floyd Nolan Jones' recent work, 'The Chronology of the Old Testament,' claims to be in what he calls the "Biblicist" school, which he described as follows:

> "The goal of the members of this school is to construct a standard chronology of the Bible from the chronological data embedded within the Hebrew Masoretic Text of the Old Testament, **independent of any outside sources**. In the past, James Ussher has been its leading proponent."[393]

Both Ussher and Jones used Biblical data alone to date from Creation to the first year of Cyrus the Great, when he issued

---

[393] Jones, Floyd Nolan, The Chronology of the Old Testament, p. 5

239

the decree ending the Babylonian captivity. They then used Daniel's 70 weeks prophecy to calculate the last 483 years prior to Christ's crucifixion. The beginning of the 70-weeks prophecy is usually linked to the 20th year of Artaxerxes. Yet, the Bible does not provide the lengths of the reigns of the Persian kings that came before Artaxerxes: Cyrus, Cambeses, Darius, and Xerxes. Both Ussher and Jones used secular data for the reigns of the Persian kings to fill in this apparent gap in the biblical data.

There is a significant period of time from the first year of Cyrus until the 20th year of Artaxerxes. Any error in the secular chronologies will automatically transfer to the biblical chronologies, essentially leaving the resulting chronology to rest partly on the inspired text, and partly on a patch-quilt of secular sources.

The reliability of the secular data, particularly the dates and list of Persian kings in Ptolemy's Canon, (the primary source for the Persian period), are highly suspect. Of the uncertainty of this period, the late Dr. Charles V. Taylor writes:

> *"Even in the latter part of the twentieth century, the history and archaeology of the second half of the Achaemenid period of ancient history of the Middle East remains insecure in many details. The standard undergraduate text for introducing this study states quite unashamedly:*
>
>> *'The entire period between the accession of Xerxes (485 BC) and the conquest of Alexander (331 BC) is*

exceedingly poor in architectural remains and building inscriptions.'

Roux is saying in effect that (1) archaeology has little to contribute here; and (2) the period was historically one of turmoil."

"The Encyclopaedia Britannica, for example, directs the reader to the article on the Greco-Persian Wars, said to have lasted 100 years. As for dating, the traditional date for the accession of Xerxes (485 BC) is based on one source only, namely Ptolemy's Canon (no connection with the Ptolemy kings!), and this is eventually aligned with General Egyptian dating, which over recent years has been revised again and again. Thus, to the extent that Egyptian dating is unreliable, so is our dating of the Mesopotamian and Persian histories."[394]

Dr. Taylor goes on to lay the blame for the inflated secular dates on a refusal to acknowledge Noah's flood as a limiting benchmark which would greatly shorten the Egyptian period from current claims. Acceptance of the secular dates for this period essentially rests on reconstructed scholarly chronologies which reject the world-wide flood and the inspired biblical genealogies. When we begin dating Egyptian history after the flood (which is the only possibility if the biblical flood account is true), all dates that rely on Egyptian dating must also be pushed much closer to our time, including the reigns of the Persian kings. Taylor continues:

---

[394] Taylor, Dr. Charles V., *The Times of the Great Kings of Persia*, EN Tech. J., vol. 3, 7988, pp. 128-134

"Dr John Osgood likewise refers to the false security of Egyptian chronology in dating the times of the Judges of Israel. Yet, as we shall see, we find startling errors even at the other end of ancient history and, Times of the Great Kings ignoring Egyptian dating as a measure, we find that the internally derived history of the Persian Empire is some 80 years too long for what appears to be the clear implication of biblical history and prophecy. Naturally, such a revision affects the dates of all previous epochs." [395]

Not only does the secular chronology of the Persian kings contradict the biblical flood, but Daniel's prophecy itself limits the Persian period to a much shorter time than secular history.

"In Daniel 11:2-4, written in the days of Cyrus the Great (Cyrus II), we read a prophecy that there will be three more kings, then a fourth, very rich and anti-Greek. After him would come a 'mighty king', whose kingdom would be broken up into four, none of the rulers of which would be his descendants. All Bible scholars agree that this refers to Alexander the Great. But then this gives us a maximum of five important Persian kings, starting with Cyrus the Great. The resultant Empire is 80 years shorter than the traditional dates suggest." [396]

The chronology presented in this book uses absolutely no secular sources, only Biblical data. As stated above, the Bible does not give definite chronological data for the period from the decree of Cyrus ending the Babylonian captivity until the

---

[395] Ibid. pp. 128-129
[396] Ibid. p. 130

reign of Artaxerxes. However, it does give the prophecy of Daniel's 70 weeks which can only be used to determine the year of the crucifixion if one knows the exact year the 70-weeks prophecy begins.

So how do we fill in the period of time from Cyrus to Artaxerxes for which the biblical data is wanting? The answer is that we don't need that data. If God took the trouble to record and preserve in His Word every single component necessary for a complete chronology from creation to the end of the Babylonian captivity, and if He also gave us in prophecy the last nearly 500 years up to the crucifixion of Jesus Christ, He would not have left a gap between these.

The problem which Ussher and others have tried to solve by supplementing Scripture with secular data is based on a faulty assumption. These chronologists were trying to get their biblical chronology to agree substantially with accepted secular chronologies regarding certain dates that were considered well-established, such as Nebuchadnezzar's destruction of Jerusalem. In order to make their biblical chronologies agree with the secular chronologies, they were forced to adopt such a gap.

Daniel's 70-weeks prophecy has a starting point, "from the going forth of the command to restore and build Jerusalem."[397] The problem is, Ezra and Nehemiah gave three or four different decrees related to the rebuilding of Jerusalem and the Temple by at least three different Persian kings. Ussher and others chose the last of these decrees as their

---

[397] Dan 9:25

starting point for the 70 weeks, which was given in the 20th year of Artaxerxes.[398] However, as will be shown later, the correct decree for the countdown of the 70 weeks is the decree of Cyrus which ended the Babylonian captivity.

The problem of missing data from Cyrus to Artaxerxes, which has plagued virtually all previous attempts to arrive at a purely biblical chronology, is the result of linking the start of Daniel's 70 weeks to the wrong decree of the wrong Persian king. The problem of missing data only exists if we attach the start of Daniel's weeks to any decree recorded in Ezra or Nehemiah apart from the very first one, that of Cyrus the Great. If we use this decree, there is no missing data to fill, because Scripture states plainly that Cyrus' decree occurred at the end of the 70 years captivity, as prophesied by Jeremiah.[399] If the underlying assumption that God gave us all the data we need to construct a complete chronology is correct, then this decree of Cyrus must be the start of the 70 weeks of Daniel. It is the only decree that allows us a chronology based exclusively on biblical data. Many more reasons for counting the 70 weeks of Daniel 9 from Cyrus' decree will be given in chapter 15.

Millennial Week Chronology on the Jubilee Calendar

One of the problems facing any attempt to reconstruct a true chronology is the apparent absence of a continuous count of years to check our calculations against. Our Gregorian calendar provides a continuous count of years, covering the last two millennia. A continuous-count calendar is very

---

[398] Neh. 2:1-10
[399] Jer. 25:11-12; Jer. 29:10

convenient. The Greeks used the Olympiads as a continuous calendar. Unfortunately, the Bible does not link any events to these calendars. Events in the Bible are usually dated from other events, such as a particular year of a king's reign, rather than tied to a continuous count of ascending years.

Yet, the Bible does provide a continuous calendar that is useful for cross-checking dates. As mentioned in the previous chapter, virtually all of the critical events in Israel's history fall on Jubilee years when we count Jubilees from creation. The birth of Abraham is in the 40th Jubilee year. The exodus is in the 50th Jubilee (a Jubilee of Jubilees). The Davidic Covenant promising the coming "Messiah" was in the 59th Jubilee year. God's promise of the rebuilding of Solomon's Temple after its destruction was in the 60th Jubilee year. And the decree of Cyrus ending the Babylonian captivity was in the 70th Jubilee year. These can hardly be a coincidence. These repeated coincidences add substantial support for one of the foundational premises of this book, that a Jubilee calendar underlies all of Biblical chronology and it begins on the first day of creation.

This foundational assumption in our chronology adds an interesting twist to the 70-weeks prophecy of Daniel. As pointed out earlier, the year of Cyrus' decree to restore Jerusalem and the Temple was given in the 70th Jubilee year. The application of the Jubilee calendar to the 70-weeks prophecy of Daniel explains why the first 69 weeks are divided into 7 weeks plus 62 weeks until Messiah is "cut off." The first 7 weeks cover a complete Jubilee cycle. Since the 50th year is intercalated into this cycle, there are actually 50 years contained in those "7 weeks" – one complete Jubilee cycle. By distinguishing an entire Jubilee cycle within the 70-weeks prophecy, we are implicitly being told that the entire prophecy is given on the Jubilee calendar outlined in Leviticus 25. And since there is an extra year (Jubilee year) intercalated after every 7 Sabbatical "weeks," the entire prophecy does not concern 490 years, as is universally assumed, but rather 500 years (including the 10 intercalary Jubilee years). Further, the year the countdown of the 69 weeks began must be a Jubilee year! The importance of these discoveries to biblical chronology cannot be overstated.

The Jubilee chronology is another verification of chiliasm which predicts six millennia under the curse. The early Christian chiliasts were absolutely right about the theory. The end of the 6th millennium is almost upon us.

Chapter 11
CREATION to ABRAHAM
1 AM – 2000 AM, the 40th Jubilee

Virtually all Biblical chronologists, both Jewish and Christian, add up the Genesis genealogies from Adam to Abraham to arrive at a date for Abraham. Most Christian chronologists put Abraham's birth in the year 2008 AM using this process. ("AM" is the abbreviation of the Latin term, "Anno Mundi" – "year of the world," counting forward from creation). But, simply adding up the years of each father when his son was born makes a faulty assumption: that each child was born on the birthday of his father. That is not realistic. There is a margin of error of 0 to 12 months for each generation.

For example, we know that Seth was born in Adam's 130th year. But, was he born the day Adam began his 130th year, a month later, six months later, or even one day before his 131st year? Adam's 130th year was 12 full months, any of which could have been Seth's birth month.

Each generation in the early Genesis genealogies must be viewed as the specified years plus an unknown number of months (between 1 and 12). Compounding over the 20 generations from Adam to Abraham, this error could be anywhere from 0 to 20 years. Of course, since births are random throughout the months, the best estimate would be the average of six months per generation.

The second problem is which year to count as the first. In our society, we consider a child to be zero years old until he has lived a full year. We consider a baby to be one year old throughout his second year of life, not his first. However, the Jews reckoned the child to be one year old throughout the first year of life. He was considered two years old after he had lived one full year, and began his second year. Thus there is no difference in saying that Adam was "130 years old" when Seth was born, or saying that Adam was in his "130th year."[400] Adam's age of 130 years was really his 130th year, which would be from his 129th birthday until his 130th birthday by western reckoning, when Seth was born.

To properly calculate the twenty generations from Adam to Abraham, we must subtract six months for each generation. We use the average of six months to account for the random birth months; and we subtract rather than add to account for inclusive reckoning, the absence of a zero-year for each person in the genealogy. Thus, using this method, Seth was born when Adam was 129.5 by western reckoning.

When we average the genealogies like this, something remarkable emerges. Noah's death and Abraham's birth occur the very same year, exactly two millennia after creation (2000 AM), which is also the 40th Jubilee.

---

[400] This principle is illustrated by circumcision "on the 8th day," while the child was "8 days old." (cf. Gen. 17:12 & Lev. 12:3).

Name	Lifespan	Age @ Son's Birth	Born AM
1. Adam	929.5	129.5 (130)	1
2. Seth	911.5	104.5 (105)	129.5
3. Enos	904.5	89.5 (90)	234
4. Cainan	909.5	69.5 (70)	323.5
5. Mahalalel	894.5	64.5 (65)	393
6. Jared	961.5	161.5 (162)	457.5
7. Enoch	364.5	64.5 (65)	619
8. Methuseleh	968.5	186.5 (187)	683.5
9. Lamech	776.5	181.5 (182)	870
10. Noah	949.5	503[401]	1051.5
11. Shem	599.5	99.5 (100)	1554.5
Flood	1	(599.5) [402]	1651 – 1652
12. Arphaxad	437.5	34.5 (35)	1654
13. Salah	432.5	29.5 (30)	1688.5
14. Eber	463.5	33.5 (34)	1718
15. Peleg	238.5	29.5 (30)	1751.5
16. Reu	238.5	31.5 (32)	1781
17. Serug	229.5	29.5 (30)	1812.5
18. Nahor	147.5	28.5 (29)	1842
19. Terah[403]	204.5	129.5 (130)	1870.5
20. Abram	174.5		2000

[401] Genesis 11:11 indicates that Noah was 500 years old, and begat Shem, Ham, and Japheth. Gen. 10:21 says that Japheth was "the elder." The boys were not triplets. Therefore Noah was 500 when Japheth "the elder" was born. The flood was in Noah's 600th year (Gen. 7:11). Shem's son, Arphaxad, was born 2 years after the flood when Shem was in his 100th year, (Gen. 11:10). Arphaxad was born in the year 1654 (2 years after the flood ended). Subtracting the 100 years of Shem's life (99.5), puts his birth in Noah's 503rd year, 3.5 years after Japheth's birth.

[402] The flood was in the 600th year of Noah (Gen. 7:11).

[403] Gen 11:26 *"Now Terah lived seventy years, and begot Abram, Nahor, and Haran."* This passage does not indicate Terah's age when Abram was born, but when Terah's first son was born. The problem is, we do not know which son was first. That it was not Abram is proven from Gen. 11:31. However, Terah died in his 205th year (204-205). Abraham left Haran the year his father died (Acts 7:4, Gen. 12:4), in his 75th year (74-75). Therefore, Terah's 130th year was Abraham's 1st year.

Noah was born in the year 1051 AM. He lived 950 years (inclusive reckoning – 949 years). Thus he died in the year 2000 AM, the same year Abraham was born. Noah's death marks the end of the second millennial "Day." Abraham's birth marks the beginning of the third millennial "Day."

Noah was in his 500th year (499 years plus some months) when God announced that his Spirit would only strive with humanity for 120 "years."[404] As the previous table shows, Noah was born in 1051.5 AM. His 500th year would cover approximately the last half of 1550 AM and first half of 1551 AM, assuming he was born early in the year. The year 1550 AM was the 31st Jubilee year, the year God announced the limit of 120 "years" for His Spirit's struggle with humanity. This suggests the possibility that God was speaking of "Jubilee years" – the particular kind of year which was present when He spoke of limiting His struggle with humanity to 120 "years."

---

[404] Gen. 5:32 – 6:3

Chapter 12
ABRAHAM to the EXODUS
2000 AM – 2500 AM, the 50th Jubilee

Isaac was born during Abraham's 100th year.[405] Isaac's birth was therefore in the latter half of 2099 AM or the first half of 2100 AM. For our purposes, we will average his birth date to the beginning of the year 2100 AM.

Four Hundred Years

From Isaac's birth to the exodus is 400 years. This is demonstrated from the following Scriptures:

> *Gen. 15:13*
> *13 Then He said to Abram: "Know certainly that **your descendants will be strangers in a land that is not theirs**, and will serve them, and they will afflict them **four hundred years**.*

This verse gives the duration of Abraham's descendants in foreign lands as "strangers" (aliens) as 400 years. Many suppose that this refers to Israel's slavery in Egypt covering 400 years. Yet, Israel could not have been in Egypt for anywhere near 400 years. Galatians 3:17 indicates that the exodus from Egypt took place 430 years after God first made the covenant with Abraham.

---

[405] Gen. 21:5

God made this covenant when Abraham still lived in Mesopotamia, before he lived in Haran.[406] Abraham lived 30 more years after God first gave him the covenant until Isaac was born.[407] Isaac lived 60 years before Jacob was born.[408] And Jacob lived 130 years before the Israelites went into Egypt.[409] This is a total of 220 years from God's covenant to Abraham until Jacob and the twelve tribes went down to live in Egypt. If Israel was in Egypt for 400 more years, it would have been 620 years from God's covenant with Abraham until the exodus, and not 430 years as Galatians 3:17 plainly states. It is apparent therefore, that the 400 years of Genesis 15:13 cannot refer exclusively to the time of Israel's sojourn in Egypt.

Also, Genesis 15:16 indicates that the exodus would be in "the fourth generation" after Israel went down to Egypt. Levi was one of the brothers who went down to Egypt – of the first generation. Levi's son, Kohath, was of the second generation. Kohath's son, Amram, was of the third generation. Amram was Moses' father, making Moses of the fourth generation from Levi.[410] Since a generation is typically about 40-60 years, the four generations of the Israelites in Egypt would be somewhere between 160 and 240 years. It would take at least eight generations to equal 400 years. Therefore, Israel was not in Egypt for anywhere near 400 years.

---

[406] Acts 7:2-5
[407] This will be proven later in this chapter.
[408] Gen. 25:26
[409] Gen. 47:9
[410] Exodus 6:14-27; 1 Chron. 6:1-3

How then should we understand the 400 years of Genesis 15:13? An accurate rendering of both the Hebrew and LXX is as follows:

> *Gen 15:13 (My translation)*
> *13 Then He said to Abram: "Know certainly that your seed will be strangers in land not their own, (and will serve them, and they will afflict them), four hundred years.*

It is apparent in both the Hebrew and LXX that the duration of 400 years describes the time Abraham's seed would be "strangers" (aliens) in a foreign land. The clause, "and will serve them, and they will afflict them," is generally descriptive of their condition. But it is the time they were "strangers" (not necessarily continual affliction) which is said to last 400 years. Abraham's seed (Isaac and his descendants) being strangers in foreign lands began the moment of Isaac's birth in Canaan. Isaac was the first promised seed. Isaac, and later Jacob, were also "strangers" in Canaan, not only the Israelites in Egypt.[411]

Abraham's seed (Isaac and Jacob) had been "strangers" in a foreign land a total of about 190 years before the Israelites went down to Egypt.[412] Their descendants (the rest of Abraham's seed – the whole nation of Israel) were afterwards "strangers" in Egypt for four generations (about 210 years). This gives the total of 400 years described in Genesis 15:13.

---

[411] Gen. 28:4, Heb. 11:8-9, 13

[412] Isaac was 60 when Jacob was born; Jacob was 130 when he went down to Egypt.

Were Isaac and Jacob "afflicted" during the time they were "strangers" in Canaan, a foreign land? Yes indeed! The "affliction" of Abraham's seed started with Hagar's and Ishmael's taunting of the boy, Isaac.[413] Isaac was also persecuted by the Philistines out of jealousy, because of God's covenant and because God blessed him so abundantly.[414] Jacob was threatened by his brother Esau who sought to kill him, causing him to flee to a foreign land for twenty years of his life.[415] Jacob was abused and unjustly made to serve by his father-in-law, Laban, during those twenty years.[416] So, Abraham's seed were "strangers" in a foreign land, and lived with "affliction" from the moment of Isaac's birth. This condition lasted until God delivered Israel out of Egypt.

Four Hundred and Thirty Years

Let's now consider the 430 year period, mentioned in Galatians 3, from the time God first made the covenant with Abraham until the exodus and giving of the Law of Moses.

> *Galatians 3:16-18*
> *16 Now to Abraham and his Seed were **the promises** made. He does not say, "And to seeds," as of many, but as of one, "And to your Seed," who is Christ. 17 And this I say, that **the law, which was four hundred and thirty years later, cannot annul the covenant that was confirmed before by God** in Christ, that it should make the promise of no effect.*

---

[413] Gen. 21:9
[414] Gen. 26:12-26
[415] Gen. 27:41-46; 31:38
[416] Gen. 31:1-20

Paul drew the 430 years, from God's promise to Abraham until the Law was given, from the following passage.

> *Exodus 12:40-41*
> *40 Now the sojourn of the children of Israel who lived in Egypt was four hundred and thirty years. 41 And it came to pass at the end of the four hundred and thirty years — on that very same day — it came to pass that all the armies of the LORD went out from the land of Egypt.*

The Hebrew word which the NKJV renders "sojourn" above literally means a "dwelling" as in a particular location.[417] The Hebrew text differs somewhat from the Septuagint and Samaritan Pentateuch in this verse. Here is the Septuagint version of verse 40.

> *Exodus 12:40 LXX* [418]
> *40 And the __dwelling__ of the sons of Israel, which dwelt __in the land of Egypt and in the land of Canaan, they and their fathers__ – four hundred thirty years.*

The location of the sons of Israel during this 430 year period is what this passage has in view. In the Septuagint, the persons spoken of include both "the sons of Israel" and "their fathers" (Isaac and Jacob). Also, the location is both "in the land of Egypt and in the land of Canaan." That the LXX is correct is proven by Paul's statement in Galatians 3:17. He wrote that the Law was given "four hundred and thirty years after" God made the promise to Abraham. The Law was given the same

---

[417] Brown Driver Briggs Hebrew Lexicon #4186
[418] The Apostolic Bible Polyglot Septuagint

year as the exodus, only seven weeks later.[419] God promised Abraham the land when he still lived in Mesopotamia.[420] So, the period of 430 years given in Exodus 12:40 and Galatians 3:17 runs from when Abraham left Ur of Mesopotamia at God's command until the year of the exodus from Egypt. The period of 400 years in Genesis 15:13 and the period of 430 years both terminate with the giving of the Law. The 30 year difference is the time between God's initial covenant with Abraham and the birth of Isaac.

It might appear to some that the Septuagint is correct (in agreement with Galatians 3:17) but the Hebrew text is mistaken by referring only to the sons of Jacob and the time spent in Egypt. However, notice that the Hebrew does not actually place the Israelites in Egypt for 430 years. The clause, "who lived in Egypt" only identifies the group, it does not point to the time of slavery in Egypt.

The clause "the children of Israel" seems at first glance to exclude Isaac and Jacob (Israel), since it refers to the location of the "children" of Jacob whom God renamed "Israel." However, in Jewish tradition, the entire nation of Israel was thought of as existing in Abraham's loins from the moment God made the promise of the covenant to Abraham. Paul explained that the entire Levitical priesthood paid tithes to Melchisedek through Abraham's tithing to Him, because they were present in Abraham's loins when he met Melchisedek.[421] From this Jewish perspective, the entire nation of Israel came

---

419 Exodus 19-20
420 Acts 7:1-5
421 Genesis 14:18-20; Heb. 7:4-9

into existence within Abraham's loins the instant God made the promise to him and he obeyed by leaving Ur of the Chaldees in response to God's promise. Thus, the "dwelling" of Israel (in Abraham's loins) changed when Abraham moved, when Isaac moved, and when Jacob moved. This is what the 430 year prophecies have in view.

The Hebrew text is correct as it stands if properly understood from this Jewish perspective. It seems that the Septuagint was embellished by the Jewish translators in order to make the Hebrew text understandable to the Greek mind. Technically, both are correct. The 430 year period in both Exodus 12 and Galatians 3 are to be counted from Abraham's leaving Ur until the exodus from Egypt.

Virtually all modern chronologists make a critical error in calculating the 400 years and the 430 years. The mistake stems from their placing the Abrahamic Covenant in Abraham's 75th year, when he left Haran after his father died, rather than when He left his home in Ur of Mesopotamia – a misreading of Genesis 12:1-4.

As previously shown, the 400 years began with the birth of Isaac, when Abraham was in his 100th year.[422] Abraham left Haran 25 years earlier, in his 75th year.[423] Most of God's appearances to Abraham occurred during the 25 year period between his leaving Haran and Isaac's birth. However, the difference between the 400 years and 430 years is 30 years, not 25 years. To solve this apparent problem, Ussher dated the

---

[422] Gen. 21:5
[423] Gen. 11:31, Acts 7:4

400 years from Isaac's being weaned (assumed to be five years old) rather than his birth. Unfortunately, this single mistake makes his chronology five years too long.

The correct solution is to date the Abrahamic Covenant five years before Abraham left Haran, when he lived in Ur of Mesopotamia. Apparently modern chronologists missed the fact that God first appeared to Abraham and gave him the promises before his leaving Haran at the age of 75. All of the promises God later repeated were first given to Abraham when he lived in Ur of Mesopotamia, before moving to Haran. That the Abrahamic Covenant was first given before Abraham lived in Haran is affirmed in both the Old Testament and the New Testament, and is critical to a proper timeline.

> *Gen 11:31*
> *31 And Terah took his son Abram and his grandson Lot, the son of Haran, and his daughter-in-law Sarai, his son Abram's wife,* **_and they went out with them from Ur of the Chaldeans to go to the land of Canaan_**; *and they came to Haran and dwelt there.*

Notice that the intention for leaving Ur in Mesopotamia was to go to Canaan, not to Haran. The temporary stop in Haran until Terah died was not their plan. The delay in Haran was most likely due to Terah's ill health. Abraham already knew about the Promised Land when he left Ur, albeit not its location. He was obeying God's call in the hope of receiving the promises by leaving Ur of Mesopotamia.

Heb. 11:8
*8 By faith Abraham obeyed when he was called to go out to the place which he would receive as an inheritance. And he went out, **not knowing where he was going**.*

Abraham's "going out" in this verse is from Ur, not from Haran. Note carefully God's words to him later, when he left Haran.

Gen. 12:1-4
*1 Now the LORD **had said** to Abram: "Get out **of your country**, From your family And from your father's house, To a land that I will show you. 2 I will make you a great nation; I will bless you And make your name great; And you shall be a blessing. 3 I will bless those who bless you, And I will curse him who curses you; And in you all the families of the earth shall be blessed."*
4 So Abram departed as the LORD had spoken to him, and Lot went with him. And Abram was seventy-five years old when he departed from Haran.

That the Abrahamic Covenant was spoken to Abraham when he lived in Ur, before living in Haran, was plainly stated by Stephen.

Acts 7:2-6
*2 And he said, "Brethren and fathers, listen: **The God of glory appeared to our father Abraham when he was in Mesopotamia, before he dwelt in Haran**, 3 and said to him, 'Get out of your country and from your relatives, and come to a land that I will show you.' 4 Then he came out of*

the land of the Chaldeans and dwelt in Haran. And from there, when his father was dead, He moved him to this land in which you now dwell.

Once we correctly establish that the Abrahamic Covenant dates from Abraham's dwelling in Ur of Mesopotamia (the land of the Chaldeans) before he lived in Haran, rather than from his departure from Haran when his father died, the reason for the 430 years becomes clear. Abraham was 75 when he left Haran. Isaac was born when he was 100, (beginning the 400-year count to the exodus). The 430 year count to the exodus begins with the Abrahamic Covenant which was first given five years before Abraham's departure from Haran, when he lived in Ur. Therefore, God's first appearance to Abraham occurred when he was 70 years old, not 75 as Ussher, Jones, and virtually all modern Christian chronologists assume. This single error makes all of their timelines five years too long.[424]

These calculations are affirmed by both ancient Christian and ancient Jewish sources. Irenaeus wrote the following in *The Demonstration of the Apostolic Preaching*:

"He appeared unto Abraham, … and said unto him: Get thee out of thy country, and from thy kindred, and from thy

---

[424] Both Ussher and Jones struggled to reconcile the 400 year statement (which ends with the exodus) with the 430 year statement (which also ends with the exodus). Because of their initial error of linking the first promise with Abraham's departure from Haran when he was 75 years old, they are forced to date the 400 year prophecy 5 years after Isaac's birth, claiming that it begins when Isaac was weaned. Yet this does not agree with the 400 year prophecy, because Isaac was an alien in the land from the moment of his birth, not his weaning.

*father's house; and come into the land that I will show thee, and there dwell. And he believed the heavenly voice, **being then of ripe age, even seventy years old**, and having a wife; and together with her **he went forth from Mesopotamia**, taking with him Lot, the son of his brother who was dead."*[425]

The ancient Jewish Chronology, *Seder Olam Rabbah* (Great Book of the Order of the World), compiled by Rabbi Yose ben Halafta in the second century AD, also placed the beginning of the Abrahamic Covenant in Abraham's 70th year.

*"Our father **Abraham was 70 years old** when he was spoken to (by God's presence) at the Covenant between the pieces as it is said: 'And it was after 430 years,' etc. After that he was spoken to he returned to Haran, stayed there five years as it is said: 'And Abraham was 75 years old when he left Haran.'"*[426]

The location of the children of Israel in foreign lands, from God's initial promise to Abraham until the exodus, was 430 years. In fact, the day of Passover when the Israelites departed from Egypt was "on that very same day"[427] (Nisan 15) that Abraham departed his homeland in Ur of Mesopotamia.

The 430 years cover the whole time of the "sojourn" of Abraham's seed. When God made the promises to Abraham,

---

[425] Irenaeus, The Demonstration of the Apostolic Preaching, 24. Translation by Armitage Robinson, D.D, Dean of Wells, London, 1920

[426] Guggenheimer, Heinrich W., Seder Olam, The Rabbinic View of Biblical Chronology, p. 8

[427] Ex 12:41

He was *"calling those things which do not exist as though they did."*[428] Abraham's seed began the sojourning with him in foreign lands, being carried by Abraham in his loins from the moment he left Ur, because he believed God's promise. Yet, the 400 years of Genesis 15 is dated from the first visible fulfillment of the promise, Isaac's birth.

Abraham was born in the year 2000 AM. God first called him and gave him the promises in his 70th year (2070 AM). Adding the 430 years puts the exodus in the year 2500 AM.
As a second witness, Isaac was born in Abraham's 100th year (2100 AM). Abraham's seed was then persecuted for 400 years, which also ends in the year 2500 AM, the year of the exodus.

The year 2500 AM is the 50th Jubilee year from creation – the first Jubilee of Jubilees (50x50=2500). Israel's being set at liberty from slavery in Egypt on the first Jubilee of Jubilees cannot be a coincidence! The God of Abraham cannot merely see and declare the future, He is orchestrating it with a precision that is astonishing! As we will see, His power and magnificence will be no less evident in the rest of the chronology.

---

[428] Rom 4:17

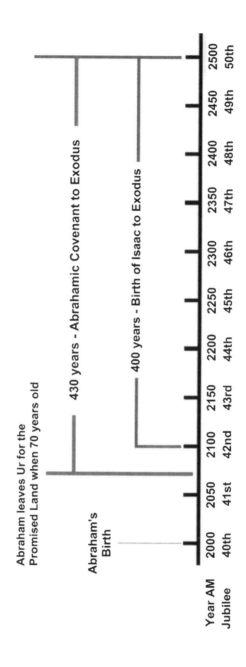

Chapter 13
The EXODUS to SOLOMON
2500 AM – 3000 AM, the 60th Jubilee

We are now faced with the first significant test of this theory – whether the Jubilee calendar actually begins at creation. If the theory is correct, the Jubilee cycles counting from creation must synchronize perfectly with the Jubilee calendar which Israel began to keep once they entered into the Promised Land. Anything less than this will falsify either the premise or the previous calculations.

God told the Israelites to begin counting the Sabbatical years and Jubilee cycles after they went into the Promised Land.[429] If we add the 40 years of wandering in the wilderness to the year of the exodus (2500 AM), we end up with the year 2540 as the year Joshua led the Israelites into the Land. If the Jews began to count the sabbatical and Jubilee years immediately, then the first Jubilee observed in the land would be in 2590, (2500+40+50). This would be ten years too early to synchronize with a continuous Jubilee calendar from creation.

Did God intend for the Israelites to begin counting sabbatical years immediately when they entered the land? The answer is no. They were to begin counting the first seven year Sabbatical cycle (which also begins the 50 year Jubilee count) when they began to farm their own land and eat of their

---

[429] Lev. 25:2

harvests.[430] The tribes did not own specific pieces of land until after Joshua conquered the people of Canaan, and had divided the inheritance by lot to all 12 tribes. This process took several years.

> *Exodus 23:29-31*
> *29 I will not drive them out from before you in one year, lest the land become desolate and the beasts of the field become too numerous for you. 30* **_Little by little I will drive them out from before you, until you have increased, and you inherit the land_***.*

Notice that they did not "inherit the land" immediately. It took five full years to defeat the Canaanites and divide the southern portion to the tribes of Judah, Ephraim, and Manasseh. Joshua 14 describes the division of the southern land.

> *Josh 14:6-11*
> *6 Then the children of Judah came to Joshua in Gilgal. And Caleb the son of Jephunneh the Kenizzite said to him: "You know the word which the LORD said to Moses the man of God concerning you and me in Kadesh Barnea. 7 I was forty years old when Moses the servant of the LORD sent me from Kadesh Barnea to spy out the land, and I brought back word to him as it was in my heart. 8 Nevertheless my brethren who went up with me made the heart of the people melt, but I wholly followed the LORD my God. 9 So Moses swore on that day, saying, 'Surely the land where your foot has trodden shall be your inheritance and your children's*

---

[430] Lev. 25:1-3, 8-10

forever, because you have wholly followed the LORD my God.' 10 And now, behold, the LORD has kept me alive, as He said, these forty-five years, ever since the LORD spoke this word to Moses while Israel wandered in the wilderness; and now, here I am this day, eighty-five years old.

Caleb was 40 years old at Kadesh Barnea, when he was one of the 12 spies.[431] Forty-five years had elapsed since then.[432] Forty of those years covered the wandering in the wilderness. Therefore, the land was divided for the southern tribes to farm after five years had transpired from their entrance into Canaan. The surveying and division of the southern land began in the 45th year, since Caleb was already 85 years old when Joshua began to divide the Land.

Yet, we learn from Joshua 18 that the northern tribes had still not received their inheritance a considerable time later because they had not gone to battle with the inhabitants of the land to defeat them. Joshua rebuked them, saying, *"How long will you neglect to go and possess the land which the LORD God of your fathers has given you?"*[433] After this, the northern tribes drove out the inhabitants and surveyed the rest of the land, after which Joshua divided it by lot to the rest of the tribes.

In Joshua 22, after all the lands were secured from Israel's enemies, and the twelve tribes had all received their allotted land inheritance, Joshua dismissed the tribal armies to go home to their inheritance and farm their own land. This is the

---

[431] Josh. 14:7
[432] Josh. 14:10
[433] Josh. 18:3

point when the Sabbatical and Jubilee cycles began to be kept by the Israelites.

Just how many years did it take to conquer the land, divide the inheritance to all 12 tribes, and dismiss the armies of Israel? Joshua does not tell us. We know it was more than 5 years, since that was how long it took to conquer and divide the southern portion. It is no stretch to assume that it took 5 more years to do the same in the northern portion, and to dismiss the armies to go to their inheritance.

Fortunately, we do not have to guess. The Apostle Paul provided a second witness for this period in the following passage.

> *Acts 13:16-19 NASB*
> *16 Paul stood up, and motioning with his hand said, "Men of Israel, and you who fear God, listen:*
> *17 "The God of this people Israel chose our fathers and made the people great during their stay in the land of Egypt, and with an uplifted arm He led them out from it.*
> *18 "For a period of about forty years He put up with them in the wilderness.*
> *19 "When He had destroyed seven nations in the land of Canaan, He distributed their land as an inheritance — **all of which took about four hundred and fifty years**."*[434]

---

[434] The KJV and NKJV, following the Textus Receptus, place the words "after these things" before "about four hundred fifty years." But, the oldest manuscripts are agreed that the correct word order should be, *"about four hundred fifty years, after these things He gave them judges, etc.,"* as in virtually all modern translations.

The 450 years described by Paul begins when God "chose our fathers." The key word here is "chose." The "chosen" or "elect" in Paul's theology refers to Abraham's descendants, never to Abraham himself. This is shown clearly in Romans 9:6-13. Paul gave a discourse on God's "choosing" (electing) some of Abraham's seed while rejecting others. He quoted God's promise to Abraham, *"In Isaac your seed shall be called."* Thus, God **chose** Isaac and rejected Esau as the conduit of His covenant. *"At this time I will come and Sarah shall have a son."* The choosing of Isaac meant the rejection of Ishmael. Paul continued by showing that God also **chose** Jacob while rejecting Esau. *"And not only this, but when Rebecca also had conceived by one man, even by our father Isaac (for the children not yet being born, nor having done any good or evil, that the purpose of God according to **election** might stand, not of works but of Him who calls), it was said to her, 'The older shall serve the younger.' As it is written, 'Jacob I have loved, but Esau I have hated.'"*

In Paul's theology, God's "choosing" (election) dealt with the particular sons of Abraham through whom God would bring to fruition His promises to Abraham. The "choosing" of Abraham's descendants through which to fulfill His promises to Abraham begins with Isaac, not with Abraham himself. In Acts 13, when Paul wrote that "God chose our fathers," he was speaking of Isaac and Jacob. He continued in the same sermon to speak directly about God's fulfilling His promise to Abraham, which He later confirmed to Isaac and then to Jacob.[435] *"And we declare to you glad tidings — that promise which*

---

[435] Gen. 28:3-4; Gen. 35:9-12

was made to the fathers. God has fulfilled this for us their children, in that He has raised up Jesus."[436]

Thus, when Paul said "God chose our fathers" he was referring to Isaac and Jacob. Thus, the 450 years mentioned by Paul begins with the birth of Isaac, the child of promise whom God "chose" over Ishmael. This was the year 2100AM. The 450 years ends when Joshua and the armies of Israel had defeated Israel's enemies and Joshua had completed dividing up the land inheritance for the 12 tribes. *"The God of this people Israel chose our fathers* [Isaac and Jacob] *… When He had destroyed seven nations in the land of Canaan, He distributed their land as an inheritance — all of which took about* **four hundred and fifty year**s.*"*

As we saw in the previous chapter, it was exactly 400 years from Isaac's birth until the exodus. It was 40 more years until Joshua and all Israel entered the Promised Land. That leaves 10 more years according to Paul's reckoning until all the land was divided, and the Israelites all went home to farm their land. Thus, we have proof that it was 50 years from the year of the exodus (the 50th Jubilee) until Israel began to farm their allotted land inheritance.

Joshua finished dividing the inheritance and dismissed the Israeli army during the year 2550 AM, the 51st Jubilee year. The next year was the first year of the first Jubilee cycle for Israel in the land. Therefore, the first Jubilee which Israel celebrated was in 2600AM, the 52nd Jubilee from creation.

---

[436] Acts 13:32-33

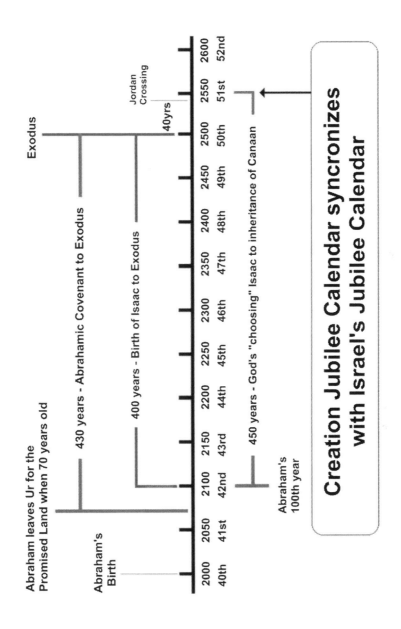

Joshua divided the last of the inheritance and dismissed the Israelite army during the year 2550 AM, which was the 51st Jubilee year from creation. The next year was counted as the first year of the first Jubilee cycle for them. Therefore, the first Jubilee year which Israel actually celebrated was in 2600 AM, the 52nd Jubilee from creation.

We have seen that Abraham's birth and Noah's death were both in the 2000th year from creation, the 40th Jubilee. Isaac was born in the next Jubilee year. God released the Israelites from slavery in Egypt on the 50th Jubilee year (year of release). Now we see that the Jubilee calendar that God commanded Israel to observe coincides perfectly with the Jubilee calendar which begins at creation. This ought to be sufficient evidence to convince any skeptic that the Jubilee calendar is God's calendar beginning at creation.

The period of the Judges is not given in precise terms in Scripture. However, it is not needed because of the following passage.

> *1 Kings 6:1-2*
> *1 And it came to pass in the four hundred and eightieth year after the children of Israel had come out of the land of Egypt, in the fourth year of Solomon's reign over Israel, in the month of Ziv, which is the second month, that he began to build the house of the LORD.*

This passage is very straight forward, dating the beginning of the construction of Solomon's Temple to 480 years after the exodus (in 2500 AM). We must use exclusive reckoning here, because the word "after" means we cannot include the year of the exodus. That brings us to the year 2980 AM as the year construction on Solomon's Temple began.

The Temple construction took seven years. After this, Solomon built his palace, taking 13 more years. This is a total of 20 years.[437]

We now arrive at the year 3000 AM, the 60th Jubilee year from creation. On this 60th Jubilee year, God appeared to Solomon with a stern warning and a promise.

> *2 Chron. 7:11-22*
> *11 Thus Solomon finished the house of the LORD and the king's house; and Solomon successfully accomplished all that came into his heart to make in the house of the LORD and in his own house.*
> *12 **Then** the LORD appeared to Solomon by night, and said to him: "I have heard your prayer, and have chosen this place for Myself as a house of sacrifice. 13 When I shut up heaven and there is no rain, or command the locusts to devour the land, or send pestilence among My people, 14 if My people who are called by My name will humble themselves, and pray and seek My face, and turn from their wicked ways, then I will hear from heaven, and will forgive their sin and heal their land. 15 Now My eyes will be open and My ears attentive to prayer made in this place. 16 For now I have chosen and sanctified this house, that My name may be there forever; and My eyes and My heart will be there perpetually.*

---

[437] 1 Kings 6:38 – 7:1; 1 Kings 9:10

17 As for you, if you walk before Me as your father David walked, and do according to all that I have commanded you, and if you keep My statutes and My judgments, 18 then I will establish the throne of your kingdom, as I covenanted with David your father, saying, 'You shall not fail to have a man as ruler in Israel.'

19 "But if you turn away and forsake My statutes and My commandments which I have set before you, and go and serve other gods, and worship them, 20 then I will uproot them from My land which I have given them; and this house which I have sanctified for My name I will cast out of My sight, and will make it a proverb and a byword among all peoples.

21 "And as for this house, which is exalted, everyone who passes by it will be astonished and say, 'Why has the LORD done thus to this land and this house?' 22 Then they will answer, 'Because they forsook the LORD God of their fathers, who brought them out of the land of Egypt, and embraced other gods, and worshiped them and served them; therefore He has brought all this calamity on them.'"

The dire prediction of the destruction of Solomon's Temple was contingent primarily on Solomon's own faithfulness. *"As for you, if you walk before Me as your father David walked..."* and *"if you turn away and forsake My statutes and My commandments which I have set before you, and go and serve other gods, and worship them,..."* We know that Solomon forsook the Lord, and caused all Israel to sin in the worship of other gods.[438] Ultimately, the destruction of Jerusalem and the Temple by Nebuchadnezzar was the result of Solomon's idolatry and

---

[438] 1 Kings 11:1-13

disobedience which set a precedent for his entire dynasty, most of which followed in his idolatrous footsteps. All of the kings of Israel (the northern kingdom) and most of the kings of Judah (the southern kingdom) followed Solomon's precedent, promoting the worship of pagan gods. Through Nebuchadnezzar, God made good on His threat to Solomon to utterly destroy the Temple he had built.

God's threat to Solomon in the 60th Jubilee year (3000 AM) was one Jubilee (50 years) after God had established the Davidic Covenant with David. The date of the Davidic Covenant is calculated backwards from Solomon's reign. Solomon began building the Temple 20 years before the 60th Jubilee in the fourth year of his reign. Therefore, Solomon began to reign 23 full years before the 60th Jubilee, when David his father died (2976 AM). David had defeated the Jebusites 33 years earlier[439] (2944 AM). He then built his own house in Jerusalem which took several years. After this he brought the Ark of the Covenant to Jerusalem[440] and God gave him the Davidic Covenant.[441] If we assume that it took David six years to build his own house and bring the Ark to Jerusalem, the Davidic Covenant would have been in the 59th Jubilee, the year 2950 AM. That it took David six years to build his house is an assumption to be sure. But it seems likely that the Davidic Covenant – which promised the coming of the Messiah to rule Israel forever on David's throne – would also be in a Jubilee year.

---

[439] 1 Kings 2:11; 1 Chron. 11
[440] 1 Chron. 15
[441] 1 Chron. 17

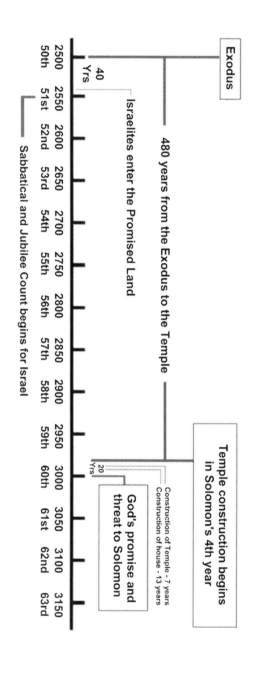

Chapter 14
SOLOMON to CYRUS
3000 AM – 3500 AM, the 70th Jubilee

This period includes the remainder of Solomon's rule, the divided kingdom – the kings of Israel and Judah – and the Babylonian captivity. Sorting out the kings of Israel and Judah is probably the most difficult puzzle for chronologists.

There are numerous problems synchronizing the parallel kings of Israel and Judah using the information in 1 & 2 Kings. There are unsolved apparent discrepancies between Kings and Chronicles, which give parallel accounts of the kings of Judah. There are also several variant readings in the manuscript evidence. Scholars agree that the methods for calculating the years were inconsistent between the northern and southern kingdoms. Even within the single northern kingdom there seems to have been inconsistencies in methods. Many attempts to reconcile all the data have been made. Yet none have solved all of the problems and apparent contradictions. This is not to say that the Scriptures are in error. They are accurate summaries of what actually occurred derived from official records of these kingdoms. However, the inconsistent methods of calculation used at different times, and complete silence about overlapping reigns or short periods when there was no king, make it virtually impossible to establish an accurate chronology of this period based on the lengths of the kings' reigns recorded in Kings and Chronicles alone.

The years given in Scripture for the kings were almost certainly calendar years[442] (from new year's day to new year's day) rather than anniversary years. Otherwise, there would have to be two separate calendars, one dating from the anniversary of that king's ascension to the throne, and the other regular calendar beginning on New Year's Day. Therefore, it is assumed that all years were regular calendar years, counting from the first month of the year which was reckoned to be that king's first year, not from the actual anniversary of the commencement of that king's reign.

There are many proposed theories regarding counting the reigns of the kings. For our purposes, the following theory will prove to be best because the total years for this period derived from this method will also be confirmed with other substantiating biblical data.

The theory used in calculating the kings in this book assumes that only whole years were counted for a particular king, and partial years were discarded. Assuming the regular civil calendar was in use (Tishri to Tishri, fall to fall), the first year of a particular king would be counted from Tishri 1 (Rosh Hashanah – New Year's Day) after he ascended the throne. If he was installed as King six months before Rosh Hashanah, the remainder of the year during which he ascended to the

---

[442] Calendar years could be counted either from Tishri to Tishri (fall to fall, as are the Sabbatical and Jubilee years), or from Nisan to Nisan (spring to spring, as on the festival calendar that began at the exodus – Ex. 12:12).

throne would not be counted as his first year, but discarded. The following whole year (Rosh Hashanah to Rosh Hashanah) would be reckoned as his first year. Likewise, if a king died during the middle of a year, his reign would be reckoned through the last full year he reigned. Thus, only whole years are counted in a particular king's reign. Partial years are discarded and not included in the total number of years a king reigned recorded in Scripture.

This system is implied by the fact that the reigns of kings are never given as X number of years plus X number of months. Only whole years are recorded in the text, implying that only whole years were being counted. It could be argued that partial years were also counted as whole years. Yet, two of the kings of Judah reigned less than one year (3 months each), and their reigns are not said to be "one year" but instead the months are given. This shows that the record keepers for the kings of Judah were not counting partial years as whole years. It is logical to conclude from these observations that partial years were never counted within the number of "years" stated for a king's reign, but only whole years, the exception being a king who reigned less than a year. These are counted in months because every king must be named in an accurate historical record.

Assuming this system to be correct, there would be an intervening calendar year between each of the kings of Judah listed. This intervening calendar year would include the partial year during which the former king died and the rest of same calendar year in which his successor assumed the throne. The transition year would not be assigned to either king as his own.

For example, if Solomon died in mid-year, his last (40th) year would be reckoned as the last full year that he reigned before he died. The year in which he died would not be counted since he reigned only a part of it. Even though his son, Rehoboam, was installed on his throne without delay, his son's reign would not be counted until after Rosh Hashanah had passed again. Therefore, the year Solomon died and Rehoboam ascended to the throne would not be counted for either Solomon or Rehoboam because neither reigned that entire year. Therefore, when adding up the kings of Judah given in 2 Chronicles, one intervening year must be added per king for this transitional year in order to arrive at an accurate total. Of course, the two kings who reigned only 3 months are not to be counted at all because they assumed the throne and died during the same intervening year in which the previous king died and the following king assumed the throne.

The following list contains the years listed in 2 Chronicles for the Davidic dynasty of the kings of Judah. According to the reckoning using the above suppositions, from the death of Solomon to the destruction of Jerusalem by Nebuchadnezzar was 413 years. The following list gives the number of years listed in 2 Chronicles for each king's reign followed by the accumulated years from Solomon's death to the end of that king's reign. This figure is derived by adding in an intervening year between each king's reign. We start by adding the year Solomon died.

Kings of Judah	Years	Acc. Years	Reference
Rehoboam	17	19[443]	2 Chron. 12:13
Abijam	3	23	2 Chron. 13:1
Asa	41	65	2 Chron. 16:13
Jehoshaphat	25	91	2 Chron. 20:31
Jehoram	8	100	2 Chron. 21:5
Ahaziah	1	102	2 Chron. 22:1-2
Athaliah (Queen)	7	110	2 Chron. 22:10-12
Joash	40	151	2 Chron. 24:1
Amaziah	29	181	2 Chron. 25:1
Uzziah	52	234	2 Chron. 26:3
Jotham	16	251	2 Chron. 27:1
Ahaz	16	268	2 Chron. 28:1
Hezekiah	29	298	2 Chron. 29:1
Manasseh	55	354	2 Chron. 33:1
Amon	2	357	2 Chron. 33:21
Josiah	31	389	2 Chron. 34:1
Jehoahaz	3 mo.	-	2 Chron. 36:1
Jehoiakim	11	401	2 Chron. 36:5
Jehoiachin	3 mo.	-	2 Chron. 36:9
Zedekiah	11	413	2 Chron. 36:11

From Solomon's death through the last full year of the last king of Judah was 413 full calendar years. Nebuchadnezzar destroyed Jerusalem the 413th year from the death of Solomon.[444] This is the beginning of the 70 years of exile and captivity in Babylon while Jerusalem lay desolate.

The previous section ended on the 60th Jubilee year, the year 3000 AM, in which God appeared to Solomon the second time warning him of both the ultimate destruction of the Temple

---

[443] 2 years are added to account for the year Solomon and Reheboam assumed the throne, plus the year Reheboam died and Abijam assumed the throne.
[444] 2 Chron. 36:10-21

and promising the restoration of Israel if they repented afterwards. This was Solomon's 23rd year after which Solomon reigned 17 more years (making a total of 40 years). [445]

Add the remaining 17 years of Solomon's reign to the 413 years for the period of the kings of the divided kingdom. This gives a total of 430 years from God's threatening to destroy Solomon's Temple until it was actually destroyed by Nebuchadnezzar. Adding the 70 years of captivity prophesied by Jeremiah[446] to the 430 years gives a total of 500 years. This is the period from God's threat to destroy the Temple and His promise to restore it (3000 AM) until the decree of Cyrus to rebuild Jerusalem and the Temple, ending the captivity[447] (3500 AM).

Four Additional Independent Lines of Evidence
There are four independent lines of additional evidence in Scripture which support the chronology presented here concerning the kings of Judah.

1. A prophecy given through Ezekiel agrees precisely with these calculations. The prophet was told to take a tile and draw on it a representation of Jerusalem. He was to symbolically act out Nebuchadnezzar's coming siege of Jerusalem by first lying on his left side for 390 days, then on his right side for 40 days, a total of 430 days. God told him that each day signified a year during which Israel and Judah

---

[445] Solomon reigned 40 years (23 years before God appeared to him, 17 years afterward), 2 Chron. 9:30.
[446] Jeremiah 25:8-11; Daniel 9:2
[447] Ezra 1

had rebelled against the Lord, and for which He was bringing Nebuchadnezzar to destroy Jerusalem and the Temple just as He had warned Solomon.[448] This is a total of 430 years.[449] It is to be reckoned from God's warning to Solomon in 3000 AM. Solomon rejected God's warning and so did most of his dynasty, as well as all the kings of Israel. This 430-year period ends with the destruction of Jerusalem. When we add the 70 years of the Babylonian captivity, we again arrive at the year 3500 AM as the end of the captivity.

2. We have confirmation from the last words of 2 Chronicles. Here the writer explained why God chose 70 years for the length of the captivity.

> *2 Chron. 36:17-21*
> *17 Therefore He brought against them the king of the Chaldeans, who killed their young men with the sword in the house of their sanctuary, … 19 Then they burned the house of God, broke down the wall of Jerusalem, burned all its palaces with fire, and destroyed all its precious possessions. 20 And those who escaped from the sword he carried away to Babylon, where they became servants to him and his sons until the rule of the kingdom of Persia, 21 to fulfill the word of the LORD by the mouth of Jeremiah,* **_until the land had_**

---

[448] Ezekiel 4

[449] The question arises as to why the 430 years is divided between 390 years for Israel and 40 years for Judah. This is best explained by the fact that the prophets which prophesied of Israel's destruction prophesied for 390 years. And God's special prophet sent to announce Judah's imminent destruction, Jeremiah, prophesied for exactly 40 years.

enjoyed her Sabbaths. As long as she lay desolate she kept Sabbath, to fulfill seventy years.[450]

God commanded a "Sabbatical" for the land every 7th year. Over a 49 year period, there were seven Sabbatical years during which Israel was forbidden from farming the land. However, after 7 Sabbatical years, there was an intercalated "Jubilee year," rounding out the 49 years to 50 years, a Jubilee cycle. In the above passage, the Babylonian captivity was said to be the accumulated 70 consecutive "Sabbatical" years which Israel had not kept. Thus, the 70 years of exile consisted of all Sabbatical years. When we extrapolate the total time period necessary for 70 Sabbatical years to occur on the Jubilee calendar, it represents a total period of 500 years when it is every seventh year, and the Jubilees are intercalated. There are exactly 70 Sabbatical years observed within 10 Jubilee cycles (500 years).

Since Israel failed to keep the Sabbatical years during a 500 year period of rebellion (which should have been calculated using God's Jubilee calendar), the accumulated 70 Sabbatical years for this whole period were all forcibly kept by God's driving Judah out for the last 70 years of that 500-year period. When counting backward the 500 years from the end of the captivity, we again arrive at God's original warning to

---

[450] It is important to notice from this passage that the 70 years captivity is to be counted from the destruction of Jerusalem and the Temple, and not from the first deportation of Nebuchadnezzar 11 years earlier, as most chronologists wrongly assume. Daniel also confirmed that Jeremiah's prophecy of 70 years was concerning the "desolations" of Jerusalem. *"I, Daniel, understood by the books the number of the years specified by the word of the LORD through Jeremiah the prophet, that He would accomplish seventy years in the desolations of Jerusalem."* (Dan. 9:2)

Solomon that He would destroy the Temple if Solomon and his sons did not obey.

3. Isaiah informs us that the 14th year of Hezekiah fell on a Sabbatical year followed immediately by a Jubilee year in Hezekiah's 15th year. The story is told in Isaiah 36-37 of the Assyrian king, Sennacherib, threatening Hezekiah and the kingdom of Judah in Hezekiah's 14th year. Hezekiah took the threatening letter to the Temple and spread it before the Lord, praying earnestly for deliverance. Isaiah was sent to Hezekiah with the promise of God's protection and a sign.

> *Isaiah 37:30-32*
> *30 "This shall be a sign to you: You shall eat this year such as grows of itself, And the second year what springs from the same; Also in the third year sow and reap, Plant vineyards and eat the fruit of them.*
> *31 And the remnant who have escaped of the house of Judah shall again take root downward, And bear fruit upward.*
> *32 For out of Jerusalem shall go a remnant, And those who escape from Mount Zion. The zeal of the LORD of hosts will do this.*

The wording here was borrowed from Leviticus 25, which contains the commandments for observing the Sabbatical year and the Jubilee year. In a normal Sabbatical year they did not farm the land, but crops would spring up on their own. But, when a Jubilee year followed the 7th Sabbatical year, there were two consecutive years when the land was not farmed.

The above passage indicates that "this year" (which was Hezekiah's 14th year)[451] was a Sabbatical year and the following year (which was Hezekiah's 15th year) was a Jubilee year. In Hezekiah's 16th year the land would return again to normal farming. The chronology presented here agrees. Hezekiah's 14th year was the year 3299 AM, a Sabbatical year. His 15th year was the year 3300 AM, the 66th Jubilee year. Why was this a sign to Hezekiah? It was a sign because Israel had long ago abandoned the Sabbatical and Jubilee observances. Because of this, God had stopped providing an abundant crop in the 6th year to last through both the Sabbatical and Jubilee years.[452] Hezekiah's sign shows that this Jubilee chronology synchronizes with Hezekiah's reign. It proves that a Jubilee cycle is 50 years, not 49 years as many incorrectly claim.

4. Jeremiah indicated that when Nebuchadnezzar had Jerusalem under siege, the year before He destroyed it and burned the Temple,[453] it was a Sabbatical year (during which all slaves were to be freed according to the Law of Moses).[454]

> *Jeremiah 34:1,8-17*
> *1 The word which came to Jeremiah from the LORD, when Nebuchadnezzar king of Babylon and all his army, all the kingdoms of the earth under his dominion, and all the people, fought against Jerusalem and all its cities, …*
> *8 This is the word that came to Jeremiah from the LORD, after King Zedekiah had made a covenant with all the people*

---

451 Isaiah 36:1
452 Lev. 25:20-22
453 Jer. 39:1
454 Ex. 21:1-2

who were at Jerusalem to proclaim liberty to them: 9 **that**
every man should set free his male and female slave —
a Hebrew man or woman — that no one should keep a
Jewish brother in bondage. 10 Now when all the princes
and all the people, who had entered into the covenant, heard
that everyone should set free his male and female slaves, that
no one should keep them in bondage anymore, they obeyed
and let them go. 11 But afterward they changed their minds
and made the male and female slaves return, whom they had
set free, and brought them into subjection as male and female
slaves.

12 Therefore the word of the LORD came to Jeremiah from
the LORD, saying, 13 "Thus says the LORD, the God of
Israel: **'I made a covenant with your fathers in the day**
that I brought them out of the land of Egypt, out of the
house of bondage, saying, 14 "At the end of seven years
let every man set free his Hebrew brother, who has
been sold to him; and when he has served you six years,
you shall let him go free from you." But your fathers did
not obey Me nor incline their ear. 15 Then you recently
turned and did what was right in My sight — every man
proclaiming liberty to his neighbor; and you made a
covenant before Me in the house which is called by My name.
16 Then you turned around and profaned My name, and
every one of you brought back his male and female slaves,
whom he had set at liberty, at their pleasure, and brought
them back into subjection, to be your male and female slaves.'
17 "Therefore thus says the LORD: 'You have not obeyed
Me in proclaiming liberty, every one to his brother and every
one to his neighbor. Behold, I proclaim liberty to you,' says
the LORD — 'to the sword, to pestilence, and to famine!'"

The chronology in this book has a Sabbatical year during Nebuchadnezzar's siege of Jerusalem just before it was completely destroyed.[455]

These four independent witnesses testify to the accuracy of the method, calculations, and underlying assumptions for the period of the kings. There were 430 years from God's threat to Solomon plus the 70 years of the captivity, for a total of 500 years. The decree of Cyrus to rebuild the Temple, ending the Babylonian captivity, was in the 70th Jubilee year, 3500 AM.[456]

Virtually all Christian chronologists since Ussher begin the seventy-year Babylonian captivity with either the end of Josiah's reign or with Nebuchadnezzar's first deportation of some Jews to Babylon at the beginning of Zedekiah's eleven-year reign. This is not because Scripture requires it, but to align their chronologies with certain secular dates which are thought to be reliable. In particular, the destruction of Jerusalem is said to have occurred in 586-587 BC. Yet, dating the captivity from anything other than the destruction of Jerusalem runs up against clear statements of Scripture.

---

[455] 3450 AM was a Jubilee year, making 3449 AM a Sabbath year. Therefore, counting backward by sevens (Sabbath years), 3428 AM was also a Sabbatical year. The Temple was destroyed in 3430 AM after a two-year siege, a few weeks before Rosh Hashanah (Jer. 52:12).

[456] In the second century, Clement of Alexandria calculated the period of the kings from the end of David's reign to the destruction of Jerusalem. *"From the reign of David to the captivity by the Chaldeans, four hundred and fifty-two years and six months."* (Clement of Alexandria, Stromata, Bk. I, ch. xxi). This matches almost perfectly the chronology presented here. There were 430 years from God's threat to Solomon until the destruction of Jerusalem. Solomon began to build the Temple after 3 years, and God appeared to him 20 years later. So, there were 453 years by our calculations, only 6 months off from Clement's.

Jeremiah's prophecy predicted Jerusalem would lie in ruins for 70 years. *"And this whole land shall be a desolation and an astonishment, and these nations shall serve the king of Babylon seventy years."*[457] 2 Chronicles 36 interpreted Jeremiah's prophecy the same way. *"As long as she [Jerusalem] lay desolate she kept Sabbath, to fulfill seventy years."*[458] Daniel concurred in his interpretation of Jeremiah: *"I, Daniel, understood by the books the number of the years specified by the word of the LORD through Jeremiah the prophet, **that He would accomplish seventy years in the desolations of Jerusalem**."*[459] The destruction of Jerusalem occurred when the last Davidic king (Zedekiah) was cut off, when the priesthood and Temple worship were abruptly ended, and Jerusalem was laid desolate in ruins. This is the only credible starting point for the 70-year Babylonian captivity from the biblical data. While modern chronologists have shortened this period to allow their date for the destruction of Jerusalem to coincide with modern dating, the early Christians did not. They counted the 70-year exile from the destruction of Jerusalem.[460]

The end of the exile in Babylon did not only conclude the 70 regular years of exile, but also 70 Jubilee years from creation. The year of Cyrus' decree was the 70th Jubilee year, a kind of double fulfillment of Jeremiah's prophecy which adds great credibility to this chronology so far.

---

[457] Jer. 25:11
[458] 2 Chronicles 36:2. See also Jer. 25:8-12
[459] Dan. 9:2
[460] Theophilus to Autolycus, Book III, ch. xxvi

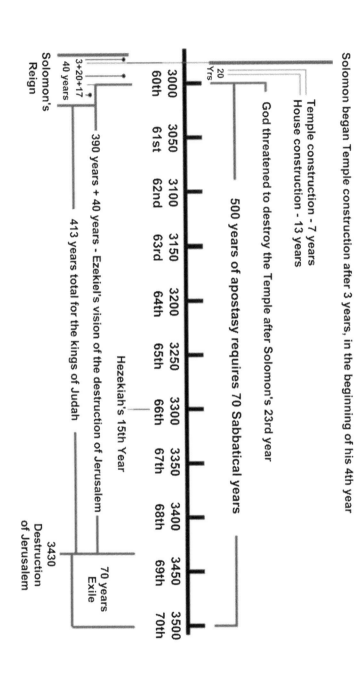

Solomon began Temple construction after 3 years, in the beginning of his 4th year

Temple construction - 7 years
House construction - 13 years

God threatened to destroy the Temple after Solomon's 23rd year

500 years of apostasy requires 70 Sabbatical years

20 Yrs

Solomon's Reign

3+20+17
40 years

390 years + 40 years - Ezekiel's vision of the destruction of Jerusalem

413 years total for the kings of Judah

Hezekiah's 15th Year

70 years Exile

3000 3050 3100 3150 3200 3250 3300 3350 3400 3450 3500
60th 61st 62nd 63rd 64th 65th 66th 67th 68th 69th 70th

3430 Destruction of Jerusalem

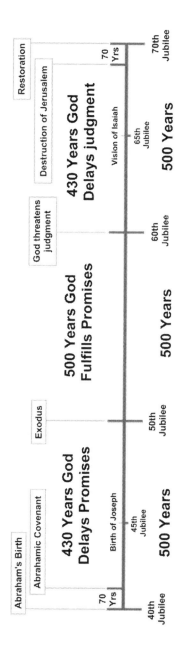

The preceding diagram illustrates the amazing symmetry of these periods of time. This is powerful evidence that human history is the product of intelligent design. And the One guiding history is the same God who appeared to Abraham and spoke through the prophets.

Chapter 15
CYRUS to the CRUCIFIXION
3500 AM – 3993 AM

We now come to what is likely to be the most controversial part of this chronology, Daniel's 70-weeks prophecy. Daniel provided us with a prophecy which covers the time from Cyrus' decree to the crucifixion of Christ – the first 69 weeks of his famous "70 Weeks" prophecy.[461] The Hebrew word translated "weeks" in this prophecy literally means "sevens" and does not necessarily refer to a period of seven days. Here, it is a period of seven years, one complete Sabbatical cycle consisting of six years of farming plus the Sabbatical year during which the land rested. The 70-weeks prophecy concerns 70 of these seven-year Sabbatical cycles.

> Dan. 9:24-27
> 24 "Seventy weeks are determined For your people and for your holy city, To finish the transgression, To make an end of sins, To make reconciliation for iniquity, To bring in everlasting righteousness, To seal up vision and prophecy, And to anoint the Most Holy.
> 25 "Know therefore and understand, That **from the going forth of the command To restore and build Jerusalem** Until Messiah the Prince, There shall be seven weeks and

---

[461] Dan. 9:24-27

sixty-two weeks; The street shall be built again, and the wall, Even in troublesome times.

26 "And after the sixty-two weeks Messiah shall be cut off, but not for Himself; And the people of the prince who is to come Shall destroy the city and the sanctuary. The end of it shall be with a flood, And till the end of the war desolations are determined.

27 Then he shall confirm a covenant with many for one week; But in the middle of the week He shall bring an end to sacrifice and offering. And on the wing of abominations shall be one who makes desolate, Even until the consummation, which is determined, Is poured out on the desolate."

Daniel's prophecy predicted the death of the Messiah after the 69th Sabbatical cycle (week) was completed, and before the 70th week begins. Also, the 69 weeks prior to Jesus' crucifixion are divided into 7 weeks plus 62 weeks. The first 7 weeks (49 years) represents a complete Jubilee cycle, since the 50th year is intercalated. This one complete Jubilee cycle was the duration of the reconstruction of Jerusalem and the Temple, including the walls which Nehemiah finished fifty years after Cyrus' decree. The following 62 weeks was the duration from the completion of Jerusalem's restoration until the cutting off of Messiah.

It is important to keep in mind that after every 7th Sabbatical year, the Jubilee year must be intercalated. During the entire 70 weeks, there are 10 intercalated Jubilee years, for a total of 500 years. Yet, since Messiah was to be "cut off" after the 69th week (before the 70th week), there were 492 full years completed from Cyrus' decree until the end of the 69th week, after which Jesus Christ was crucified in the 493rd year. This number is calculated by multiplying the 70 weeks of years (7x70=490), then adding the 10 intercalated Jubilee years (490+10=500), and subtracting the last week (7 years) which occurs after Jesus' crucifixion (500-7=493).

Daniel's prophecy was given during the Babylonian captivity, after Nebuchadnezzar had destroyed Jerusalem. Daniel predicted a restoration of Jerusalem (vs. 25) followed by a second destruction of Jerusalem after Messiah was cut off. The second destruction of Jerusalem in verse 26 occurs after the 69th week, but before the 70th week. We know that the second destruction of Jerusalem was in AD 70, forty years after Jesus' crucifixion. Since the final "week" occurs after the second destruction of Jerusalem, it must be separated from the other 69 weeks by at least 40 years (the duration between Jesus' crucifixion and the destruction of Jerusalem). This necessary gap in Daniel's prophecy is the age in which we now live, and will be addressed fully in the next chapter. For now we need to turn our attention to the starting point of the 70-weeks prophecy, *the going forth of the command to restore and build Jerusalem.*

Cyrus' Decree Begins the 70-Weeks Countdown

The beginning point of the prophecy is the command of Cyrus ending the Babylonian captivity. Using the decree of Cyrus as the trigger for the 70-weeks prophecy is immediately rejected by conservative Christians on two counts: First, it flows counter to the secular historical dates that are considered to be well established (that the fall of Jerusalem was in 586/587 BC). But as we have already demonstrated, the secular dates are highly suspect, and depend on assumptions that Egyptian history began long before the flood, hence denying Noah's flood and denying the prophecy of the five Persian kings in Daniel 11:2-4.

Second, many claim that it does not meet the commencement criteria in Daniel 9:25, *"from the going forth of the command to restore and build Jerusalem."* The claim is made that Cyrus only ordered the rebuilding of the Temple, not the city or its walls. Also, since specific mention is made of the construction of the "wall" in Daniel's prophecy, these chronologists look to Artaxerxes' command to Nehemiah as the only one which qualifies because it mentions the rebuilding of the wall.

Yet, a careful look at Daniel's prophecy reveals that the "wall" statement does not refer to the command itself, but only states that the wall would be constructed at some point "in troublesome times" afterwards. Note carefully the wording of Daniel's prophecy. *"Know therefore and understand, that from the going forth of the command to restore and build Jerusalem until Messiah the Prince, there shall be seven weeks and sixty-two weeks; The street shall be built again, and the wall, even in troublesome times."* The command itself does not mention the wall. The comments about the wall's construction are editorial, describing what will ultimately follow the command. The only criterion is that the specified command includes the rebuilding of Jerusalem. If the wall's construction must be a part of this decree, then so also must the last clause, *"even in troublesome times."* No one would suggest that the Persian king decreed "troublesome times" for his construction project! Therefore, the "wall" comment is only an editorial description of what would follow, and not the decree itself. Regardless of which decree we attach this prophecy to, the latter statement about the wall's construction would still be true.

The objection that the command of Cyrus only concerned the rebuilding of the Temple and not the city of Jerusalem is simply false. While it is true that the wording of the decree as given in the first chapter of Ezra and the last chapter of 2 Chronicles mentions only the rebuilding of the Temple, these quotations from Cyrus' decree are clearly selective, not exhaustive treatments of the entire decree.

> *2 Chron. 36:23*
> *23 Thus says Cyrus king of Persia:*
> *All the kingdoms of the earth the LORD God of heaven has given me. And He has commanded me to build Him a house at Jerusalem which is in Judah. Who is among you of all His people? May the LORD his God be with him, and let him go up!*

That this is not the entire decree is plain because Ezra gives a longer version of it.

> *Ezra 1:2-4*
> *2 Thus says Cyrus king of Persia:*
> *All the kingdoms of the earth the LORD God of heaven has given me. And He has commanded me to build Him a house at Jerusalem which is in Judah. 3 Who is among you of all His people? May his God be with him, and let him go up to Jerusalem which is in Judah, and build the house of the LORD God of Israel (He is God), which is in Jerusalem. 4*

And whoever is left in any place where he dwells, let the men of his place help him with silver and gold, with goods and livestock, besides the freewill offerings for the house of God which is in Jerusalem.

That even Ezra's version is only an excerpt, and not the entire decree given by Cyrus, is proven by Isaiah's prophecy about Cyrus some 200 years earlier.

Isaiah 44:24-28
24 Thus says the LORD, your Redeemer, And He who formed you from the womb:
"I am the LORD, who makes all things, Who stretches out the heavens all alone, Who spreads abroad the earth by Myself; 25 Who frustrates the signs of the babblers, And drives diviners mad; Who turns wise men backward, And makes their knowledge foolishness; 26 Who confirms the word of His servant, And performs the counsel of His messengers; Who says to Jerusalem, 'You shall be inhabited,' To the cities of Judah, 'You shall be built,' And I will raise up her waste places; 27 Who says to the deep, 'Be dry! And I will dry up your rivers;
*28 **Who says of Cyrus, 'He is My shepherd, And he shall perform all My pleasure, <u>Saying to Jerusalem, "You shall be built</u>," And to the temple, "Your foundation shall be laid".'"***

If Cyrus did not decree both the rebuilding of the Temple and the city of Jerusalem, then Isaiah's prophecy was in error. Clearly, Isaiah was not mistaken, and the decree of Cyrus included the rebuilding of Jerusalem, whether or not this was included in Ezra's excerpted quotation.

Furthermore, Josephus wrote that Cyrus' decree was in response to his being shown Isaiah's prophecy. He was greatly impressed with the God of Israel who called him by name two centuries before he was born. Cyrus immediately decreed both the rebuilding of Jerusalem and the Temple.

> *"Accordingly, when Cyrus read this* [Isaiah's prophecy about him], *and admired the Divine power, an earnest desire and ambition seized upon him to fulfill what was so written; so he called for the most eminent Jews that were in Babylon, and said to them, that he gave them leave to go back to their own country, and* **to rebuild their city Jerusalem, and the temple of God***, for that he would be their assistant, and that he would write to the rulers and governors that were in the neighborhood of their country of Judea, that they should contribute to them gold and silver for the building of the temple, and besides that, beasts for their sacrifices."*[462]

Josephus then quoted Cyrus' own comments about his decree in a letter written by him:

> *"King Cyrus to Sisinnes and Sathrabuzanes sendeth greeting. I have given leave to as many of the Jews that dwell in my country as please* **to return to their own country, and to rebuild their city, and to build the temple of**

---

[462] Josephus, Antiquities, Book XI, ch i

God at Jerusalem on *the same place where it was before.*
... "[463]

Shortly after Cyrus' death, the construction of Jerusalem was opposed by the people of the surrounding area. Ezra wrote about the first letter of opposition sent to Ahasuerus (Cambyses, Cyrus' son), but does not give the content.[464] However, Josephus provides the text of this letter. It is clear from the letter that the Jews were not only rebuilding the Temple, but also the city of Jerusalem and its walls.

> *"To our Lord Cambyses. We thy servants, Rathumus the historiographer, and Semellius the scribe, and the rest that are thy judges in Syria and Phoenicia, send greeting. It is fit, O king, that thou shouldst know that those Jews which were carried to Babylon are come into our country, and* ***are building that rebellious and wicked city, and its market-places, and setting up its walls****, and raising up the temple; know therefore, that when these things are finished, they will not be willing to pay tribute, nor will they submit to thy commands, but will resist kings, and will choose rather to rule over others than be ruled over themselves."*[465]

According to Josephus, Cambyses replied with the following letter:

---

[463] Josephus, Antiquities, Book XI, ch. i
[464] Ezra 4:6
[465] Josephus, Antiquities, Book XI, ch. i

*"Cambyses the king, to Rathumus the historiographer, to Beeltethmus, to Semellius the scribe, and the rest that are in commission, and dwelling in Samaria and Phoenicia, after this manner: I have read the epistle that was sent from you; and I gave order that the books of my forefathers should be searched into, and it is there found that **this city** hath always been an enemy to kings, and its inhabitants have raised seditions and wars. We also are sensible that their kings have been powerful and tyrannical, and have exacted tribute of Celesyria and Phoenicia. **Wherefore I gave order, that the Jews shall not be permitted to build that city**, lest such mischief as they used to bring upon kings be greatly augmented."*[466]

Ezra recorded another similar disruption of the building of Jerusalem in the early years of Artaxerxes, again caused by a similar letter sent to the Persian king.

Ezra 4:11-22
11 To King Artaxerxes from your servants, the men of the region beyond the River, and so forth:
*12 Let it be known to the king that the Jews who came up from you have come to us at Jerusalem, **and are building the rebellious and evil city, and are finishing its walls and repairing the foundations. 13 Let it now be known to the king that, if this city is built and the walls completed**, they will not pay tax, tribute, or custom, and the king's treasury will be diminished. 14 Now because we receive support from the palace, it was not proper for us to see the king's dishonor; therefore we have sent and informed*

---

[466] Ibid.

the king, 15 that search may be made in the book of the records of your fathers. And you will find in the book of the records and know that this city is a rebellious city, harmful to kings and provinces, and that they have incited sedition within the city in former times, for which cause this city was destroyed.

16 We inform the king that if this city is rebuilt and its walls are completed, the result will be that you will have no dominion beyond the River.

17 The king sent an answer: To Rehum the commander, to Shimshai the scribe, to the rest of their companions who dwell in Samaria, and to the remainder beyond the River: Peace, and so forth.

18 The letter which you sent to us has been clearly read before me. 19 And I gave the command, and a search has been made, and it was found that this city in former times has revolted against kings, and rebellion and sedition have been fostered in it. 20 There have also been mighty kings over Jerusalem, who have ruled over all the region beyond the River; and tax, tribute, and custom were paid to them. 21 __*Now give the command to make these men cease, that this city may not be built until the command is given by me.*__

22 Take heed now that you do not fail to do this. Why should damage increase to the hurt of the kings?

Years later, Artaxerxes gave Nehemiah permission to resume the construction of Jerusalem and its walls.

Neh. 2:1-8

1 And it came to pass in the month of Nisan, in the twentieth year of King Artaxerxes, when wine was before him, that I took the wine and gave it to the king. Now I had never been sad in his presence before. 2 Therefore the king said to me, "Why is your face sad, since you are not sick? This is nothing but sorrow of heart."

So I became dreadfully afraid, 3 and said to the king, "May the king live forever! Why should my face not be sad, when the city, the place of my fathers' tombs, lies waste, and its gates are burned with fire?"

4 Then the king said to me, "What do you request?"

So I prayed to the God of heaven. 5 And I said to the king, "If it pleases the king, and if your servant has found favor in your sight, I ask that you send me to Judah, to the city of my fathers' tombs, that I may rebuild it."

6 Then the king said to me (the queen also sitting beside him), "How long will your journey be? And when will you return?" So it pleased the king to send me; and I set him a time.

7 Furthermore I said to the king, "If it pleases the king, let letters be given to me for the governors of the region beyond the River, that they must permit me to pass through till I come to Judah, 8 and a letter to Asaph the keeper of the king's forest, that he must give me timber to make beams for the gates of the citadel which pertains to the temple, __for the city wall__, and for the house that I will occupy." And the king granted them to me according to the good hand of my God upon me.

It is quite clear that Artaxerxes' decree in his twentieth year, giving leave to Nehemiah, permitted the resumption of what had already been authorized by Cyrus but had repeatedly been stalled by the opposition of Israel's enemies. Artaxerxes' decree was not the initial decree to rebuild Jerusalem and its walls after the Babylonian captivity. Several years before Artaxerxes' permission to Nehemiah to complete the rebuilding of the walls, Ezra the priest had thanked God for giving Israel mercy in the sight of kings of Persia, to rebuild the Temple, the city of Jerusalem, and the walls. *"For we were slaves. Yet our God did not forsake us in our bondage; but He extended mercy to us in the sight of the kings of Persia, to revive us,* **to repair the house of our God, to rebuild its ruins, and to give us a wall in Judah and Jerusalem**.*"*[467] Therefore, the decree of Artaxerxes cannot be the initial decree for the rebuilding of Jerusalem. The decree of Cyrus in his first year is the only possible start for the 70-weeks prophecy since it is the only decree for which we have a definite date in Scripture, and because it is the first decree to meet all the criteria in Daniel's prophecy.

Daniel 9 actually confirms this interpretation that the 70 weeks are to be counted from Cyrus' first year. Daniel's visitation by Gabriel to reveal the 70 weeks was in the first year of Darius the Mede.[468] It was Cyrus the Persian who defeated the Babylonians, and immediately began to rule over the entire kingdom. Yet, Cyrus granted Darius the Mede, father of his wife, immediate local jurisdiction over the newly

---

[467] Ezra 9:9
[468] Daniel 9:1

acquired territory of Babylon.[469] Cyrus' years in Scripture are reckoned from his conquering of the Babylonians, when he first absorbed the Jewish nation in Babylonian exile into his newly expanded kingdom. It was Cyrus who defeated the Babylonians, not Darius the Mede. Hence, the first year of Darius, when Cyrus gave him local jurisdiction over Babylon, was also the first year of Cyrus' reign over the Jews. Darius was installed as the local ruler, while Cyrus ruled over the entire Persian Empire. And since the decree of Cyrus ending the Babylonian exile was in his first year,[470] it is evident that Daniel's 70-week prophecy was delivered to him at the time Cyrus made the decree to rebuild Jerusalem and the Temple. In other words, Gabriel was dispatched to inform Daniel that the captivity had just ended. Cyrus had just issued the decree from the first day Daniel began praying,[471] which was precisely the end of 70 years from the complete destruction of Jerusalem.[472]

Daniel 9 bears this out. In the beginning of the chapter, Daniel stated that this occurred in the first year of Darius (which is also the first year of Cyrus). Daniel informs us that he had been studying the prophet Jeremiah, specifically the prophecy that the captivity would last 70 years, dating this from the destruction of the city. No doubt, Daniel's prayer of

---

[469] Kelly Santee, Darius the Mede: His Identity Revealed
http://www.presentruth.com/2008/06/darius-the-mede-his-identity-revealed/
[470] Ezra 1:1
[471] Daniel 9:2
[472] Most chronologists, including Ussher, count the 70 years from the first deportation of captives to Babylon (Dan. 1:1), which took place about 20 years before Jerusalem was destroyed by Nebuchadnezzar. However, several Scriptures indicate clearly that the 70 years was for the desolation of Jerusalem (2 Chron. 36:17-21; Jer. 25:8-11; Dan. 9:2).

repentance for Israel which follows was because he knew that the 70 years since the destruction of Jerusalem had expired that very day! So, he began to fast and pray on behalf of Israel's sins, and for the restoration of Jerusalem, on the very day that the 70-year exile was prophesied by Jeremiah to end.

> *"I pray, let Your anger and Your fury be turned away from Your city Jerusalem, Your holy mountain; because for our sins, and for the iniquities of our fathers, Jerusalem and Your people are a reproach to all those around us. Now therefore, our God, hear the prayer of Your servant, and his supplications, and for the Lord's sake cause Your face to shine on Your sanctuary, which is desolate. O my God, incline Your ear and hear; open Your eyes and see our desolations, and the city which is called by Your name; for we do not present our supplications before You because of our righteous deeds, but because of Your great mercies. O Lord, hear! O Lord, forgive! O Lord, listen and act!* **Do not delay for Your own sake, my God**, *for Your city and Your people are called by Your name."* [473]

The reason Daniel asked God not to *"delay for Your own sake"* was because of His promise that the desolation of Jerusalem would last 70 years. If it went more than 70 years, which is what all other interpretations require, then God would have "delayed" and not honored His word through Jeremiah! Note Daniel's prayer refers to both the city and the House of God.

Gabriel appeared 21 days after Daniel began to fast and pray. Note carefully Gabriel's announcement to Daniel.

---

[473] Dan 9:16-19

306

> *"In the beginning of your supplication **the word was issued** and I have come to tell you. For you are a man greatly loved. Therefore consider the matter and understand the vision. Seventy sevens have been determined upon your people and upon the holy city ... And thou shalt know and understand, that **from the issuing of the word** for the restoration and the building of Jerusalem until Messiah the prince ..."*[474]

Virtually all commentators assume that "the word" which was "issued" at the beginning of Daniel's fasting referred to a command given to the angel to visit Daniel. Yet, the same words are used in reference to the issuing of the "word" to rebuild Jerusalem. Gabriel was dispatched to inform Daniel that Cyrus had issued the decree already. Daniel could start counting down the 70 weeks from the first day of his fast!

We learn in the early part of the book that Daniel adopted a diet reflective of his state of mourning immediately from the beginning of his transport to Babylon. Daniel was taken captive by Nebuchadnezzar the same year that Jeremiah prophesied that the exile would last 70 years.[475] Daniel began his diet of mourning when he reached Babylon. "Thus Daniel continued until the first year of King Cyrus"[476] (the year the captivity ended). So Daniel's diet of mourning began when Jeremiah prophesied of the upcoming destruction of Jerusalem and 70 years of exile that would follow, and it ended with the 21 day fast recorded in Daniel 9, at the time of

---

[474] Daniel 9:23-24a LXX my translation
[475] Cf. Jer. 25:1-14 & Daniel 1:1-2
[476] Daniel 1:21

Cyrus' decree. Why would Daniel stop his diet of mourning in the first year of Cyrus unless the order had been given to restore Jerusalem (the subject of his prayer), and the countdown had begun to the coming of the Messiah, both for which Daniel longed?

Some of the early Christians also believed that the 70-weeks prophecy of Daniel began with the decree of Cyrus, from the time when Daniel received the message from Gabriel. Tertullian wrote: *"We shall count, moreover, from the first year of Darius, as at this particular time is shown to Daniel this particular vision; for he says, 'And understand and conjecture that at the completion of thy word I make thee these answers.' Whence we are bound to compute from the first year of Darius, when Daniel saw this vision."*[477] The first year of Darius was the first year of Cyrus, as has been shown.

Dating the 70-weeks prophecy from the decree of Cyrus frees us entirely from reliance on non-biblical sources in establishing our chronology. Secular historical research involves a great deal of speculation, and is open to a wide variety of interpretations depending on the presuppositions of the interpreters. Modern scholarship, even Christian scholarship, seems willing to adopt historical dates that are based on a chronology that denies the flood and contradicts the Bible. New archeological discoveries frequently overturn long-established historical "facts." But the Word of God remains unchanged. It is "sufficient" so that the man of God may be "thoroughly equipped."[478] That equipment includes

---

[477] Tertullian, Answer to the Jews, ch. viii
[478] 2 Tim. 3:16-17

the chronological timeline of God's dealings with mankind, which He has so painstakingly preserved for us in His Word.

Daniel's 70 Sabbatical cycles (weeks) were broken into three parts, 7 Sabbatical cycles, 62 Sabbatical cycles, and 1 Sabbatical cycle. The last cycle of 7 years is the tribulation. The deliberate distinction between the first 7 Sabbatical cycles and the remaining 62 Sabbatical cycles (prior to the death of the Messiah) are proof that the 70 weeks are to be counted from Jubilee to Jubilee. The first section of "7 weeks" (50 years) marks a complete Jubilee cycle within the prophecy, and synchronizes it with the Jubilee calendar established at creation.

The 70-weeks prophecy of Daniel begins on the 70th Jubilee year from creation, the year Cyrus decreed the end of the captivity and the rebuilding of Jerusalem and the Temple. The first Jubilee cycle consisted of the first "seven weeks" in the prophecy, and was the duration of time from Cyrus decree until the Temple and Jerusalem's walls were completed by Nehemiah (covering the books of Ezra and Nehemiah). Adding the remaining "62 weeks" (442 years) we arrive at the end of the year, 3992 AM.

The next day was Rosh Hashanah (Tishri 1) 3993 AM which began the fall festivals. This is when Jesus began to announce that He was going away. Jesus was crucified six months later, on Passover; *"After sixty and two weeks Messiah shall be cut off..."*[479] in the middle of the year 3993 AM.

---

[479] Daniel 9:26

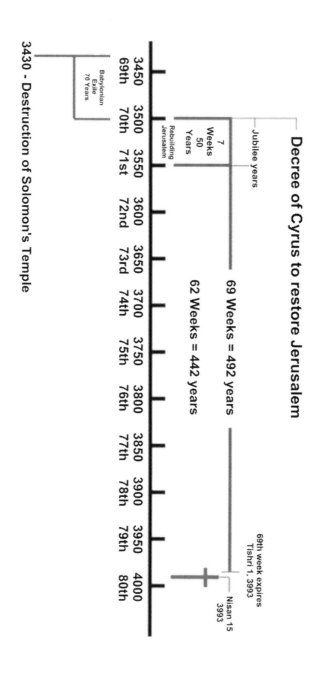

Chapter 16
CRUCIFIXION to KINGDOM
3993 AM – 6000 AM, 120th Jubilee

To complete the Jubilee chronology, the gap between the 69th and 70th weeks must be clearly defined. We have two witnesses to the duration of this period. The first witness is Hosea.

> *Hosea 5:14-6:2 LXX[480]*
> *14 For I am as a panther to Ephraim, and as a lion to the house of Judah. And will seize by force, and **I will go**, and **I will take, and there shall not be one rescuing**.*
> *15 **I shall go and return unto My place until of which time they should be removed from view** and they shall seek My face.*
> *6:1 In their affliction they will rise early to me, saying, "We should go and return to the Lord our God, for He snatched us away, and He will heal us. He shall strike, and He shall dress our wounds.*
> *2 **He will heal us after two days, on the third day we shall arise, and we shall live before Him**.*
> *3 And we shall know, and shall pursue to know the Lord. As dawn readied, we shall find Him; and He shall come to us as rain, early and late, to the earth.*

---

[480] Apostolic Bible Polyglot, Septuagint

The word "Day" in God's vocabulary sometimes means a millennium, particularly in prophecy, as has been shown. That is clearly the case with this prophecy because taking "days" as twenty-four hour periods would be absurd in this context.

Many suppose that the book of Hosea refers exclusively to the Assyrian destruction of the northern kingdom of Israel in Hosea's day. Yet, the New Testament quotes from Hosea and applies the interim between the destruction and restoration of Israel to the present age.[481] Also, notice that the destruction and wounding is to both Ephraim and Judah. The Assyrian captivity concerned only the northern tribes, not Judah.

Verses 14-15 describe a sequence of two major events: God's "going away" followed by Israel's being "removed from view." The former refers to Christ's going back to heaven; the latter refers to the destruction of Jerusalem 40 years later. After "two days" (2 millennia) Israel would repent, and God would restore them "on the third day."

The question is, when did this period of two millennia begin? It began the moment the 69th Sabbatical cycle ended,[482] in the beginning of the year of the crucifixion, on Rosh Hashanah, 3993 AM. The "two days" is precisely the length of the gap between the 69th and 70th weeks of Daniel.

Jesus attended the fall feasts in Jerusalem six months before His crucifixion, as described in John 7:1 – 10:21. It was at the

---

[481] cf. Hos. 1:10-11; Hos. 2:23 & Rom. 9:22-26; Rom. 11:30; 1 Pet. 2:10
[482] Daniel 9:24-27

fall festival season (Rosh Hashanah, Yom Kippur, and Sukkot) that Jesus first began to announce that He was "going away." This was a direct reference to Hosea's prophecy that He would "go and return unto My place" and God's judgment would follow by Jerusalem being removed from His sight.[483]

John 7
2 Now the Jews' Feast of Tabernacles was at hand. ...
10 But when His brothers had gone up, then He also went up to the feast, not openly, but as it were in secret. 11 Then the Jews sought Him at the feast, and said, "Where is He?"
...
32 The Pharisees heard the crowd murmuring these things concerning Him, and the Pharisees and the chief priests sent officers to take Him. 33 Then Jesus said to them, "__I shall be with you a little while longer, and then I go to Him who sent Me. 34 You will seek Me and not find Me, and where I am you cannot come__."
35 Then the Jews said among themselves, "__Where does He intend to go that we shall not find Him?__ Does He intend to go to the Dispersion among the Greeks and teach the Greeks? 36 What is this thing that He said, '__You will seek Me and not find Me, and where I am you cannot come__'?"

John 8:21
21 Then Jesus said to them again, "__I am going away, and you will seek Me, and will die in your sin. Where I go you cannot come__."

---

[483] Matt. 23:37-39; Matt. 24:2; Luke 19:42-44

The fulfillment of Hosea's prophecy, and the start of the two millennia, begins when Jesus made His announcement: "_**I shall go and return unto My place**_,"[484] at the exact time that the 69th week ended.

Just days before His crucifixion, Jesus referred to Hosea's prophecy again.

> _Matt. 23:37-39_
> _37 "O Jerusalem, Jerusalem, the one who kills the prophets and stones those who are sent to her! How often I wanted to gather your children together, as a hen gathers her chicks under her wings, but you were not willing! 38 See! Your house is left to you desolate; 39 **for I say to you, you shall see Me no more till you say, 'Blessed is He who comes in the name of the LORD**!'"_

Jesus was crucified on Passover, six months after He began announcing His departure and the 69th week ended. Remember, the "weeks" are Sabbatical cycles which must begin and end on Rosh Hashanah (New Year's Day) in the fall. Daniel said that Messiah would be cut off "after" the period of 7 plus 62 weeks. It was six months after.

The last two millennia began the day after the 69th Sabbatical cycle expired, on Tishri 1, 3993 AM, six months before the crucifixion. Jesus was crucified and then returned to His place at the Father's right hand.

The conclusion of the 70th week brings the dawn of the 120th Jubilee and Christ's Kingdom. Jesus' crucifixion was 7 years

---

[484] Hosea 5:15

short of a Jubilee year (after 69 weeks). Therefore, the end of the two millennia from His "going away" cannot include the 70th week. In other words, the second coming of Jesus Christ, and the "last trumpet"[485] of the 120th Jubilee will occur 2007 years from the beginning of the crucifixion year. The seven-year tribulation follows the "two days" interval. Otherwise, the 6,000th year and the 120th Jubilee would not coincide.

The Second Exile: 70x7 + 70x7 + 70x7 + 70x7 = 1960 Years

There is a second witness to the gap in Daniel's 70-weeks prophecy. Remember, Daniel 9 indicated two events which would take place after the 69th week but before the 70th week. These were the crucifixion of Christ and the second destruction of Jerusalem. The "two days" prophecy of Hosea gives us the duration of the gap from Christ's crucifixion in AD 30. But, Leviticus 26 gives us the duration of this gap counting from the destruction of Jerusalem 40 years later, in AD 70.

Some scholars place the crucifixion in the year AD 33. If this date is correct, there would only be 37 years from the crucifixion until the destruction of Jerusalem in AD 70. One significant reason for rejecting the AD 33 date comes from the Talmud which states that certain bad omens began occurring regularly at the Temple 40 years before its destruction, and continued for the entire 40 years between AD 30 and AD 70.

- On Yom Kippur (Day of Atonement), lots were cast for the two goats. *"And Aaron shall cast lots upon the two goats; one lot for the Lord, and the other lot for the*

---

[485] Cf. Lev. 25:9 & 1 Cor. 15:52

scapegoat."[486] The "lots" were two small stones, a black one with the words, "For Azazal" (the scape-goat), and a white one with the words, "For the Lord." The white stone always used to come up in the right hand of the High Priest, indicating that the Lord had chosen His goat for a sacrifice. But for the last 40 years, it no longer did.

- After the High Priest offered the blood of the goat within the Holy of Holies, and the scape goat was turned loose in the wilderness, a cord dyed red and hung on the Temple would always miraculously turn white as a sign that God had accepted the sacrifice for Israel. For the last 40 years it no longer turned white on Yom Kippur.
- For the last 40 years, the oil lamp of the menorah closest to the Holy of Holies refused to burn.
- For the last 40 years the huge double doors of the Temple would open by themselves.

All of these things spelled the same message: the glory of God had departed from the Temple.

> "Our Rabbis taught: During the last forty years before the destruction of the Temple the lot ['For the Lord'] did not come up in the right hand; nor did the crimson-coloured strap become white; nor did the westernmost light shine; and the doors of the Hekal would open by themselves, until R. Johanan b. Zakkai rebuked them, saying: Hekal, Hekal, why wilt thou be the alarmer thyself? I know about thee that thou wilt be destroyed, for Zechariah ben Ido has already

---

[486] Lev.16:8

prophesied concerning thee: Open thy doors, O Lebanon, that the fire may devour thy cedars."[487]

These things began to occur from the time Jesus was crucified. If Jesus was crucified in AD33 as some claim, these bad omens would have been occurring at the Temple regularly throughout Jesus' entire ministry. The New Testament tells us that a very significant omen occurred in the Temple at the moment of Jesus' death – the tearing of the veil. We would expect these bad omens to coincide. This is sufficient reason to conclude that when the veil was torn at Jesus' crucifixion, these things also began to occur. There were, therefore, 40 years between the crucifixion and the destruction of the Temple.

Scripture repeatedly predicted two exiles of Israel from the Land – the Babylonian exile prophesied by Jeremiah, and the Roman exile prophesied by Daniel[488] and Jesus.[489] Scripture also predicted two returns from exile back to the Land, [490] the one decreed by Cyrus, and the other implemented by the Messiah at His coming. The duration of the Babylonian exile was prophesied by Jeremiah – 70 years.[491] The duration of the second Roman exile is given in Leviticus 26 – 1960 years.

Immediately after God commanded Israel to observe the Sabbatical and Jubilee year cycles, He told them what their

[487] Talmud, Yoma 39b.
http://www.yashanet.com/library/temple/yoma39.htm
[488] Daniel 9:26
[489] Luke 21:24
[490] Isa. 11:11; Isa. 61:7 (LXX); Luke 21:24 & Rom. 11:25-27
[491] Jer. 25:11

punishment would be if they did not obey Him – exile from the Land.

> *Lev. 26:31-35*
> *31 I will lay your cities waste and bring your sanctuaries to desolation, and I will not smell the fragrance of your sweet aromas.*
> *32 I will bring the land to desolation, and your enemies who dwell in it shall be astonished at it.*
> *33 I will scatter you among the nations and draw out a sword after you; your land shall be desolate and your cities waste.*
> *34 Then the land shall enjoy its sabbaths as long as it lies desolate and you are in your enemies' land; then the land shall rest and enjoy its sabbaths.*
> *35 As long as it lies desolate it shall rest — for the time it did not rest on your sabbaths when you dwelt in it.*

2 Chronicles actually cites this passage in order to explain why the Babylonian exile lasted 70 years.

> *2 Chron. 36:15-21*
> *15 And the LORD God of their fathers sent warnings to them by His messengers, rising up early and sending them, because He had compassion on His people and on His dwelling place. 16 But they mocked the messengers of God, despised His words, and scoffed at His prophets, until the wrath of the LORD arose against His people, till there was no remedy.*
> *17 Therefore He brought against them the king of the Chaldeans, who killed their young men with the sword in the*

house of their sanctuary, and had no compassion on young man or virgin, on the aged or the weak; He gave them all into his hand. 18 And all the articles from the house of God, great and small, the treasures of the house of the LORD, and the treasures of the king and of his leaders, all these he took to Babylon. 19 Then they burned the house of God, broke down the wall of Jerusalem, burned all its palaces with fire, and destroyed all its precious possessions. 20 And those who escaped from the sword he carried away to Babylon, where they became servants to him and his sons until the rule of the kingdom of Persia, 21 to fulfill the word of the LORD by the mouth of Jeremiah, **until the land had enjoyed her Sabbaths. As long as she lay desolate she kept Sabbath, to fulfill seventy years.**

The 70 years of the Babylonian exile was to allow for 70 consecutive Sabbatical years compressed together (without the intervening 6 year periods of planting and harvesting). Seventy Sabbatical years normally covers a 500-year period (including the Jubilee years). As previously shown, it was precisely 500 years from God's initial threat to Solomon until the return from exile by the decree of Cyrus. God fulfilled His threat to the letter.

Yet, in Leviticus 26, God warned that He would multiply their initial judgment by a factor of 7 if afterward they still did not obey Him. *"And if ye still refuse to hearken to me, then will I chasten you yet **even seven times more** for your sins."*[492] The word rendered "seven times" means a multiple of seven, and "more" means in addition to the initial punishment which

---

[492] Lev. 26:18 LXX

was the first exile to Babylon. Therefore, God threatened to multiply the 70 year captivity by 7, making a total of 490 years of exile. But, He did not stop there. In verse 21 He said that if they still do not obey He would add the seven-fold judgment (490 years) a second time, making a total of 980 years. In verse 24, He warned them the third time, saying if they still do not obey He would add the seven-fold judgment (490 years) a third time, making a total of 1,470 years of exile. Finally, in verse 28, God warned them that if they still did not obey, in His fury He would add the seven-fold judgment (490 years) a fourth time, making a total of 1,960 years for the second exile.

The 1960 year period was the limit that God prescribed for Israel's punishment. After this, He promised to remember His covenant with Abraham concerning the Land inheritance. *"But if they confess their iniquity and the iniquity of their fathers, with their unfaithfulness in which they were unfaithful to Me, and that they also have walked contrary to Me, and that I also have walked contrary to them and have brought them into the land of their enemies; if their uncircumcised hearts are humbled, and they accept their guilt — then I will remember My covenant with Jacob, and My covenant with Isaac and My covenant with Abraham I will remember; I will remember the land."*[493]

The Abrahamic Covenant granted the Land (from the Nile to the Euphrates rivers) to Abraham and his Seed as an unconditional perpetual inheritance, no strings attached. This is the promise that Christians, who have become *"Abraham's*

---

[493] Lev 26:40-42

seed and heirs according to the promise,"[494] are to look forward to as our hope.[495]

The second exile began forty years after Jesus' crucifixion when the Romans destroyed Jerusalem, as predicted by both Daniel[496] and Jesus.[497] If the secular historical dates are correct, this exile began in the Jewish year which covers the fall of AD 69 to the fall of AD 70. Add the 1,960 years of Israel's second exile and we have the year 2029-2030. This is when the 70th week will begin – on Rosh Hashanah 2029. It will conclude on Yom Kippur 2036, **IF** the calendar-date of AD 30 for the crucifixion, and the calendar-date of AD 70 for the destruction of Jerusalem, are accurate.

We have with these dates the convergence of a two-fold witness for the duration of the gap between the 69th and 70th weeks. The first witness counts two millennial Days (2000 years) from Jesus' crucifixion until the beginning of the 70th week – the first event Daniel mentioned within this gap. The second witness dates from the second destruction of Jerusalem by the Romans, plus 1960 years, to the beginning of the 70th week – the second event Daniel described within this gap. Both independent methods of calculating this period put the start of the 70th week on Rosh Hashanah, 2029. This means that the second coming at the end of the 70th week will be on Yom Kippur, AD2036, assuming the Gregorian dates for these events are correct. It must be Yom Kippur (Day of

---

[494] Gal. 3:16,26-29
[495] Heb. 6:13-20
[496] Daniel 9:26
[497] Luke 19:41-44; Luke 21:20-24

Atonement) because this is when the Jubilee trumpet is blown announcing the 120[498]th Jubilee year.

The Purpose of the 70th Week Following the Exile

At the end of God's threat to Israel of the 1960-year second exile in Leviticus 26, He spoke of their collective repentance.

> *"But if they confess their iniquity and the iniquity of their fathers, with their unfaithfulness in which they were unfaithful to Me, and that they also have walked contrary to Me, and that I also have walked contrary to them and have brought them into the land of their enemies; if their uncircumcised hearts are humbled, and they accept their guilt — then I will remember My covenant with Jacob, and My covenant with Isaac and My covenant with Abraham I will remember; I will remember the land."*[499]

At this point, God will reconfirm the Mosaic covenant for one Sabbatical cycle[500] (the last of the 70 weeks), during which He will accept the penitent offerings of Israel in the rebuilt temple.[501] This is what Daniel meant when he wrote: "Then he shall strengthen the covenant for one week."[502] God's two prophets will prophesy in Jerusalem for the first 3.5 years of this final week. But, they will be killed and the sacrifices stopped by the Antichrist in the middle of that week. He will then enter the Temple, taking his seat as God. His image will be erected in the Temple, and he will demand worship under

---

[498] Lev. 25:9
[499] Lev 26:40-42
[500] Daniel 9:27
[501] Deut. 30:1-6; Mal. 4:4-6; Rev. 11:1-11
[502] Daniel 9:27

penalty of death.[503] This is the "abomination of desolation" that Jesus spoke about.[504]

There is a common theory among modern Christians that the "covenant" to be confirmed which begins the 70th week is some sort of peace treaty between the Antichrist and the Jews. This is not the case. 2 Thessalonians 2 states plainly that the Man of Sin will be "revealed" when he takes his seat in the Temple claiming to be God. This corresponds to the "abomination of desolation" which Daniel placed in the middle of the 70th week. Therefore, the Man of Sin will not have been revealed at the beginning of this 7-year period.

The early Christians' copies of Daniel 9:27 were slightly different than our copies of the Septuagint, as the following quote of Daniel by Hippolytus shows.

> *"Behold, too, the Lord's kindness to man; how even in the last times He shows His care for mortals, and pities them. For He will not leave us even then without prophets, but will send them to us for our instruction and assurance, and to make us give heed to the advent of the adversary, as He intimated also of old in this Daniel. For he says, "*<u>*I shall make*</u>* a covenant of one week, and in the midst of the week* <u>*my sacrifice*</u>* and libation will be removed." For by one week he indicates the showing forth of the seven years which shall be in the last times. And the half of the week the two prophets, along with John, will take for the purpose of proclaiming to all the world the advent of Antichrist, that is*

---

[503] Rev. 13
[504] Matt. 24:15

to say, for a "thousand two hundred and sixty days clothed in sackcloth;" and they will work signs and wonders with the object of making men ashamed and repentant, even by these means, on account of their surpassing lawlessness and impiety."[505]

The Hebrew text and our copies of the LXX do not specify who the person is who confirms the covenant for 7 years. Grammatically, it could either refer to the Messiah or the prince who shall come (Antichrist). Yet, Revelation 11:1-3 seems to support the above rendering, that it is God's daily sacrifice, and that God will accept this Temple worship as an act of genuine repentance by Israel.

> *Rev. 11:1-3*
> *1 Then I was given a reed like a measuring rod. And the angel stood, saying, "Rise and measure the temple of God, the altar, and those who worship there. 2 But leave out the court which is outside the temple, and do not measure it, for it has been given to the Gentiles. And they will tread the holy city underfoot for forty-two months. 3 And I will give power to my two witnesses, and they will prophesy one thousand two hundred and sixty days, clothed in sackcloth."*

God's two prophets plainly encourage the Temple worship which includes animal sacrifices on the altar. This is acknowledged by the measuring of the Temple and those worshiping at the altar apparently under the direction of the two witnesses. Therefore, it seems that the Temple worship during the first half of the 70th week is something acceptable

---

[505] Hippolytus, Frag. xxi

to God, and done at His direction. The "covenant" that is to be renewed for a limited period of "one week" is the same covenant that was formerly made obsolete by the coming of the New Covenant.[506]

Why will God renew the Mosaic covenant for seven years when it is clear that animal sacrifices "could never take away sin?"[507] The answer is to be found in the closing words of the Jewish Bible, a final warning to the Jewish nation.

> *Malachi 4:1-6*
> *1 "For behold, the day is coming, Burning like an oven, And all the proud, yes, all who do wickedly will be stubble. And the day which is coming shall burn them up," Says the LORD of hosts, "That will leave them neither root nor branch. 2 But to you who fear My name The Sun of Righteousness shall arise With healing in His wings; And you shall go out And grow fat like stall-fed calves. 3 You shall trample the wicked, For they shall be ashes under the soles of your feet On the day that I do this," Says the LORD of hosts.*
> *4 "__Remember the Law of Moses__, My servant, Which I commanded him in Horeb for all Israel, With the statutes and judgments. 5 __Behold, I will send you Elijah the prophet Before the coming of the great and dreadful day of the LORD.__ 6 And he will turn The hearts of the fathers to the children, And the hearts of the children to their fathers, Lest I come and strike the earth with a curse."*

---

[506] Heb. 8:13
[507] Heb. 10:4,11

Isn't it strange that the Old Testament ends with a prophecy of the second coming of Christ to reign and the promise of sending Elijah the prophet (both of which are themes of the book of Revelation), yet instructs the readers to obey the Law of Moses? You would think that in the context of the end times the instruction would point Israel away from the Law to Christ. Yet, it instead points them to something that was made obsolete long ago by the coming of the new Covenant. Why? This question and the question of renewing of the Covenant for one "week" both have the same answer. It is found in the Law of Moses – a promise that cannot expire or be terminated.

> *Deut. 30:1-6*
> *1 "Now it shall come to pass, when all these things come upon you, the blessing and the curse which I have set before you, and you call them to mind among all the nations where the LORD your God drives you, 2 and you return to the LORD your God and obey His voice, according to all that I command you today, you and your children, with all your heart and with all your soul, 3 that the LORD your God will bring you back from captivity, and have compassion on you, and gather you again from all the nations where the LORD your God has scattered you. 4 If any of you are driven out to the farthest parts under heaven, from there the LORD your God will gather you, and from there He will bring you. 5 Then the LORD your God will bring you to the land which your fathers possessed, and you shall possess it. He will prosper you and multiply you more than your fathers. 6 And the LORD your God will circumcise your heart and the heart of your descendants, to love the LORD your God with all your heart and with all your soul, that you may live.*

This promise is what Paul had in mind when writing about the restoration of Israel in the last days.

> *Rom. 11:25-36*
> *25 For I do not desire, brethren, that you should be ignorant of this mystery, lest you should be wise in your own opinion, that blindness in part has happened to Israel until the fullness of the Gentiles has come in. 26 And so all Israel will be saved, as it is written:*
> *"The Deliverer will come out of Zion, And He will turn away ungodliness from Jacob; 27 For this is My covenant with them, When I take away their sins."*
> *28 Concerning the gospel they are enemies for your sake, but concerning the election they are beloved for the sake of the fathers. 29 For the gifts and the calling of God are irrevocable. 30 For as you were once disobedient to God, yet have now obtained mercy through their disobedience, 31 even so these also have now been disobedient, that through the mercy shown you they also may obtain mercy. 32 For God has committed them all to disobedience, that He might have mercy on all.*
> *33 Oh, the depth of the riches both of the wisdom and knowledge of God! How unsearchable are His judgments and His ways past finding out!*
> *34 "For who has known the mind of the LORD? Or who has become His counselor? 35 Or who has first given to Him And it shall be repaid to him?"*
> *36 For of Him and through Him and to Him are all things, to whom be glory forever. Amen.*

A day of national repentance is coming for Israel – the 70th week of Daniel. Those found truly repentant, desiring to be restored to God, will do exactly what Malachi commands them to do – "remember the Law of My servant Moses." Many will return to the Law, clinging to the promise in the Law of Moses of the restoration of Israel. For the first 3.5 years they will offer sacrifices in national repentance. Then the genuineness of their repentance will be tested by fire for the last 3.5 years, as Antichrist stops the sacrifices, defiles the Temple, and persecutes them. Finally, Jesus will appear to save them at the end of the 70th week after 6000 years since Adam first sinned and was expelled from Eden.

The 70th week must follow (not precede) the end of the 2000 years from Jesus' crucifixion and the 1960 years from the destruction of Jerusalem. Remember, Jesus was crucified seven years short of the 80th Jubilee year, at the end of the 69th week. So there are 2007 years needed from the crucifixion until the 120th Jubilee, the year of Christ's return. Remember, Hosea's prophecy said that "after 2 days," "on the third day" God would restore Israel. Thus, the 70th week remains to be fulfilled after the expiration of the 2000 years from Jesus' going away, and the 1960 years from the destruction of Jerusalem.

Using the Jubilee chronology presented here to predict the date for the second coming is only as reliable as the Gregorian calendar dates with which we link it, the dates for Jesus' crucifixion (AD 30) and the destruction of Jerusalem (AD 70). These dates should not be assumed to be infallible. Any error in these secular dates skews the date for the second coming by that amount. In any case, historians almost unanimously put the destruction of Jerusalem in AD 70, and the year of Jesus' crucifixion is recognized by many if not most scholars as AD 30.[508] These two major events are not likely to be off by more than a few years. If they are correct, the 70th week will begin on Rosh Hashanah, September 11, 2029. Jesus will return on Yom Kippur, October 1, 2036, six-thousand years exactly from Adam's sin and expulsion from Eden. This assumes, of course, that our Jubilee calendar is correct.

---

[508] Some scholars claim that Jesus was crucified in AD 33. However, if this is correct, there would be no harmony between the "2 days" prophecy of Hosea and the 1960 year from Leviticus 26. That is, there would not be 40 years between the crucifixion and the destruction of Jerusalem, but only 37 years. Also, there are problems with Jesus' age when He began His ministry. Luke's Gospel states that Jesus was beginning His 30th year when John baptized Him (Luke 3:32). His ministry exceeded three Passovers (about 3.5 years). That agrees with an AD 30 crucifixion, but is problematic for an AD 33 crucifixion because it would require a birthdate in the year 1, which is too late because Herod (who threatened to kill all of the babies under 2 years), died before that year. Jesus was almost certainly born in September of 3 BC. (See my **Mystery of the Mazzaroth** book for the evidence).

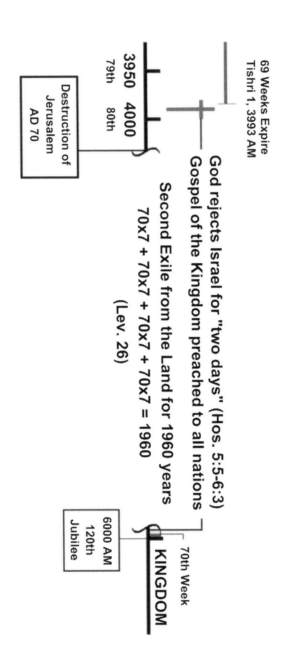

69 Weeks Expire
Tishri 1, 3993 AM

3950   4000
79th   80th

Destruction of
Jerusalem
AD 70

God rejects Israel for "two days" (Hos. 5:5-6:3)
Gospel of the Kingdom preached to all nations

Second Exile from the Land for 1960 years
70x7 + 70x7 + 70x7 + 70x7 + 70x7 = 1960

(Lev. 26)

6000 AM
120th
Jubilee

70th Week

KINGDOM

Chapter 17
From NOW until THEN

There are almost two decades before the beginning of the 70th Week of Daniel, as of the completion of this book. During this time many things must occur. According to Revelation, there is another world empire that will arise before the Antichrist comes to power.

Revelation 17-18 describes a woman riding a seven-headed beast. The woman is identified as Rome. *"And the woman whom you saw is that great city which reigns over the kings of the earth."*[509] John used the present tense of the verb "reigns" indicating that the woman was currently reigning over the kings of the earth when John wrote Revelation. Rome is the only possible candidate. The whole interpretation of this vision was explained by the angel to John as follows:

> *Revelation 17:7-18*
> *7 But the angel said to me, "Why did you marvel? I will tell you the mystery of the woman and of the beast that carries her, which has the seven heads and the ten horns. 8 The beast that you saw was, and is not, and will ascend out of the bottomless pit and go to perdition. And those who dwell on the earth will marvel, whose names are not written in the Book of Life from the foundation of the world, when they see the beast that was, and is not, and yet is.*

---

[509] Rev 17:18

> 9 *"Here is the mind which has wisdom: The seven heads are seven mountains on which the woman sits. 10* **There are also seven kings. Five have fallen, one is, and the other has not yet come. And when he comes, he must continue a short time.**
> *11* **The beast that was, and is not, is himself also the eighth, and is of the seven,** *and is going to perdition."*

This prophecy explains that there are seven kingdoms preceding the reign of Antichrist. Five of those kingdoms had already fallen before John's time. They were the world kingdoms which had dominated the nation of Israel – Egypt, Babylon, Persia, Greece, and Syria. The sixth kingdom which was present in John's day was Rome. Rome's kingdom has continued up to the present time through the Roman Catholic Church – an earthly kingdom in Christian disguise. The seventh kingdom had not yet come in John's day. Yet, the kingdom of the Beast is not the seventh kingdom itself, but the eighth kingdom which is of the seven.

This raises the question, what is the seventh kingdom that intervenes before the kingdom of Antichrist? Various commentators have offered different proposals, including:

- the Ottoman Empire of the Muslims
- the British Empire
- Germany's Third Reich
- the United States
- A future one-world government

Of these, the Ottoman[510] and British Empires hardly qualify, since the seventh empire is said to only continue "a short time." The Ottoman Empire lasted 623 years, from 1299 – 1922. The British Empire lasted over 300 years. America also seems unlikely since she has lasted over 200 years. Besides, all of the other kingdoms listed had direct rule over the nation of Israel. America has not.

Of the remaining two possibilities, Germany's Third Reich fits the criterion of existing only a "short time." Yet, despite the atrocities against the Jews, Nazi Germany never governed the nation of Israel either – the common thread for all the other nations listed. For this reason, in the author's opinion, Nazi Germany was not the seventh kingdom.

That leaves a future short-lived kingdom. Without question, we are heading now for a one world government that will attempt to synthesize democracy and socialism. All of the current signs point to this. The reelection of Barack Obama, who openly advanced a socialist agenda in his first term, is proof that the majority of Americans prefer a nanny-state to freedom and self-reliance. America has reached the tipping point where the people are prepared to cannibalize this once

---

[510] Joel Richardson has offered some compelling research in favor of the Antichrist's kingdom emerging from a revival of the Ottoman Empire. (See: The Islamic Antichrist, WND publications). There is no doubt that Islam will play a very important role in the final kingdom, given all of the parallels between Islamic eschatology about the coming of the Twelfth Imam, Muhammad al-Mahdi, and Christian eschatology about the Antichrist. Yet, rather than Islam being the religion of the Antichrist, as Richardson claims, it may be that Islamic eschatology will merely be the conduit for Muslims to receive the Antichrist. In a similar way, apostate Judaism and apostate Christianity are being prepared to accept the Antichrist through their own false eschatologies.

great nation for their own personal gain. It is only a matter of time before the American economy collapses from the strain of entitlement spending financed by debt, and with it the economies of virtually all the nations of the world. A world government with a single currency is the only option.

The middle-east is also about to explode. The revolutions in Egypt, Libya, and Syria, compounded by Iran's acquisition of nuclear weapons, Israel's constant harassment by Iran-backed Hamas, and President Obama's shunning of Israel and its security needs, leaves Israel with no choice but to go it alone in a preemptive attack on its perceived enemies. Once the middle-east war begins, oil prices will skyrocket. The economies of most of the free world cannot sustain this "perfect storm." As economic pressures increase, the nations will descend into chaos and anarchy.

From the ashes will arise what has been planned for centuries, the supposed world-wide socialist utopia. The world will be subdivided into ten states within a United States of the World. This newly formed world kingdom will settle the conflict over Israel, and permit the rebuilding of a Jewish Temple next to the Islamic Dome of the Rock. Jerusalem holy sites will be given a special status, and the three mono-theistic religions (Judaism, Christianity, and Islam) will be merged based on their common elements (with the help of willing apostate religious leaders from all three religions). Those who will not go along, who insist on the mutually exclusive claims of each religion, will be considered enemies of the state and terrorists.

Nebuchadnezzar's golden image had feet and toes of iron mixed with clay. The early Christian pastor, Hippolytus, commented on the last kingdom – the feet – as follows:

> *"As these things, then, are destined to come to pass, **and as the toes of the image turn out to be democracies**, and the ten horns of the beast are distributed among ten kings, let us look at what is before us more carefully, and scan it, as it were, with open eye. The "golden head of the image" is identical with the "lioness," by which the Babylonians were represented. "The golden shoulders and the arms of silver" are the same with the "bear," by which the Persians and Medes are meant. "The belly and thighs of brass" are the "leopard," by which the Greeks who ruled from Alexander onwards are intended. The "legs of iron" are the "dreadful and terrible beast," by which the Romans who hold the empire now are meant. The "toes of clay and iron" are the "ten horns" which are to be. The "one other little horn springing up in their midst" is the "antichrist." The stone that "smites the image and breaks it in pieces," and that filled the whole earth, is Christ, who comes from heaven and brings judgment on the world.*

> *"But that we may not leave our subject at this point undemonstrated, we are obliged to discuss the matter of the times, of which a man should not speak hastily, because they are a light to him. For as the times are noted from the foundation of the world, and reckoned from Adam, they set clearly before us the matter with which our inquiry deals. For the first appearance of our Lord in the flesh took place in*

Bethlehem, under Augustus, in the year 5500;[511] and He suffered in the thirty-third year. And 6,000 years must needs be accomplished, in order that the Sabbath may come, the rest, the holy day "on which God rested from all His works." For the Sabbath is the type and emblem of the future kingdom of the saints, when they "shall reign with Christ," when He comes from heaven, as John says in his Apocalypse: for "a day with the Lord is as a thousand years." Since, then, in six days God made all things, it follows that 6,000 years must be fulfilled. And they are not yet fulfilled, as John says: "five are fallen; one is," that is, the sixth; "the other is not yet come."

Writing nearly 1800 years ago, Hippolytus saw the seventh world kingdom as a conglomeration of ten democracies. Yet, John described the kingdom of the Beast as the eighth, but of the seven. Thus, the seventh kingdom will be transformed into the eighth when the Antichrist – the "little horn" – comes up after the ten and takes control from them. The ten presidents of this ten-democracy world government will give their kingdoms to the Beast. Then the final 3.5 years of his reign of terror will commence.

Revelation 17:12-17
12 "The ten horns which you saw are ten kings who have received no kingdom as yet, but they receive authority for one hour as kings with the beast. 13 These are of one mind, and they will give their power and authority to the beast. 14 These will make war with the Lamb, and the Lamb will

---

[511] Hippolytus was using the incorrect dates in the Septuagint for the genealogies in Genesis.

overcome them, for He is Lord of lords and King of kings; and those who are with Him are called, chosen, and faithful."
15 Then he said to me, "The waters which you saw, where the harlot sits, are peoples, multitudes, nations, and tongues. 16 And the ten horns which you saw on the beast, these will hate the harlot, make her desolate and naked, eat her flesh and burn her with fire. 17 For God has put it into their hearts to fulfill His purpose, to be of one mind, and to give their kingdom to the beast, until the words of God are fulfilled."

God will put it in the hearts of these ten presidents to turn their own states over to the Beast. It is therefore apparent that they will govern for a "short time" before the Antichrist comes to power. At the mid-point of the 70th week, these ten kings will destroy Rome, and then immediately turn over their kingdoms to the Beast.

In describing this final kingdom that will quickly morph into the Beast's empire, Daniel described it as iron mixed with clay, forming an unstable substance.

Daniel 2:41-44
41 Whereas you saw the feet and toes, partly of potter's clay and partly of iron, the kingdom shall be divided; yet the strength of the iron shall be in it, just as you saw the iron mixed with ceramic clay.
42 And as the toes of the feet were partly of iron and partly of clay, so the kingdom shall be partly strong and partly fragile.

43 As you saw iron mixed with ceramic clay, they will mingle with the seed of men;[512] but they will not adhere to one another, just as iron does not mix with clay.

44 And in the days of these kings the God of heaven will set up a kingdom which shall never be destroyed; and the kingdom shall not be left to other people; it shall break in pieces and consume all these kingdoms, and it shall stand forever.

The nature of the seventh kingdom will be both strength and fragility. No doubt it will enforce the emerging socialist agenda with force. Yet, democracies are inherently fragile. When the people rise up against it, a government cannot survive for long. The socialist utopian fantasy, which will appear in the guise of democracy, will not work because the various peoples will not adhere to one another. Racial, religious, and economic divisions will tear this kingdom apart. It will be short lived.

God's two prophets will prophesy for 3.5 years prior to the revealing of Antichrist.[513] Their calling down plagues upon this seventh kingdom will also bring it to its knees.[514] It is the arrival of the Beast from the abyss, and his killing of the two prophets who tormented the people of earth, that will propel him to power and acceptance as their deliverer.

---

[512] The LXX has, "so shall it be among the seed of men."

[513] The two prophets will be killed by the Beast when he ascends out of the abyss, (Rev. 11:7).

[514] Rev. 11:1-13

Between now and then we can expect the emergence of a socialist – democratic world government, with the whole world being divided into ten regions, with ten co-regents. National sovereignty will become a thing of the past. Laws will be dictated by a world Congress with representatives from all nations. Christians who refuse to cooperate with the new world religion – a merging of Judaism, apostate Christianity, and Islam – will be increasingly persecuted and denied basic civil rights. All of this is coming in the next two decades.

What can Christians do about it? How can we hang on to the old America based on a constitution, freedom, and individual responsibility? We cannot. What is coming is impossible to change. God has predetermined it. The best advice is to get out of the way of this monolithic machine.

The Christian hope is not the salvaging of the United States of America as we remember it, governed by the Constitution and Bill of Rights. It is the arrival of Christ's Kingdom. We cannot stop the evil men and demonic powers that are driving this agenda. They are on a leash held by God Himself. We can only hope to survive until our King arrives to wipe the wicked multitudes off of the face of the earth and bring the Kingdom of the Messiah – a Kingdom of perfect justice.

> *Psalm 37:1-40*
> *1 Do not fret because of evildoers, Nor be envious of the workers of iniquity.*
> *2 For they shall soon be cut down like the grass, And wither as the green herb.*

3 *Trust in the LORD, and do good; Dwell in the land, and feed on His faithfulness.*

4 *Delight yourself also in the LORD, And He shall give you the desires of your heart.*

5 *Commit your way to the LORD, Trust also in Him, And He shall bring it to pass.*

6 *He shall bring forth your righteousness as the light, And your justice as the noonday.*

7 *Rest in the LORD, and wait patiently for Him; Do not fret because of him who prospers in his way, Because of the man who brings wicked schemes to pass.*

8 *Cease from anger, and forsake wrath; Do not fret — it only causes harm.*

9 *For evildoers shall be cut off; But those who wait on the LORD, They shall inherit the earth.*

10 *For yet a little while and the wicked shall be no more; Indeed, you will look carefully for his place, But it shall be no more.*

11 *But the meek shall inherit the earth, And shall delight themselves in the abundance of peace.*

12 *The wicked plots against the just, And gnashes at him with his teeth.*

13 *The Lord laughs at him, For He sees that his day is coming.*

14 *The wicked have drawn the sword And have bent their bow, To cast down the poor and needy, To slay those who are of upright conduct.*

15 *Their sword shall enter their own heart, And their bows shall be broken.*

16 *A little that a righteous man has Is better than the riches of many wicked.*

17 For the arms of the wicked shall be broken, But the LORD upholds the righteous.

18 The LORD knows the days of the upright, And their inheritance shall be forever.

19 They shall not be ashamed in the evil time, And in the days of famine they shall be satisfied.

20 But the wicked shall perish; And the enemies of the LORD, Like the splendor of the meadows, shall vanish. Into smoke they shall vanish away.

21 The wicked borrows and does not repay, But the righteous shows mercy and gives.

22 For those blessed by Him shall inherit the earth, But those cursed by Him shall be cut off.

23 The steps of a good man are ordered by the LORD, And He delights in his way.

24 Though he fall, he shall not be utterly cast down; For the LORD upholds him with His hand.

25 I have been young, and now am old; Yet I have not seen the righteous forsaken, Nor his descendants begging bread.

26 He is ever merciful, and lends; And his descendants are blessed.

27 Depart from evil, and do good; And dwell forevermore.

28 For the LORD loves justice, And does not forsake His saints; They are preserved forever, But the descendants of the wicked shall be cut off.

29 The righteous shall inherit the land, And dwell in it forever.

30 The mouth of the righteous speaks wisdom, And his tongue talks of justice.

31 The law of his God is in his heart; None of his steps shall slide.

32 *The wicked watches the righteous, And seeks to slay him.*

33 *The LORD will not leave him in his hand, Nor condemn him when he is judged.*

34 *Wait on the LORD, And keep His way, And He shall exalt you to inherit the land; When the wicked are cut off, you shall see it.*

35 *I have seen the wicked in great power, And spreading himself like a native green tree.*

36 *Yet he passed away, and behold, he was no more; Indeed I sought him, but he could not be found.*

37 *Mark the blameless man, and observe the upright; For the future of that man is peace.*

38 *But the transgressors shall be destroyed together; The future of the wicked shall be cut off.*

39 *But the salvation of the righteous is from the LORD; He is their strength in the time of trouble.*

40 *And the LORD shall help them and deliver them; He shall deliver them from the wicked, And save them, Because they trust in Him.*

Chapter 18
PREPARATION

Jesus' command to those whom He would make ruler over His household was discussed at length in the first chapter. Those pastors who refuse to prepare Christ's flock will be punished severely. There is ample time for faithful shepherds to begin feeding the sheep under their care the necessary food so they will not be caught off guard by the end-time events. But, if they begin to "eat and drink with the drunken,"[515] and abuse Christ's flock for their own gain and security, they will be cut in two and thrown in with the unbelievers at Jesus' return.[516]

This concept should not be shocking to any pastor who knows his Bible. It is consistent with Old Testament prophecy.

> *Isa. 56:9-12*
> *9 All you beasts of the field, come to devour, All you beasts in the forest.*
> *10 His watchmen are blind, They are all ignorant; They are all dumb dogs, They cannot bark; Sleeping, lying down, loving to slumber.*
> *11 Yes, they are greedy dogs Which never have enough. And they are shepherds Who cannot understand; They all look to*

---

[515] Drunkenness is a metaphor for willful self-deception and willful ignorance. See Isa. 28:7-9; Isaiah 29:9 & 1 Thess. 5:7-8.
[516] Luke 12:42-48

their own way, Every one for his own gain, From his own territory.

12 "Come," one says, "I will bring wine, And we will fill ourselves with intoxicating drink; Tomorrow will be as today, And much more abundant."

Jer. 25:34-37

34 "Wail, shepherds, and cry! Roll about in the ashes, You leaders of the flock! For the days of your slaughter and your dispersions are fulfilled; You shall fall like a precious vessel.

35 And the shepherds will have no way to flee, Nor the leaders of the flock to escape.

36 A voice of the cry of the shepherds, And a wailing of the leaders to the flock will be heard. For the LORD has plundered their pasture, 37 And the peaceful dwellings are cut down Because of the fierce anger of the LORD.

Ezek. 34:7-10

7 'Therefore, you shepherds, hear the word of the LORD: 8 "As I live," says the Lord GOD, "surely because My flock became a prey, and My flock became food for every beast of the field, because there was no shepherd, nor did My shepherds search for My flock, but the shepherds fed themselves and did not feed My flock" — 9 therefore, O shepherds, hear the word of the LORD! 10 Thus says the Lord GOD: "Behold, I am against the shepherds, and I will require My flock at their hand; I will cause them to cease feeding the sheep, and the shepherds shall feed themselves no more; for I will deliver My flock from their mouths, that they may no longer be food for them."

Zech. 11:17
17 "Woe to the worthless shepherd, Who leaves the flock! A sword shall be against his arm And against his right eye; His arm shall completely wither, And his right eye shall be totally blinded."

The principal danger for Christ's sheep in the next several years is deception. There is a time of trouble on the horizon, a time far worse than anything else this world has ever seen or will ever see.[517] The roaring lion is going to molest the Christian churches on a scale never seen before. The flocks are going to be scattered, and the sheep will become his prey. According to Jesus, the majority of His followers will fall away and forsake Him in the time of trouble.

Matt 24:3-14
3 Now as He sat on the Mount of Olives, the disciples came to Him privately, saying, "Tell us, when will these things be? And what will be the sign of Your coming, and of the end of the age?"
4 And Jesus answered and said to them: "Take heed that no one deceives you. 5 For many will come in My name, saying, 'I am the Christ,' and will deceive many. 6 And you will hear of wars and rumors of wars. See that you are not troubled; for all these things must come to pass, but the end is not yet. 7 For nation will rise against nation, and kingdom against kingdom. And there will be famines, pestilences, and earthquakes in various places. 8 All these are the beginning of sorrows.

---

[517] Daniel 12:1; Matt. 24:21-22

> *9 "Then they will deliver you up to tribulation and kill you, and you will be hated by all nations for My name's sake. 10 And then many will be offended, will betray one another, and will hate one another. 11 Then many false prophets will rise up and deceive many. 12 And because lawlessness will abound, the love of many will grow cold. 13 But he who endures to the end shall be saved.*

This is one of the most frightening passages of Scripture in the entire New Testament. It describes the mass apostasy of the majority of Christians. The fatal deception of Christians comes in four ways:

- False christs will deceive many Christians (v. 5)
- Persecution will be too much for the spiritually weak (vss. 9-10)
- False "prophets" will seduce many Christians away from the truth (vs. 11)
- The abandonment of Jesus' commandments will cause the majority of Christians to lose their love (agape) for Christ (vs. 12)

The apostasy will become so powerful that few Christians will overcome it. The deception will flow partly from counterfeit miracles and counterfeit "spiritual gifts" which have tapped into a demonic spiritual power claiming to be the Holy Spirit. The deceptions will come through false prophets employing lying signs and wonders. *"For false christs and false prophets will rise and show great signs and wonders to deceive, if possible, even the elect. See, I have told you beforehand."*[518]

---

[518] Matt 24:24-25

Some wrongly suppose that the clause, "if possible, even the elect" implies that it is not possible to deceive the elect. That is simply false. The words, "to deceive, if possible, even the elect," describe the sinister motives and intentions of the false prophets when they employ false signs and wonders. The reason the false prophets use false signs and wonders is in the hope that they will be able to deceive some of the elect. The grammar does not support the impossibility of this, but just the opposite.

Only those who stand firmly on God's Word, resisting the flood of false prophets and teachers with their lying signs and wonders, will endure to the end and be saved. It is the responsibility of pastors to educate and strengthen the flock under their care so that they will be able to "endure to the end." This is done by giving them the proper food at the proper time.

God has provided in His Word all of the necessary equipment for His people. Jesus' sheep must begin to prepare now to face it head on. Most cannot prepare unless their pastors "shepherd" them in the way Jesus Christ, the Good Shepherd, would do. Unfortunately, many pastors are "hirelings" and will flee when they see the wolf coming.[519]

For almost two millennia, Christian intelligentsia has hidden the chiliasm of the earliest Christian apologists and martyrs, disparaging them as quirky and simple-minded men. Yet, these were the giants of the early churches, the pastors who successfully navigated and steered their congregations

---

[519] John 10:12-13

through wave after wave of intense Roman persecutions. In the process, they fought off and defeated the flood of Gnostic heresies. They were flawed men to be sure, but faithful custodians of what they had been handed down by the Apostles. These men faced intense persecution and martyrdom boldly. Satan could not touch them.

Who should we as pastors look to for inspiration? It should be these great men who stared down wild beasts and endured the flames of the pyre to preserve the Apostolic Faith for future generations. If we, as pastors of Christ's flock, are going to be found faithful at Jesus' coming, perhaps we ought to take a second look at the rest of what the early Christian giants had to say on other theological topics – on baptism, on free will, on the future inheritance of the redeemed, on the danger of falling from the faith, and on preparation for facing the Antichrist. It's time to discard all the theological "fables" we have turned to for soothing the "itching ears" of those who pay our salaries. We must take a stand for the unvarnished truth no matter the cost. Taking a stand is costly to be sure. But not taking a stand will prove to be much more costly – being cut in two and cast in with the unbelievers.

Knowing what is coming beforehand is beneficial only if Christians have wise counsel on how to become prepared. The knee-jerk reaction is to store up lots of food, or start building a bunker. Yet, God does not want His people to react out of fear, but out of confidence and firm trust in Him. Fear is an indicator that we are unprepared. God does not want us to rely on our own strength, wisdom, or finances. He wants us to walk by faith, trusting His promises to supply our needs.

He wants the knowledge of these things to drive us to our knees, to reexamine our relationship with Him. He wants us to throw off our worldly entanglements so that when the shout is given, *"Behold the Bridegroom comes, go out to meet Him,"*[520] we will be ready to abandon everything and take a leap of faith into the waiting arms of our Savior. If we hesitate, it could spell disaster. *"Remember Lot's wife."* [521]

The most important aspect of preparation is spiritual, not physical. The end-time tribulation is a final call to repentance as John indicated: *"'Let us be glad and rejoice and give Him glory, for the marriage of the Lamb has come, and **His wife has made herself ready.'** And to her it was granted to be arrayed in fine linen, clean and bright, for the fine linen is the righteous acts of the saints."*[522] The ones who will survive and thrive in the last trial are those who have *"**cleansed themselves** of all filthiness of the flesh and spirit, perfecting holiness in the fear of God."*[523] *"These are the ones who come out of the great tribulation, **and washed their robes and made them white in the blood of the Lamb**. Therefore they are before the throne of God, and serve Him day and night in His temple. And He who sits on the throne will dwell among them. They shall neither hunger anymore nor thirst anymore; the sun shall not strike them, nor any heat; for the Lamb who is in the midst of the throne will shepherd them and lead them to living fountains of waters. And God will wipe away every tear from their eyes."*[524] We must stop our sinful habits now. We

---

[520] Matt. 25:6
[521] Luke 17:32
[522] Rev. 19:7-8
[523] 2 Cor. 7:1
[524] Rev. 7:14-17

must let go of materialism now. We must take up our cross and follow Jesus now. We must begin to walk by faith now.

Jesus promised at the end of the Sermon on the Mount that if we obey His teaching in that sermon, He will make sure we survive the coming storm. We ought to cling to these words, and hammer them home to our congregations.

> *Matt. 7:24-27*
> *24 "Therefore whoever hears these sayings of Mine, and does them, I will liken him to a wise man who built his house on the rock: 25 and the rain descended, the floods came, and the winds blew and beat on that house; and it did not fall, for it was founded on the rock.*
> *26 "But everyone who hears these sayings of Mine, and does not do them, will be like a foolish man who built his house on the sand: 27 and the rain descended, the floods came, and the winds blew and beat on that house; and it fell. And great was its fall."*

This sermon contains a series of commandments of Jesus Christ, what Paul later called "the Law of Christ."[525] Only those who are living by these commandments of Jesus will escape the coming storm. The rest will be overcome by it.

Jesus also promised in that sermon to meet all of our physical needs IF we seek His Kingdom first. This requires the total abandonment of the things of this world.

---

[525] Isa. 42:4; Gal. 5:2

Matt 6:25-34

25 "Therefore I say to you, do not worry about your life, what you will eat or what you will drink; nor about your body, what you will put on. Is not life more than food and the body more than clothing? 26 Look at the birds of the air, for they neither sow nor reap nor gather into barns; yet your heavenly Father feeds them. Are you not of more value than they? 27 Which of you by worrying can add one cubit to his stature? 28 "So why do you worry about clothing? Consider the lilies of the field, how they grow: they neither toil nor spin; 29 and yet I say to you that even Solomon in all his glory was not arrayed like one of these. 30 Now if God so clothes the grass of the field, which today is, and tomorrow is thrown into the oven, will He not much more clothe you, O you of little faith?

31 "Therefore do not worry, saying, 'What shall we eat?' or 'What shall we drink?' or 'What shall we wear?' 32 For after all these things the Gentiles seek. For your heavenly Father knows that you need all these things. 33 But seek first the kingdom of God and His righteousness, and all these things shall be added to you. 34 Therefore do not worry about tomorrow, for tomorrow will worry about its own things. Sufficient for the day is its own trouble."

These promises and many others will provide the anchor for our faith in the days ahead. The most important first steps now are learning to walk by faith, and seeing God's provision now as we abandon materialism and put His Kingdom first.

How do we learn to walk by faith? It only comes by taking progressively larger leaps of faith based on God's promises.

We must risk personal and financial ruin, staring down our fear in order to act boldly on God's Word, just as Abraham did. As we see Him respond to our faith in small ways, we learn to trust Him in bigger things and to take bigger leaps of faith based on His promises. We must get to the place where nothing matters except our hope of Jesus' coming to establish His Kingdom. When this hope is real and tangible, and when we begin to hate the present world system and all its allurements, fear is driven out and faith takes its place.

The early Christian pastors had plenty to say about preparing spiritually for the end times. Cyprian's comments below, while written nearly 2000 years ago, are typical. These words were intended for the Christians living in the very last days.

> *"For you ought to know and to believe, and hold it for certain, that the day of affliction has begun to hang over our heads, and the end of the world and the time of Antichrist to draw near, so that we must all stand prepared for the battle; nor consider anything but the glory of life eternal, and the crown of the confession of the Lord; and not regard those things which are coming as being such as were those which have passed away. A severer and a fiercer fight is now threatening, for which the soldiers of Christ ought to prepare themselves with uncorrupted faith and robust courage, considering that they drink the cup of Christ's blood daily, for the reason that they themselves also may be able to shed their blood for Christ. For this is to wish to be found with Christ, to imitate that which Christ both taught and did, according to the Apostle John, who said, 'He that saith he abideth in Christ, ought himself also so to walk even as He*

walked.' Moreover, the blessed Apostle Paul exhorts and teaches, saying, 'We are God's children; but if children, then heirs of God, and joint-heirs with Christ; if so be that we suffer with Him, that we may also be glorified together.'

"For there comes the time, beloved brethren, which our Lord long ago foretold and taught us was approaching, saying, 'The time cometh, that whosoever killeth you will think that he doeth God service. And these things they will do unto you, because they have not known the Father nor me. But these things have I told you, that when the time shall come, ye may remember that I told you of them.' Nor let any one wonder that we are harassed with increasing afflictions, when the Lord before predicted that these things would happen in the last times, and has instructed us for the warfare by the teaching and exhortation of His words. Peter also, His apostle, has taught that persecutions occur for the sake of our being proved, and that we also should, by the example of righteous men who have gone before us, be joined to the love of God by death and sufferings. For he wrote in his epistle, and said, 'Beloved, think it not strange concerning the fiery trial which is to try you, nor do ye fall away, as if some new thing happened unto you; but as often as ye partake in Christ's sufferings, rejoice in all things, that when His glory shall be revealed, ye may be glad also with exceeding joy'."[526]

"Nor let any one of you, beloved brethren, be so terrified by the fear of future persecution, or the coming of the threatening Antichrist, as not to be found armed for all

---

[526] Cyprian, Epistle LV, 1,2

things by the evangelical exhortations and precepts, and by the heavenly warnings. Antichrist is coming, but above him comes Christ also. The enemy goeth about and rageth, but immediately the Lord follows to avenge our sufferings and our wounds. The adversary is enraged and threatens, but there is One who can deliver us from his hands. He is to be feared whose anger no one can escape, as He Himself forewarns, and says: 'Fear not them which kill the body, but are not able to kill the soul; but rather fear Him which is able to destroy both body and soul in hell.' And again: 'He that loveth his life, shall lose it; and he that hateth his life in this world, shall keep it unto life eternal.' And in the Apocalypse He instructs and forewarns, saying, 'If any man worship the beast and his image, and receive his mark in his forehead or in his hand, the same also shall drink of the wine of the wrath of God, mixed in the cup of His indignation, and he shall be tormented with fire and brimstone in the presence of the holy angels, and in the presence of the Lamb; and the smoke of their torments shall ascend up forever and ever; and they shall have no rest day nor night, who worship the beast and his image'."

"For the secular contest men are trained and prepared, and reckon it a great glory of their honor if it should happen to them to be crowned in the sight of the people, and in the presence of the emperor. Behold a lofty and great contest, glorious also with the reward of a heavenly crown, inasmuch as God looks upon us as we struggle, and, extending His view over those whom He has condescended to make His sons, He enjoys the spectacle of our contest. God looks upon us in the warfare, and fighting in the encounter of faith; His

angels look on us, and Christ looks on us. How great is the dignity, and how great the happiness of the glory, to engage in the presence of God, and to be crowned, with Christ for a judge! Let us be armed, beloved brethren, with our whole strength, and let us be prepared for the struggle with an uncorrupted mind, with a sound faith, with a devoted courage. Let the camp of God go forth to the battle-field which is appointed to us. Let the sound ones be armed, lest he that is sound should lose the advantage of having lately stood; let the lapsed also be armed, that even the lapsed may regain what he has lost: let honor provoke the whole; let sorrow provoke the lapsed to the battle. The Apostle Paul teaches us to be armed and prepared, saying, "We wrestle not against flesh and blood, but against powers, and the princes of this world and of this darkness, against spirits of wickedness in high places. Wherefore put on the whole armor, that ye may be able to withstand in the most evil day, that when ye have done all ye may stand; having your loins girt about with truth, and having put on the breastplate of righteousness; and your feet shod with the preparation of the Gospel of peace; taking the shield of faith, wherewith ye shall be able to quench all the fiery darts of the wicked one; and the helmet of salvation, and the sword of the Spirit, which is the word of God.'"[527]

Jesus suffered with courage and determination, completing His heavenly task. The Apostles showed the same resolve, shedding their blood to conclude their assigned mission. Many of the early Christian pastors quoted in this book also went to their executions in the Roman persecutions with a

---

[527] Cyprian, Epistle LV, 7,8

steadfast faith and resolve. These have all set the bar very high for us with their courage and resolve. Now, we have been handed the baton; we have the final leg of the race to complete. Will we measure up to the challenge to prepare Christ's churches for the end-game, or will we keep peddling the popular fables of comfort and ease until the storm washes away the foundations? There will be a victorious Church to meet Christ at His coming, the Bride "who has made herself ready." The question is: Will it include you?

Mystery of the Mazzaroth presents an entirely new theory on the meaning of the Zodiac – a prophetic calendar counting down to the end of the age and Messiah's Kingdom. If you enjoyed The TIME of the END, you will equally enjoy this companion volume.

Made in the USA
San Bernardino, CA
22 March 2016